GOVERNING IN FAITH
Foundations for Formation

GOVERNING IN FAITH

Foundations for Formation

John Henry Thornber
& Michael Gaffney

Connor Court Publishing
Ballarat

Published in 2014 by Connor Court Publishing Pty Ltd.

Copyright © 2014 John Henry Thornber & Michael Gaffney

ALL RIGHTS RESERVED. This book contains material protected under International and Federal Copyright Laws and Treaties. Any unauthorized reprint or use of this material is prohibited. No part of this book may be reproduced or transmitted in any form or by any means, electronic or mechanical, including photocopying, recording, or by any information storage and retrieval system without express written permission from the publisher.

Connor Court Publishing Pty Ltd.
PO Box 224W
Ballarat VIC 3350
sales@connorcourt.com
www.connorcourt.com

ISBN: 9781925138016 (pbk.)

Cover Photograph: Cape Finisterre, west coast of Galicia, Spain, taken by Michael Gaffney, 2013.

Cape Finisterre, which derives its name from the Latin *finis terrae*, meaning "end of the earth", is the final destination for many pilgrims who walk the Camino, otherwise known as the Way of St. James.

Lying on the western coast of continental Europe, Finisterre has had spiritual and geographical significance since ancient times. For many, it is a place of reflection to consider 'what lies beyond the horizon'. For the courageous, skilful and faithful, it is a place of departure for the New World.

For those involved in the governance of Church ministries, Cape Finisterre can serve as a type of metaphor. Our pilgrim journey has taken us to this point, to the edge. We cannot go back. We cannot stand still. And going further means we are sailing into unchartered waters. It carries enormous risks as well as opportunities. It requires a brave and warm heart, relevant expertise and a mature faith.

Our book has been written to assist those wishing to continue the journey.

Printed in Australia

CONTENTS

	About the Authors	vii
	Acknowledgements	ix
	Preface	x
	Glossary	xiv
1	Changing Contexts for Canonical Governance and Formation	1
2	Forming Professionals for Mission and Ministry	33
3	Identifying Formation Needs	69
4	Mature and Self-Aware Canonical Governors: The Human Dimension	88
5	'Called' and Committed Canonical Governors: The Spiritual Dimension	104
6	Informed and Reflective Canonical Governors: The Intellectual Dimension	132
7	Discerning and Responsible Canonical Governors: The Pastoral Dimension	168
8	Developing a Framework for Formation	194
9	Forming Foundations for the Future	222
	References	243
	Appendices	266

About the Authors

The inspiration for this book came from the authors' personal histories and their professional interests and research in governance in Church ministries.

John Henry Thornber

John Henry Thornber is a member of the Congregation of Christian Brothers, a Religious Institute of the Catholic Church. He has been an educator for some 40 years as a teacher in primary and secondary schools, subject coordinator, sports master, year coordinator, principal and diocesan school office consultant. Over recent years, he has been involved in governance developments for the Congregation in New South Wales, and on the National Planning Committee for Schools Governance for the future governance of Christian Brothers' schools in Australia. John Henry has a PhD from the Australian Catholic University on the topic of formation needs for 'canonical governors', i.e. individuals responsible for leading ministries in ways that are faithful to their mission in light of Church law.

Michael Gaffney

Michael Gaffney is a lay person with over thirty years' experience in education as a teacher, school and school system executive member, and university academic. He is Professor of Education at the University of Canberra, and formerly Professor of Educational Leadership at the Australian Catholic University. Mike works as a researcher and consultant to Australian governments and school systems in areas of educational leadership, policy and governance. He has worked extensively as a policy advisor and decision maker engaged at the interface of school, parish, diocese and government in promoting the mission of Catholic education in both secular and sacred contexts.

Through their respective backgrounds, these authors have an informed appreciation of the complexities surrounding the nature of mission and governance in the education, health and social welfare ministries of the Catholic Church, and especially the formation needs of people involved in the governance of these ministries.

Acknowledgements

We wish to thank Associate Professor Patrick McArdle, Director of the Centre for Catholic Identity and Mission at the Australian Catholic University for his help, particularly with theological questions and viewpoints, and other colleagues from ACU including Evan Wills who made an indispensable contribution to survey development and distribution, Dr. Roger Vallance who provided challenging insights into the nature and use of the statistical tools, and Vicki Bourbous, who as the Library Liaison Officer at Strathfield Campus helped enormously with searching the literature on these somewhat obscure and under-researched areas of governance and formation. We were also greatly assisted by Dr. Vincent Wacher who not only helped us make sense of the statistical results but made their presentation so much easier to interpret, and Dr. Guenter Plum with his keen eye for detail in the editing of the original research work.

We are also grateful to those who gave their time to undertake the survey and offered to be interviewed for the research underpinning this book. Their support was more than matched by the encouragement they offered regarding what they saw as the important issues surrounding formation for governance in the Church and the potential contribution of the research for addressing those issues. In particular, we are grateful to Emeritus Professor Francis Morrisey OMI who was an extremely helpful mentor with canonical advice and support throughout the project.

Finally we would like to thank John Henry's religious congregation, the Christian Brothers for the opportunity and support and particularly thank his community at Chatswood, New South Wales, Australia for their ongoing encouragement. And our heartfelt thanks and appreciation goes to Mike's wife Elisabeth for her extraordinary support and encouragement through the years of research and writing that have gone into this book.

John Henry Thornber
Michael Gaffney

Preface

The fall in the number of religious staying in or joining religious life has become a significant issue for the governance of Church ministries, especially those in health, aged care, education and social welfare. Lay people fill most roles in senior management and increasingly are being called to governance responsibilities. These accelerating levels of involvement of the laity in the ecclesial world had not been envisaged by the Council Fathers of Vatican II and were not reflected in the revised Code of Canon Law. In the minds of many, governance informed by, and under the jurisdiction of Canon Law, i.e. canonical governance, had always been and presumably would forever be the role and responsibility of the clergy and religious. How times are changing. The scale, complexity and importance of governance roles in Church ministries raise the question of what constitutes appropriate formation of the laity for undertaking such roles. This book is designed to answer that question. It is based on our research into the formation needs of lay people to undertake roles in canonical governance.

This research involved the study of Church documents used in formation for priesthood – Pastores Dabo Vobis (Pope John Paul II, 1992) and for ecclesial lay workers – Co-Workers in the Vineyard of the Lord (United States Conference of Catholic Bishops, 2005). These documents provided the basis for identifying the key areas (or dimensions) of formation, and for designing a survey to investigate the existing and desired traits of canonical governors. The survey items invited respondents to nominate agreement or otherwise on the desirability of certain traits of canonical governors and the extent to which they perceived those traits in practice. The survey was administered online, and offered to people with expertise in canonical governance and related areas. Responses came from seven countries, the majority from Australia and the United States of America. The survey was followed with a series of interviews with respondents who had strong backgrounds in Canon Law, theology and formation.

The findings supported the need for a framework for formation for canonical governance as consisting of four related dimensions – human, spiritual, intellectual, and pastoral. Survey respondents and interviewees provided much valuable advice and opinion about the content and desirability of the traits associated with each of the dimensions. Of particular interest was the discrepancy between the levels of desirability of various traits and the perceived enactment of those traits. Interviewees expressed concern at these discrepancies, especially the perceived lack of understanding by those with canonical governance responsibilities about how the Church operates (ecclesiology), how the purpose and mission of the ministry is understood (missiology), and who has authority in the Church and how this authority is exercised in governance processes (Canon Law).

From these findings, we believe that it is time for a framework for formation of canonical governors to be articulated and understood by bishops, leaders of religious institutes, current and prospective canonical governors, and those responsible for their formation. This book has been written with these folk in mind.

In Chapter 1, we provide an outline of the changing context of Church governance since the Second Vatican Council. Changes in society, in the number and role of priests and religious, and in the involvement of the laity challenge us to consider different models and possibilities for the Church. The implications of these changes are explored in Chapter 2 which focuses on issues surrounding the formation of lay people professionally involved in Church ministries. We introduce the notion of a framework incorporating four dimensions of formation: human, spiritual, intellectual and pastoral; and highlight some of the key concepts associated with each, including the nature of human maturity, transcendence and vocation, theological reflection, and pastoral development. The framework is considered in depth in Chapter 3 as a means of identifying the formation needs of canonical governors. The processes of survey development, distribution and analysis are explored, including the wording and selection of items to measure the desirability and existence of particular traits of canonical governors. The nature and themes resulting from the factor analysis of survey responses is also covered. In Chapters 4 to 7, we report the responses to traits in each of the dimensions. Each chapter treats a different dimension of traits associated with the role of canonical governors. Differences among the survey respondent groups are investigated as well as the patterns in the responses that were identified through factor analysis. We discuss the implications of the survey responses as seen through the eyes of the interviewees, and identify a series of salient and desired characteristics of canonical governors, namely that such individuals are committed to their role; are confident, respectful, just and compassionate; have a sense of vocation and their baptismal call; are informed about Catholic intellectual tradition; are reflective about the nature of God and the Church; and understand their responsibility for the stewardship of the Catholic identity of their ministry.

In light of the literature and research findings from earlier chapters, we develop a framework for formation in Chapter 8. This framework draws on Vatican II documents about formation – *Optatam Totius* (Abbott, 1966f) on priestly formation and *Apostolicam Actuositatem* (Abbott, 1966b) on lay formation, along with the previously noted documents: *Pastores Dabo Vobis* (Pope John Paul II, 1992) and *Co-Workers in the Vineyard of the Lord* (United States Conference of Catholic Bishops, 2005). Our view is that an appropriate framework for formation should have the following features:

1. A broad and clearly defined scope and terminology.
2. A recognised and valid base in ecclesial literature and related Church teaching.
3. A means of identifying formation needs.

4. A set of principles to underpin the process of formation needs and the design of formation programs.

In Chapter 9, Forming Foundations for the Future, we outline the principles that need to underpin the content and design of formation programs, and conclude with a series of questions for planning and evaluating such programs.

At this critical time in the life of the Church, we believe the ideas and approaches to formation outlined in this book can provide a worthwhile resource for those charged with the responsibility for enlivening and sustaining Church ministries in health, aged care, education and social welfare. This is not just about running an effective and efficient not-for-profit organisation. It is about something deeper, it is about meaning and mission, it is about governing in faith. We wish those who are called to this work, every success.

John Henry Thornber
Michael Gaffney
(Authors)

Glossary

Baptism: The sacrament of rebirth by which one becomes a member of the Church and a new creature in Christ (McBrien, 1994).

Bishop: A cleric appointed by the Roman Catholic Pope to lead a diocese in the Church. The bishop is responsible for the governance and spiritual life of the faithful in the diocese. Bishops are the link to the first apostles commissioned by Jesus Christ to lead the Church from the period called 'Apostolic Times' (Roman Catholic Church, 1983, Code of Canon Law, Cns 375, 376).

Code of Canon Law: The promulgated law (1983) of the Roman Catholic Church for the good order of the operation of the Church (Latin Rite) to assist it to achieve the mission of the founder, Jesus Christ (Coriden, 2004).

Canonist: A person who has undertaken studies in the law of the Roman Catholic Church – Canon Law – and is qualified to offer advice on the law (Coriden, 2000).

Canonical Governance: The carrying of the responsibility of the ministry in the light of Code of Canon Law of the Roman Catholic Church.

Canonical Governor: A person given responsibility in accordance with Canon Law to maintain the requirements of a ministry, theologically and canonically, for the Church's mission.

CICLSAL: Congregation for Institutes of Consecrated Life and Societies of Apostolic Life. The Vatican body responsible for the oversight and approval of religious institutes and Public Juridic Persons for the governance of ministries

Congregation Leaders: People appointed as leaders of Religious Institutes under Canon Law (Roman Catholic Church, 1983, Code of Canon Law, Cns 617-630).

Ecclesiology: The branch of Theology that studies the Church, its meaning and operations (McBrien, 1994)

Formator: One who undertakes to prepare others for the responsibilities of a future task – in this case, preparation of another for the responsibilities of canonical governance.

Governance: The role of responsibility for and stewardship of the purpose and meaning of an organisation in the light of the relevant law (canonical or civil) and the expounded mission of the organisation (Chait, Ryan, & Taylor, 2005, p. 3).

Lay People or Laity: People who have a membership of Christian life because they have been baptised. This means all Christians, including clerics; lay people are usually described as the members of the faithful have not been ordained to the ministerial authority of priesthood (Hahnenberg, 2003, pp. 12-18).

Ministry: The public activity of a baptised follower of Jesus Christ flowing from the Spirit's charism and an individual personality on behalf of the Christian community to proclaim, serve, and realise the kingdom of God (O'Meara, 1999, p. 150).

Mission: The purpose for which an organisation exists. Mission "is proclaiming, serving, and witnessing to God's reign of love, salvation, and justice" (Schroeder, 2008, p. 3).

Missiology: The branch of Theology which studies how mission is understood and enacted - also called Theology of Mission (Bevans & Gros, 2009).

Moral Person: An entity which comes into existence without any legislator (Morrisey, 2009).

Priest: A man (in the Roman Catholic Church) ordained and empowered to lead the religious rites of the Church. The role has been a basic requirement for governance over several hundred years (Roman Catholic

Church, 1983, Code of Canon Law, Cns 273-289). Bishops, priests and deacons are defined as the clergy or 'clerics'.

Public Juridic Person (PJP): An entity which is created by a legislator. Canon Law gives the juridic person status to the entity in the Church in the same manner that corporation law allows for such entities in civil law. In the Catholic Church, the person's goods are deemed to be owned by the Church (Morrisey, 2009, p. 18). It is identified by the abbreviation PJP.

Religious Institute: A body which has been approved by the Church to allow for "the Consecrated and Apostolic Life" (Coriden, 2004, pp. 99-106).

Religious (The), or **members of religious institutes**: The members who voluntarily join the Religious Institute usually live a life in common, take vows, and engage in ministries in the name of the Church. They have conducted significant ministries in health, education, welfare, and aged care but find now that, in general, they can no longer do so for a range of reasons.

Sponsorship: The formal relationship between a recognised Catholic organisation and a legally formed entity entered into for the sake of promoting and sustaining the Church's mission in the world (Smith, Brown, & Reynolds, 2006, p. ii Foreword). However, it is also seen as "an evolving concept" (CHAUSA, 2007b, p. 6). The term is often used in Catholic Healthcare governance in the USA, and has a similar meaning to the term 'canonical governance' used in this book as it usually embraces canonical governance in the responsibilities.

Stewardship: Acknowledgement that resources are held and administered in sacred trust (Grant & Vandenberg, 1998, p. 122).

Theologian: A scholar, an academic, a highly trained specialist with a wide knowledge of Christian tradition and the history of doctrine and with a number of linguistic and hermeneutical skills (Bevans, 2002, p.

18). Where theology is understood as a study of the search for God, theologians serve an auxiliary role to assist people in their search for meaning in life (Bevans, 2002).

Theology: The ordered effort to understand, interpret, and systemise the experience of God and of Christian faith. It is "faith seeking understanding" (Anselm, in McBrien, 1994).

Second Vatican Council or Vatican II: The Council of the Catholic Bishops of the world held between 1962 and 1965 which addressed issues for the Church and provided 16 major documents for change and development for the future of the Church.

Vatican: An independent nation, headquarters of the Roman Catholic Church.

All Scripture quotations are from *The New American Bible* with *Revised New Testament* (Confraternity of Christian Doctrine, 1988).

What good is it my brothers and sisters, if you say you have faith but do not have works? Can faith save you? If a brother or sister is naked and lacks daily food, and one of you says to them, "Go in peace; keep warm and eat your fill." And yet you do not supply their bodily needs, what is the good of that? So faith by itself, if it has no works, is dead.

James 2:14-18.

1
Changing Contexts for Canonical Governance and Formation

One hundred years ago, the religious were running Catholic hospitals and schools with little or no government funding but with enormous amounts of support from the local laity and parish communities. Fifty years ago in the time of Vatican II, the seminaries, convents and novitiates were full. Today, the hospitals and schools in Australia and other Western countries rely on government funding for their recurrent and capital needs and are staffed almost exclusively by lay people from variety of faith backgrounds – how times have changed! The 'Catholic world', like the wider social world has experienced a rapid cultural shift. The former assumptions about how things are and how things will and should be, simply no longer hold.

Nowhere are these changes more apparent than in the increasing role of the professional laity in the governance of the large and complex Church ministries of health, education and social welfare. In previous times, it was a given that the important strategic decisions about the purpose and priorities of the ministry would be made by 'the Bishop' or 'Father' or 'Brother' or 'Mother Superior' – and it was not uncommon for such deliberations to take place around the meal tables of presbyteries, monasteries, and convents! As the numbers of religious, especially those involved in the governance of the ministries, continues to fall across most Western countries, increasing numbers of lay people are being called to assume responsibility and exercise stewardship for those ministries – both civilly and canonically. For many in the Church, this is new territory. The increasing involvement and responsibility of the laity to maintain the requirements of a ministry, theologically and canonically, for the mission of the Church raises some critical questions: Are these people up to the task? Is the Church hierarchy ready and willing to accept them? What personal attributes and expertise should these individuals possess? What questions do they have about their roles? What are their needs? How might they be 'formed' to take on these roles, and how might such processes be similar – and different, from those that have been done before with brothers, sisters and priests?

Governance in the Catholic Church is changing. One feature that is most certainly different is the new governance structures, referred to as emerging Public Juridic Persons (PJPs). These are entities that are created by a legislator and can exist under civil law as well as Canon Law. The Church, through the authority of Canon Law, gives PJP status to an entity in the same manner that governments, through the exercise of civil law, recognise the PJP status of companies established through corporation law. In the 1983 code (Morrisey, 2009) there have been three forms of PJP established under Canon Law: dioceses, parishes, and religious institutes. The new code also allowed for the establishment of alternative PJPs without a great deal of explanation of what they might look like (Canons 114-116). In recent times, new forms of PJP have emerged. Some have been established by a single religious institute. Others have been created by several religious institutes working partnership. Whatever their configuration, these new bodies are being designed to enable continuation of the ministry and therefore require committed, informed, knowledgeable and skilled people to serve in governance roles.

Granting PJP status to a body created under the Code of Canon Law enables it to act 'in the Church's name'. Put simply, this means that its ministry will rightfully be recognised as 'Catholic'. These PJPs consequently have the authority to govern 'Catholic' hospitals, schools, and social welfare agencies. In this book we refer to the 'natural' persons that, for example, sit on the boards of PJPs as canonical governors.

These people may be members of the PJP appointed in their own right, or representatives of members if the creation of the PJP in question allows for other PJPs to be members (Austin, 2011; Morrisey, 2009). In either case, these canonical governors have a key stewardship role for the mission and sustainability of the ministry

Our purpose in this book is to describe the nature and needs for formation for people called to become members of the PJPs in the Catholic Church. In doing so, we deliberately refer to the role of canonical governor as a calling in to leadership to carry out the mission given by Jesus Christ to be a messenger of God's love in the world. In responding to this call, canonical governors are assumed to be believers in the Christian message. But what do we know of these people? How might we find out? And when we do, how do we prepare and support them to understand and fulfill their responsibilities for the mission of the Church in these changing times? These are questions that will be addressed in forthcoming chapters. For the moment, let's take a look back from where we have come, and consider what is needed in these changing times in Church governance.

Changing Times in Church Governance

The event that gave articulation to changes affecting the Church was the Second Vatican Council (1962-1965). This Council, to which all Catholic bishops were invited, was called by Pope John XXIII within 90 days of his election. From the Council came pronouncements calling for changes in how the Church saw itself, and how it interacted with the world. In making these calls, the bishops were not casting out what was believed – even though to some it seemed that this was the case. Rather, they were proclaiming a preference for an alternative ecclesiology, i.e. a different way of understanding the Church, its meaning and operations, from what was the current predominant way of seeing the Church (Bevans and Schroeder, 2004; Cunningham, 1986). The Council re-examined the traditions of the Church and called for a new approach to how the Church proclaimed the good news of Jesus Christ in a way that was more appropriate to the current times (Kirkwood, 2012b), while also honouring ancient ways for interpreting the Christian message (Bevans and Schroeder, 2004).

The responses to the bishops' calls for change were tumultuous (Arbuckle, 1993). What was proclaimed by the Council had little preparation for being heard by the people in the Church, whether they were members of the clergy or the laity. In particular, there was scant attention given to planned systems for formation of ministers to implement the changes (Confoy, 2008; Schuth, 1999). The consequences have taken decades to come to light and have been intensified by changes which have taken place in the secular world, including the raising of the education level of the people in the Church (which has seen an increase in questioning of doctrines and procedures), and the increasing complexity of living evidenced by science enabling life to be extended through medical development, computers revolutionising communications, and globalisation changing markets and means and forms of production (Cleary, 2007; Morrisey, 2011).

In a concomitant to these changes, the last 30 years of the twentieth century saw a huge decline in the number of priests and religious in Western countries through departures from 'religious life' (Reid, Dixon, and Connolly, 2010) and a dramatic fall in the numbers coming forward to join. The religious had conducted ministries in health, education and welfare which were for the good of people and a significant element of evangelisation, the spreading of the good news of Jesus Christ (Grant and Vandenberg, 1998). The Church had established governance structures to enable these religious, operating in established religious institutes, to conduct the ministries in the name of the Church. However, the fall in the number of religious, the aging of their members and the increased complexity of the professionalism and administration of the ministries, have seen lay people increasingly undertake leadership and managerial roles in the ministries (Kirkwood, 2012b). Throughout this time, the responsibility for governance of the ministries, both canonically and civilly, remained with the religious institutes. However in the last twenty years, the capacity of the religious institutes to fulfil responsibilities in this area has fallen and seen the creation of new entities with lay people undertaking greater responsibility for governance (Austin, 2011; Grant and Vandenberg, 1998; Kelly and Mollison, 2005; Schweickert, 2002).

Canonical governance has been described as the stewardship of the Church's resources for mission (see Grant and Vandenberg, 1998, p. 122). For centuries in the eyes and mind of Church leaders, governance belonged to those 'in sacred orders' (Canon 129§1). This has traditionally meant priests and bishops, not the laity (Rinere, 2003), although this has been contested from time to time. For example, canon lawyers debate the meaning of the phrasing in the Code in Canon 129#2 – 'lay members of Christ's faithful can cooperate in the exercise of this same power in accordance with the law', and how broadly this canon might be interpreted (Beal, 1995; Coriden, 2000; Di Pietro, Undated; Huels, 2000; Sweeney, 2005). While these debates continue, lay persons are increasingly being thrust into canonical governance roles with significant stewardship responsibilities. This is because Leaders of religious institutes wish to ensure that the ministries for which they have responsibility have governance 'handed over' appropriately in order that such ministries continue to serve the mission of the Church (Grant and Vandenberg, 1998; Gray, 2005).

While the leaders of religious institutes have their canonical authority in governance of their institute recognised in Canon 596§3, there is uncertainty in how this power can be passed to new governance entities, i.e. Public Juridic Persons, a term for corporate existence in the Roman Catholic Church under Canon Law (Morrisey, 2009, p. 17), which have lay people accountable under Canon 129§2. A major complication is that the understanding of 'governance' in the Church is changing as the Church encounters this new context (Wood, 2009).

The peak body for Catholic health agencies in North America, the Catholic Health Association of the USA (CHAUSA), has recognised such complications and argues that these changing circumstances call for a 'renewed understanding of what constitutes ecclesial ministry and new manifestations of ministerial grace appropriate to our time' (CHAUSA, 2005, p. 25). In other words, they along with others (Arbuckle, 1995; Fox, 2005, 2010; Hahnenberg, 2003; Kirkwood, 2012a, 2012b; Lakeland, 2007; Morrisey, 2002, 2011; Ranson, 2006; Wood, 2003) maintain that the Church needs to adapt from what was taken for granted as the traditional domains and roles of priests and religious in canonical governance and embrace the growing leadership role of the laity. In doing so, they contend that this would be a 'specific affirmation of the vocation all Christians share to witness to the Gospel by deeds of love and service in the world and within the Church' (CHAUSA, 2005b, p. 25).

An important consideration in addressing this challenge is the perceptions of stakeholders about the desired characteristics of those involved in canonical governance, how these characteristics are currently evident, and the type of formation needed to bridge any discrepancies between the actual and the desired characteristics. The stakeholders include bishops in light of their canonical responsibility for all ministries in their diocese (Canons 678; 790), the religious institutes who have been stewards of the ministries (P. Smith, 2006a), and those working in the ministries and who see them as expressions of the mission of bringing the good news of God's love to all people (Bevans, 2009; Karam, 2008; Morrisey, 2002). Recent literature on Church governance indicates that the formation needs for those newly called to canonical governance are yet to be appropriately identified and planned for (Cleary, 2009; Morrisey, 2002; Sweeney, 2005). The nature and analysis of stakeholder perceptions covered in this book is designed to inform this work.

The following sections of this chapter outline the changes in the

Catholic Church and society which led to the creation of new forms and organizations for ministry, including the evolution of the legal notion of a PJP. This historical overview provides the context for our investigation of the nature of formation for canonical governance.

Changes in the Church from Vatican II

The major influence on changes in the Church over the past 50 years has been Vatican II. Within ninety days (!) of his election as Pope in 1958, Pope John XXIII announced to a group of Cardinals his intention of calling a council of all the bishops of the world. The Pope explained that he was motivated 'solely by a concern for the good of souls and in order that the new pontificate may come to grips, in a clear and well-defined way, with the spiritual needs of the present time' (Alberigo and Komonchak, 1995, p. 1). In his opening speech at Vatican II, he spoke of the role of the Council in strengthening the Church so that "she will look to the future without fear. In fact, by bringing herself up to date where required, and by the wise organisation of mutual cooperation, the Church will make men, families, and peoples really turn their minds to heavenly things" (Pope John XXIII, 1962).

The outcomes of Vatican II have both challenged and affirmed the Catholic faithful. Moreover, these outcomes combined with breathtaking social and technological changes in the secular world to produce consequences for the Church that were unimagined in 1965. Several important documents from Vatican II have continued to influence developments in the Church in this topic as it responds to these changes in the wider society. These include *Lumen Gentium* (Abbott, 1966e) on the nature of the Church, *Perfectae Caritatis* (Abbott, 1966g) on the renewal of religious life, *Apostolicam Actuositatem* (Abbott, 1966b) on the apostolate and role of the laity in the Church, *Optatam Totius* (Abbott, 1966f) on priestly formation, *Ad Gentes* (Abbott, 1966a) on the missionary activity of the Church, and *Gaudium et Spes* (Abbott, 1966d) on the role of the Church in the modern world. These documents looked at the Church in a fresh manner. The theological underpinnings of long standing practices were examined. In some cases, this led to a jettisoning of approaches that had been used for centuries. The historical timeline detailing significant Papal events and the release of these documents is shown Figure 1.1.

Figure 1.1 Timeline of events and release of Vatican II documents

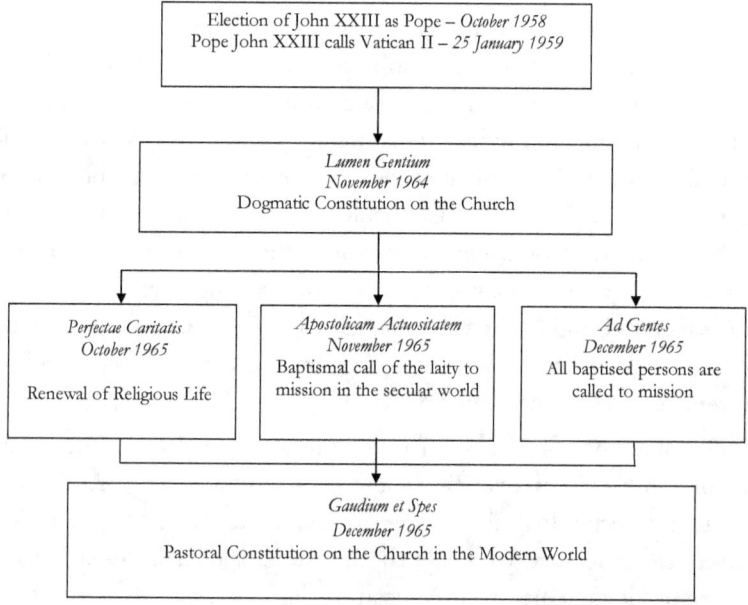

In its final document *Gaudium et Spes* (The joys and hope) on the Pastoral Constitution of the Church in the World, Vatican II recognised that cultural change and modernity were relevant factors in the Church coming to terms with the world. This was in stark contrast to the traditional philosophical approach of centuries past that had assumed stability and perpetual order. This latter perspective has since been criticised as defensive, deductive, neo-scholastic and ahistorical (Gallagher, 2003). For example, Arbuckle (1993) has pointed out that while neo-scholasticism had a coherent intellectual framework, it had one serious disadvantage in that "it was so self-contained that its supporters saw no need to listen to and learn from other philosophies" (p. 23).

In moving away from neo-scholastic philosophy, Vatican II recognised modernity. Toulmin (in Walter Brueggemann, 1993, p. 4) describes modernity as an approach which identifies "the kinds of knowledge that qualify as real knowledge in the horizon of this moment". He identified the characteristics of modernity as a move

- from *oral* to *written*, so that what is reliable is what is written;
- from *the particular* to *the universal*, so that real truth is what is true everywhere;
- from *local* to *general*, so that real truth had to be the same from locale to locale; and
- from *the timely* to the *timeless*, so that real truth is unchanging.

This description of modernity fitted with the approach that the Church had adopted over the centuries with regard to the universality and timelessness of truth. However, much of the substance of *modernity* (as understood by those in the secular world at least) had been created outside the framework of Church authority, and ecclesiastical claims about what could be regarded as true and universal held diminishing sway since the Age of Enlightenment. In other words, the scientific, geographical, industrial developments from the 16th century onwards did not fit the world view which the Church had continued to proclaim into the 20th century. To further complicate matters, proclamations in the documents of Vatican II came at a time when modernism itself was coming to an end as a way of seeing the world, at least in the Western cultures (Gallagher, 2003). So in the years following Vatican II, we had a situation where the Church was opening up to the world, while at the same time the world itself was changing. The impacts of these simultaneously changing Church and Western world cultures have been profound.

Culture has been defined as a 'pervasive pattern of meanings embodied in symbols, a system of conceptions expressed in symbolic forms by means of which [people] communicate, perpetuate, and develop attitudes toward life' (Geertz, cited in Arbuckle, 1993, p. 37). The Mass in Latin, fish on Fridays, Lenten fasts, and sodalities are all examples of cultural elements that gave people meaning. Changes to these elements such as the Vatican II call for liturgy in the vernacular disturbed how people made meaning of their place and participation in the Church. Put simply, changes to cultural practices and symbols change the understanding that people have of their culture. For many in the Church, these are changes that are being continually worked through – in some areas extended, and in some areas reversed!

Debate about changing Church culture came to a dramatic head at Vatican II on the vote as to whether the role of Mary, the Mother of God, would be dealt with in *Lumen Gentium* through describing Mary's role in the Church, or in a separate document focusing on Mary's role in salvation as a mediator between God and humanity. This debate resulted in the closest vote in the council – 1,114 to 1074. Twelve months later, the final document was passed with just five voting against it. Since then, many people have reflected encouragingly on this result. For example, Johnson (2003, p. 127) has noted that:

> Seen theologically, the mentality of non-historical, authoritarian orthodoxy accompanied by a piety that focused on the world to come was out voted by the forces for renewal that called the church to enter into history and engage the social and political implications of the gospel.

This example and the associated tensions involved highlight the difficulty as well as the possibility of cultural change in the Church. The lessons from this narrative provide hope that the cultural changes necessary for meaningful involvement of the laity in canonical governance are possible.

The changes in theological and cultural outlook from Vatican II impacted on Catholic identity in a manner that caused turmoil for many – from those who looked for change and tried to enact it in their lives and communities, to those who sought to maintain the structures and practices of the past at all cost (Leckey, 2006, p. 37). Anthropologist Arbuckle (1993) has described the period as one of chaos, but also as one that was culturally inevitable. Vatican II had proclaimed change, but there was no formation planning in place to enact the changes. Seminaries continued to form priests under the pre-Vatican II model, with little instruction on how or what to change (Confoy, 2008; Schuth, 1999). As a result, what people understood, valued and took for granted as the identity and culture of the Catholic Church, as Arbuckle (1993, p. 36) explains, 'crashed in the late 1960s and early 1970s beyond anything that could have ever been imagined back in 1961'. Changing practices in liturgy and piety led to confusion in theology, religious life, parish life and teaching (Arbuckle, 2010; Gallin, 2000). There was less certainty about what it meant to be Catholic. Significant numbers of the Church leaders continued using authoritarian approaches, but from the late 1960s, many of the laity and lower clergy were not listening (Greeley, 2004, p. 82). Their more extensive education and the questioning approach of that education saw them more openly defiant of Church authority and capable of articulating their own claims. Theologically and spiritually, there was a move from an emphasis on *transcendence* (i.e. that God is above and apart from the material world) to *immanence* (i.e. that God exists in all parts of the created universe) in the ensuing search for holiness (Taylor, 1999). This is recognised in the description of holiness from Fr Richard Lennan (2005, p. 401) as "express[ing] the life of grace, the life of God within us. That life which the tradition associates most directly with the Holy Spirit is a gift from God". In this sense, the task is to make 'holiness' evident in the here and now.

Hence, we have a context where the existence of God and the nature of holiness are being looked at differently. While Vatican II had acknowledged that the world had changed, and that, consequently, the Church needed to change if it were to engage world for the sake of mission, there was a further shift occurring in thinking about the secular world. This has been described as a move from *modernism* to *postmodernism*.

Postmodernism is based on the idea that reality is constructed as we try to understand it, i.e. from our own 'personal reality'. The principles of postmodernism contradict those of the Enlightenment and modernity. For example, postmodernists are sceptical of explanations which claim to be valid for all groups, cultures, traditions, or races, and instead focus on the relative truths of each person (Arbuckle, 2013). The implications for canonical governance and formation are that in moving from the universal to the local and the individual, formation needs to be flexible enough to build in the needs of individuals and local communities and their understandings of Catholic identity. Thus we can see how the characteristics of modernity from Toulmin's model (as described in Brueggemann, 1993, p. 6) need to be reversed when looking at the world from a postmodernist perspective. For example, Brueggemann argues that a range of shifts in thinking and action are involved, namely from *written* to *oral*, from *universal* to *particular*, from *general* to *local*, and from *timeless* to *timely*. Accordingly, thinking and knowing in a postmodern world is characterised by contextualisation, localisation and pluralism (Brueggemann, 1993, p. 8).

The implications of postmodern thinking on canonical governance are significant. Those undertaking these leadership roles need to understand their responsibility to know and reflect upon Scripture and Church teaching, while also exercising the freedom and courage to read the signs of the times and act accordingly – as was called for in *Gaudium et Spes* (Abbott, 1966a). Arbuckle (2007b) highlights this very point in proffering The Good Samaritan parable as the essential model for Catholic identity in the ministry of health care.

The postmodernist approach of moving away from certainty to questioning sources encouraged the re-reading of the core Christian biblical texts and looking at them in context rather than as universals.

This saw the development of Narrative Theology as an approach to interpreting the Scriptures (Brueggemann, 1997). This approach involves asking questions such as to why was the story remembered. Who was the audience? Why was it written and re-interpreted? This seeking of the meaning of the ancient documents in their context fitted well with the call to interpret them for the present. This is seen as a positive consequence of the advent of postmodernism. One implication of a postmodernist perspective for formation of leaders for canonical governance is that the questions for interpreting scripture need to be relevant for the narrative of the ministries, their relationship to Church, and most importantly to the audience, their needs and their capacity to read the signs of the times in the light of the history.

The Changing Role of Religious Institutes

Following the call for change in *Lumen Gentium*, the bishops of Vatican II went on to explore its implications in *Perfectae Caritatis*. These related to the need for religious to *be involved in a process of renewal*, which encouraged 'a continuous return to the sources of all Christian life and to the original inspiration behind a given community'; and to *adapt* which involved 'an adjustment of the community to the changed conditions of the times' (Abbott, 1966g, p. 168). *Perfectae Caritatis* was directive over a wide range of matters affecting religious life, including governance, manner of living and praying, preparation for ministry and dress (Confoy, 2008). These calls were far-reaching and, as with other areas of Vatican II proclamation, the religious were ill-prepared for implementing the changes envisaged (Confoy, 2008). Combined with the revolutionary cultural changes occurring in the Western world at this time, Arbuckle (1987, p. 3) contends:

> Many religious and their communities went into a state of cultural malaise, confusion or anomie – or what is popularly called 'culture shock'. This triggered off the movement

in which thousands withdrew from religious life and the priesthood.

As well as the withdrawal of the religious, there was a significant decline in the number seeking to join religious communities. The call for change from Vatican II had consequences far beyond what had been envisaged and in very different directions (Reid et al., 2010). One of those 'different directions', or unintended consequences, has been the call (and in fact, the necessity) for lay people to undertake civil and canonical governance roles in education, health and welfare ministries which the religious had built up for the mission of the Church. At the same time, religious institutes recognised that they could no longer maintain the diversity and level of involvement in these ministries and set about re-imagining and redesigning their roles. This has been most evident in their efforts in the areas of induction and formation of lay staff, and in pastoral outreach activity – for example in underprivileged communities and Third World countries.

This re-imagining of their role has been taking place since Vatican II, where the bishops reaffirmed the role of religious as men and women who, as a result of a call from the Holy Spirit, sought to lead their lives following Christ in a particular way with vows of poverty, chastity and obedience with the goal of personal holiness and salvation. This way was usually in a community life with the purpose of building up of the Church through the ministries of prayer, teaching, healing, caring in missionary situations, the following of migrants to new lands, and going to places where the Christian message has not been heard. In keeping with the tradition of the Church's social teaching and mission, the service of members of religious institutes has been directed to the poor and misplaced. The bishops saw that such a life as a necessary role to play in the circumstances of the present age, and stated this in *Perfectae Caritatis* (Abbott, 1966g, n. 1).

Historically, new forms of religious life have emerged in response to new needs in the Church and the world. This is succinctly summed up by Schweickert (2002, p. 1) who describes successive incarnations of religious life as involving 'the virgins and widows, the desert ascetics, the monastics, the mendicants, the apostolic congregations, [and] the ministerial orders'. The 16th to 20th centuries saw a large increase in the number of religious and a significant expansion of the ministries (Seasoltz, 2003). One of the changes that accompanied these developments was the dispensing of the services "not by individuals on a one to one basis, but through large-scale institutions" (Wittberg, 2006, p. 9). This framework of institution, both in service and in community living, was the dominant mode of life for those joining religious life until the dramatic changes brought about by the confluence of the postmodernist world and Vatican II since the mid 1960s.

Over the past 50 years, the *framework of institution* for brothers and nuns has been augmented, and in some cases replaced by a *framework of smaller groups and individuals*. Wittberg (2006) noted that most religious traditions have a group of people she refers to as *religious virtuosi* whose role is focused on attaining and helping others to attain some form of inner spiritual perfection or holiness. This group increased significantly in the Catholic tradition in the 19th and 20th centuries and the members were particularly engaged in the ministries of health and education. This shift has increasingly involved religious stepping back from the 'front line delivery' of traditional ministries, and taking a more pronounced stewardship role, especially over matters of understanding and adherence to the special spirituality, or charism, underpinning the ministry work authorised by, and carried out in the name of the religious institute. These 'religious virtuosi' have also been involved as canonical governors whose role is to assume direct responsibility for maintaining the requirements of the ministry, theologically and canonically for the mission of the Church. Current trends indicate that these forms of ministry involvement are now becoming less common, with the consequent issue of whether lay person governors are willing and able to be the new virtuosi. As the religious move on, questions of canonical leadership and formation needed for the task of continuing the ministries need to be addressed.

Changing Relationships between Religious Institutes and Bishops

Under Canon Law, religious institutes can be established by the Holy See or by a diocesan bishop (Canon 579). Whatever the origins, an Institute may only operate in a diocese with the permission of the diocesan bishop (Austin, 2011). It is important to note that the religious and their ministries are in the service of the Church which operates through a diocese under the leadership of the bishop who has the responsibility to coordinate "all apostolic works and actions, with due respect for the character and purpose of each institute and the laws of its foundation" (Canon 680). Religious institutes also have rights under Canon Law. However, there is a need for some "fluidity" when addressing matters where the law is not clear as to who has authority to make certain appointments (Cusack, 2006). History has examples of where religious who had been invited into a diocese by a bishop, then saw the need to leave when the bishop seemed not to support the character and purpose of the institute. On the other hand, there is a long history of religious working with deep commitment to the ministry and the people of the diocese in harmony with their bishop, as the hierarchical leader with pastoral responsibility for the people of his diocese. Changes in the governance of the ministries are seeing bishops needing to relate to different types of canonical governor. These people may not come from a particular institute but rather from newly established PJPs which may consist of various religious institutes and related agencies, and are led by a combination of religious and lay people, or increasingly, lay people. These circumstances have profound implications for both parties.

To appreciate some of these implications, let's take a step back to consider why the religious institutes developed the ministries in the first place. The religious have ministered to people's needs in the name of the Church for the purpose of the mission and the salvation of the soul of the individual who joined the life. According to Schneiders (2001), these individuals joined the order because they wanted to dedicate their life to God and to their neighbour. In many cases this was because they were inspired by the example of the religious they knew.

The ministries of many of the religious institutes are strategies to achieve the mission, for example, the Congregation of Christian Brothers' Constitution 24 (1996) states that the brothers 'are missioned by the Church for the evangelisation of youth, particularly the materially poor'. While the Congregation was not specifically 'missioned' to conduct schools – that was one of the significant aspects of ministry by which it has sought to be true to the mission. In times past, this also involved running teachers' colleges to prepare brothers to teach in Christian Brothers' schools. This work of integrating congregational life and ministry was the usual pattern for religious institutes of pre-Vatican II era. The interaction of the life and the ministry shaped the meaning system of the congregation (Cleary, 2007) and provided the means for the charism of the congregation to be recognised and treasured. The post-Vatican II era is proving to be something quite different for religious institutes. In short, they are at increasing risk of losing the connection with their ministries, and consequently their connection with their meaning system and their charism (Wittberg, 2006).

The combination of Vatican II's call to change and the broader societal changes since the 1960s has been seen as the reason why so many priests and religious decided to leave in the years following Vatican II (Confoy, 2008). In the midst of these impacts on religious life were writers who spoke of the need to *rethink* (Turner, 1986), to *re-evaluate* (Schneiders, 1986) and to *refound* (Arbuckle, 1987; Wittberg, 1991) religious life. These calls have been made courageously and sometimes with painful consequences. Various images used have been used to describe the nature of the context and what has to be done, for example *crossroads* (Schweickert, 2002), *journey* (Barnett, 2005) and *letting go* (Gottemoeller, 1991; Grant and Vandenberg, 1998). In each case, these writers are dealing with changes in the meaning and purpose of religious life when it is no longer focused on the institutional ministries that the members had taken for granted. In fact, they recognise that the ministries' needs have moved beyond the skills and capacities of the remaining members of the religious institutes – yet the congregation still had the canonical and civil responsibility for the institutions which were providing the ministries. Consequently they argue that the challenge for the religious is to find ways to ensure that the ministries are governed well (but differently!) and continue to faithfully serve the mission of the Church (Fox, 2008; Gottemoeller, 2005; Hehir, 2008; McArdle, 2010).

As we move into the 21st century, emerging needs in the Church and the means for dealing with them are expected to be much less institutionalised (Schneiders, 2001; Wittberg, 2006). Leaders of the religious institutes need to ensure that the sacred tasks in ministry for which the institute has held responsibility in the name of the Church, are passed to others who understand what is being asked of them. How others understand what is being asked of them, and how they respond, depends on their faith and their understanding of theology and the Church. In contrast to the particular charism and model of theology and Church adopted by particular religious institutes, emerging arrangements for canonical governance are likely to display much more diversity. This is because the members will be increasingly drawn from the laity with varying degrees of familiarity with particular religious institute traditions. Hence the challenge will be foster understanding and cohesion around the more general (and fundamental) topic of Catholic identity. A key component of these endeavors invariably involves consideration and appreciation of different ways of understanding theology and viewing and engaging with the Church.

Valuing Different Models of Theology and Church

As the mission of the Church is the good news of God's kingdom, a significant element of the context is an understanding of God, expressed in the theology. Macquarrie (in Lennan, 1998, pp. 13-

14) set out the elements and study of theology as proceeding from a religious faith'. Macquarrie claimed that this proceeding required an understanding of 'faith', that it is a human activity; is not the preserve of any one religion; and is done by people who bring their personal faith into dialogue with an already existing tradition. From this base, Lennan (1998) proposed that the dimensions of Catholic theology are to:

- embrace the human desire to seek meaning;
- encompass the conviction that God can be known by human beings and that God is known to us most fully in Jesus Christ;
- believe God's life giving presence continues in history through the Holy Spirit, the Spirit of the risen Jesus who sustains the Church and moves the human heart to be open to God, particularly the God revealed in the Bible;
- believe faith in Jesus is lived within the community of the Church and that those in authority within the Church – the College of Bishops under the leadership of the Pope – have a particular responsibility for nurturing the Church in unity; and
- believe faith leads to shaping the understanding of self and neighbour, and seeking engagement with the world in mission.

This approach to theology shapes the practices, liturgical expressions and doctrines which gave life to meaning systems in the Catholic Church (Cleary, 2007). These in turn influence how we understand and express what it means to be a church and a member of the Church. These questions are complex, for while we may agree (in faith) on the following of Jesus in bringing the good news of God's kingdom to the world, we may differ on what this means in practice.

The study of how we and others understand the Church is called 'ecclesiology'. McBrien (1994, p. 1238) has defined ecclesiology as 'the theological study of the Church'. One means of approaching such study is through considering different models (or images) of the Church. For example, Dulles (1987) has nominated the following:

- The Church as Institution.
- The Church as Mystical Communion.
- The Church as Sacrament.
- The Church as Herald.
- The Church as Servant.

Dulles (1987, p. 11) refers to these models as 'avenues [to] approach to the mystery of the Church'. We believe this thinking is crucial because without an awareness of the different ways of 'being church', individuals and groups can become dogmatic that their model is the only way of getting to God and doing God's work.

Just as there are different ways of understanding the Church, there are also different approaches to theology, or the study of God. In the Catholic tradition, three major approaches (or types) have been identified. An overview of these approaches over the life of the Church and their historical origins has been developed by Gonzales (in Bevans and Schroeder, 2004, p. 37) as shown in Figure 1.2.

Figure 1.2 Ways of approaching theology

	Type A Theology	Type B Theology	Type C Theology
Origin	Carthage	Alexandria	Antioch
Culture	Roman	Hellenistic	Near Eastern
Key Figure	Tertullian	Origen	Irenaeus
Key Word	Law	Truth	History
Trajectory	Augustine Anselm of Canterbury Aquinas Protestant Orthodoxy Fundamentalism Neo-Thomism	Abelard Schleiermacher Liberal Protestantism Mohler Lonergan Rahner	Francis of Assisi Early Luther Wesley Barth Teilhard de Chardin Gutierrez
Christology	Person: High	Person: Premodern: High Modern: Low	Person: Low
Ecclesiology	Institution	Mystical Communion Sacrament	Herald/Servant
Eschatology	Futurist Individual	Realised Individual	Inaugurated Historical
Salvation	Spiritual	Premodern: Spiritual illumination Modern: Holistic	Holistic
Anthropology	Negative Hierarchical	Positive Premodern: Hierarchical Modern: Equality	Positive Premodern: less Hierarchical Modern: Equality

Culture	Premodern: Classicist	Premodern: Classicist	Premodern: Classicist
	Counter-cultural or translation models	Modern: Empirical Anthropological model	Modern: Empirical Praxis or moderate counter-cultural models
Figures in Mission	Francis Xavier	Cyril and Methodius. Matteo Ricci, Max Warren, John Mbiti	East Syrian Monks Francis of Assisi Liberation theologians

Source: Gonzales (in Bevans and Schroeder, 2004, p. 37)

The key point is that each type of theology has ancient origins and traditions in the Church, and that over time particular types of theology fluctuate in prominence. For example, Bevans and Schroder (2004) argue that the dominant theology of the 19th and 20th centuries was Type A. They warn that the danger of any dominant mode of theology is that it can deem alternative views not only unorthodox, but also wrong or heretical.

Type A is based on the dictum: 'keep the law and the law will keep you'. The emphasis is on the Church as an institution that can exert control. The High Christology language of the 'god-ness' or divinity of Jesus, the 'God-man', is emphasised rather than the humanity of Jesus. While the belief is that humanity is basically good, the capacity to get it wrong is emphasised. Hence the law is there to command rather than guide followers to spiritual fulfillment. O'Meara (1999) claims that Type A had been the major influence for most of the history of the Church:

> For fifteen hundred years a structure of the Christian churches, the form (often the sole form) of the diversity

has been not Christ and his Body, not the Spirit with its gifts, but clergy and laity (pp. 158-159).

Vatican II re-imagined the Church, not with something entirely new, but with an emphasis on alternative ancient traditions, as Bevans and Schroeder (2004, pp. 65-66) explain:

> In many ways, the ecclesiology of the Second Vatican Council was influenced by Type B theology. The revolution at the council was the move from an understanding of the church as a hierarchical, perfect society ... to an understanding of the church as a community, the people of God mystically united to Christ.

What's more, Bevans and Schroeder (2004) suggest that the seeds of Type C were also there in *Ad Gentes* – Decree on the Church's Missionary Activity and in *Gaudium et Spes* – The Pastoral Constitution on the Church in the Modern World.

The consequences of these Vatican II documents on formation for governance and other forms of ministry were not immediately evident. Much of the formation taking place was still based on Type A ecclesiology. In fact Arbuckle (1993) argued that significant changes were not apparent until the early 1990s; and that even at that time he was expressing fears about the 'restorationist' activity going on in the Church, designed to bring the world back to Type A orthodoxy (pp. 18-20).

The call of Vatican II saw the move away from the neo-scholastic theology which had dominated church thinking, practice and governance for centuries. The postmodernist world saw the development of practical theologies (D'Orsa and D'Orsa, 2010; Lynch, 1998; Tracy, 1983). These ways of understanding God were viewed as diverse and local rather than global, as Lynch (1998, p. 168) explains:

> local theologies give priority to criteria drawn from the cultural or political experience of particular groups rather

than to the more traditional academic and, usually, male dominated categories that presented themselves as timeless and independent of any one culture.

This stance on pluralism acknowledged the perspectives of women, the poor and the indigenous. It also explored the perspective of the laity finding God in the secular world as well as in their increasing ecclesial role (Muldoon, 2009). This breadth of perspectives was highlighted by Ormerod (1997) in his overview of the approaches of noted theologians including Kung, Moore, Schillebeeckx, Rahner, Lonergan, Metz, Guiterrez, Boff, Fiorenza, Johnson and Ruether. Significantly, while his analysis presented the diversity in starting points, contexts and conclusions, it nevertheless demonstrated the unity of belief among the people of the Church.

Bevans (2002) emphasised a similar point in his analysis of the contextual approaches to theology, described in terms of the following models:

- Translation.
- Anthropological.
- Praxis.
- Synthetic.
- Transcendental.
- Countercultural.

Our purpose in referring to these models is to highlight the point that there is no single way of studying and understanding God. Consequently leaders in the Church, including canonical governors, need to be aware of the different approaches and be able to determine what is most relevant and useful in their particular situation when reading the signs of the times for their ministry.

The Changing Role of Laity in the Church

Just as the bishops wrote a section on Religious Life in *Lumen Gentium* and then dealt more fully with this theme in *Perfectae Caritatis*, they used the same approach reflecting on the role of the laity in the Church in the world. The Decree on the Laity was entitled *Apostolicam Actuositatem*. The radical idea expressed in this document was the statement of the responsibility of all Christians, not just the clergy, for the spreading of the good news and the bringing about of the kingdom of God (Leckey, 2006). This aspect of renewal placed the proclamation of the salvific mission of the Church through the sacraments of baptism and confirmation, rather than primarily through the sacrament of orders which had been the view dominating the operation of the Church.

This was a significant shift in thinking in that it recovered the role of all Christians and dignified the place of all members of the Church as carriers of the good news (Leckey, 2006; Muldoon, 2009). Moreover, it articulated that the place of carrying out this task was in the secular world. Hagstrom (2003, pp. 155-156) has expressed the distinctive contribution of the laity in the following terms:

> The laity's relationship to the world gives the lay apostolate a special character. The emphasis here is on identity, not function ... The laity, because of their secular character, make the Church present and operative in the world in a way distinct from that of clerics and religious.

The Vatican proclamation of the laity's role in their family, workplace and social life contributed to the development of a theology of the laity which had been growing through the work of theologians, including Yves Congar who viewed Church ministries as activities of the whole community of believers (Fox, 2003, p. 140; Lynch, 1998, p. 173). This renewed understanding of the community of the Church as the 'People of God' was given further depth in *Apostolicam Actuositatem* as the bishops fleshed out what they had said in *Lumen Gentium*, as noted by Hagstrom (2003, p. 156).

If the life of the laity in the world is *in itself* an instrument of the Church's mission, then the everyday activities of the laity can take on a redemptive value. Thus, temporal activities are not simply a *means* but also an *end* in themselves to exercising the apostolate of the laity.

In these writings, the secular nature of the life of the laity is being expressed as a theological reality. And, it is through this life that the laity can deepen their relationship with God and carry the message of hope to the world. Associated with this thinking is the question about formation of the laity especially those in professional and in volunteer roles in the Church. This relates to the need for formation, and to form and content of formation programmes for the laity. This is new territory in the Church, especially where it relates to laity with responsibilities for the governance and management of Church ministries.

Prior to Vatican II, theology (in the Catholic Church at least!) had been almost exclusively taught by clergy in seminaries to men in priestly formation. Since then, more programmes in theology have been established and made more widely available to religious and lay people (Leckey, 2006, p. 10). These developments have been particularly significant for those seeking to become teachers and principals in Catholic schools; nurses, doctors and administrators in Catholic hospitals; and counsellors, case workers, and directors in Catholic social welfare agencies. In addition, there have been growing numbers of lay people who have become academics in theology, not only at the universities, but also at the seminaries themselves. This has occurred in the decades following Vatican II when the number of religious was falling dramatically in the Western world and their work and leadership in the ministries was being carried out increasingly by lay people. Their contribution has since become vital to the mission of the Church.

The Coming of New Leadership in Ministry

While inspiring to many, the call of Vatican II provided little readiness and few strategies for the changes to be enacted. Ricoeur, who had authored the phrase 'hermeneutics of suspicion', explained that 'if you want to change behavior, you must first change imagination'. The bishops had written the words, as a starting point to *change imagination*, but the confusion that their call had on existing imagination of many in the Church is taking some decades to clear. People have needed time and guidance to interpret what had been said and then to consider how to implement the ideas, priorities, and principles associated with the Vatican II documents. This has been especially evident in countries where increasingly educated Catholic lay people continue to seek new ways of taking up the call (Wood, 2003). Put simply, in the years following Vatican II, many set about creating a range of pathways with much enthusiasm and generosity – but with limited formation in the new understanding of ancient traditions.

We are currently in a period where the scale and scope of involvement of lay people in Church ministries is unprecedented. The questions of leadership, governance, canonical integrity and formation to sustain the mission are now critical. Moreover, enthusiasm and generosity needs to be underpinned by thorough understanding of the meaning, purpose and principles of the ministry in which we are engaged, together with a deep knowledge of ourselves and an informed appreciation of the gifts we bring to this work in the Church.

Grant and Vandenberg (1998) have set out the history of the movement from ministries governed and operated by religious institutes to ministries where lay people are in management and governance roles. They use the term 'sponsorship' to refer to the governance roles taken up by those (religious and lay) people who as members of a recognised Catholic organisation enter into a formal relationship with their diocese (through the bishop), their parish (through the priest) and/or a religious institute (through the Congregational Leader) for the purpose of promoting and sustaining the Church's mission (Smith, Brown and Reynolds, 2006). Because of its association with commercial advertising, the term 'sponsorship' has caused confusion in certain quarters. For these reasons we have decided to use the term 'canonical governance', as referring to the carrying of the responsibility of the ministry in the light of the Code of Canon Law of the Roman Catholic Church. Thus, we equate the phrase 'sponsorship of ministries', for example as used in the North American health sector (CHAUSA, 2007b), with the concept of 'canonical governance of a PJP'.

The evolution of management, organizational structure and governance of Church ministries, based on the initial work done by Grant and Vandenberg relating to Catholic healthcare, is shown in Table 1.1. It summarizes the changes from when all roles were done by the members of the religious institutes to the present. As these changes progress, we are seeing increasing professionalization, specialisation and involvement of the laity as workers, managers, administrators and governors of Church ministries.

Table 1.1
Evolution of Management, Organizational Structure, and Governance Arrangements of Church Ministries

Period	Management	Organisation Structure	Governance Arrangements	
			Decision-Making Entity	Canonical Governance (Sponsorship)
Pre-1960	Local superior as Chief Executive Officer	Stand alone, independent healthcare facilities; schools run and governed by congregations	Local superior and council	Term not defined, identified with religious

1960s	Predominantly religious, few lay persons; appointments by the religious congregation leadership	Beginnings of centralised services in education and health, generally through motherhouse offices	All-religious boards; emergence of lay advisory boards in hospitals and schools	Beginning of formal definition: tied to appointments of chief executives and boards; synonymous with presence of religious
1970s	Increasing numbers of lay people in executive positions in schools and hospitals	Development of healthcare systems, generally based within single congregation	Formally constituted boards of religious and laity serving together	Emerging role of the laity in influencing canonical governance; withdrawal of congregational sponsorship
1980s	Partnership of religious and laity serving in executive leadership	Alliances, networks and multi-congregation; arrangements; health systems; college university consortia	Boards with increasing integration of lay and religious roles	Searching for means for linking management and canonical governance responsibilities
1990s	Professional management; full incorporation of laity into ministry	Large integrated regional and national health and education systems; school mergers	Emergence of professional boards (including remuneration for board members)	Development of models for distinctive governance responsibilities of lay and religious
2000 and beyond	Continuing professional management in hospitals, schools and school systems	Continuing consolidation of health and education ministries at the systemic and local levels	Emergence of governing boards with fiduciary and canonical responsibilities	Increasing range of models for lay involvement and fewer solely religiously governed (i.e. sponsored) organizations

Based on Grant and Vandenberg (1998)

The detail in Table 1.1 is based on the original work of Grant and Vandenberg (1998), and incorporates our insights about the evolution of health and education ministries in Australia since 1960. It is interesting to note that the trends that Grant and Vandenberg predicted are being realised. In 2011, CHAUSA reported that 85 per cent of members of Catholic Health Association USA who currently do not have lay canonical governors expect that by 2016 they are most likely to have moved to that position (Catholic Health World, 2011a). This finding emphasizes that lay people are becoming more and more involved at all levels of the ministries, as religious relinquish, or are unable to fill various roles. This is evident in the pattern of moving from operational tasks as teachers and nurses to management responsibilities as principals and hospital administrators, and then to governance roles. Along with these changes, the religious institutes that ran Church ministries lost their ability to stand alone. The resulting mergers with other Catholic entities (for example other religious institutes) have seen some ministries lose their distinctive charism. This has brought about the need to identify that which made the entity 'Catholic' in the first place, and which authorised it as to serve the mission of the Church as an ecclesial ministry (Wood, 2009). Most significantly, these changes have seen lay people engaged not only in the secular world (as envisaged by *Apostolicam Actuositatem*), but also in Church ministries as ecclesial workers. In other words, lay people are not only out there serving the mission, but are increasingly taking on roles in the Church where they have a responsibility of canonical stewardship towards it!

In these circumstances, the significance of the question of formation for canonical governors cannot be underestimated. In fact the size of the Catholic health systems in the USA and Australia, as shown in Table 1.2, is a case in point. The senior executives of these organizations not only have the responsibility for the fiscal viability and the professional quality of the services provided, but also the stewardship of the mission from which those services derive their meaning and existence.

Table 1.2
Examples of Catholic Health Systems

Organization	Annual Revenue[1.] stated	Employees	Reference
Ascension Health	15.5 billion	113,500	Ascension Health (2011)
Trinity Health	7.0 billion	53,000	Trinity Health (2011)
Catholic Health East	4.1 billion	54,000	Catholic Health East (2011)
Catholic Healthcare	44.5 million	3,454	Catholic Healthcare Limited (2011)

Sources: Annual Reports from 2010-11.
Note 1. Annual revenue is stated in $US, unless otherwise stated.

Figures on USA health systems show that 6 of the 20 largest systems are Catholic and had revenues between $US 3 and 13.9 billion in 2010 (Modern Healthcare, 2011). These examples indicate the enormity of what is being asked of people who are invited to be stewards of these Church ministries as canonical governors.

Recapping the changing context for Church governance

In this chapter, we have presented an overview of the changing Church and societal contexts for canonical governance and formation. The election of Pope John XXIII and his call for a Second Vatican Council (Vatican II) initiated the Church's renewal and response to a world that is evolving from modernism to postmodernism. The documents from Vatican II interacted with this changing world with significant implications for religious institutes and laity alike, and for the future of Church ministries and the mission they serve.

Allied with these trends was the revision of the 1917 Code of Canon

Law (also initiated by Pope John XXIII), the authorisation of the new code in 1983, and the subsequent changes to various canons related to the language of legal entities, in particular the meaning and possible new forms of PJPs.

New possibilities for canonical governance are raising new questions about the role of the laity, and the stewardship of Church ministries. The particular challenges around the formation of people to undertake these roles are addressed in the next chapter.

2
Forming Professionals for Mission and Ministry

Emerging forms of governance in the Church are creating new opportunities and demands for leaders of Church ministries. In times past, priests, sisters and brothers experienced years of formal preparation in religious spirituality prior to taking on leadership roles (Fox, 2010b; Oakley and Russett, 2004; Wood, 2003). These days, leadership roles in the governance of Church ministries are increasingly being undertaken by lay people with varying degrees of spiritual preparation. As a consequence, the nature and need for formation is more complex, especially in light of the changes that continue to take place in the Church and the wider society. New ways of leading ministries need to be developed, recognised and supported – and these new ways will inevitably involve people formed in lay spirituality. While some programmes have been developed in the United States of America and Australia for the formation of lay leaders, the general focus of these programmes has been for those in senior management rather than board members, or governors. Currently there are a few formation programmes for lay persons who hold canonical authority and have responsibility for ensuring and promoting the mission for which the Church organisation was created in first place. To add to the complexity, it is worth noting that these same people often hold the civil responsibility as well!

In this chapter, we outline those aspects of Canon Law regarding the role of the laity and discuss the need for fresh understandings about Church governance and the nature of formation. We discuss the meaning of the term *formation* and what this implies for lay people in governance roles through considering the two Church documents, *Pastores Dabo Vobis*

(John Paul II, 1992) on priestly formation and *Co-Workers in the Vineyard of the Lord* (USCCB, 2005) on the formation of lay people for roles in the Church. Through analyzing these documents we make the case for a framework for formation based upon four dimensions: human, spiritual, intellectual and pastoral, and for seeing formation as relating to the 'whole person', i.e. the combination and relationships between those dimensions.

New understandings and pathways to governance

Over the centuries, Church governance has been very much the domain of clerics and religious. Formation programmes were designed and delivered to prepare them to run the ministries effectively and efficiently, and to exercise canonical responsibility over them– in other words, to ensure that the ministries were 'Catholic' in the legal-authoritative sense of the term. For example, the 1917 Code of Canon Law reserved jurisdiction, or governance to clerics (Austin, 2011; Beal, 1995). In contrast, lay people have traditionally been given little to no authority in canonical governance, and consequently have been seen as having little to no need for formation for such roles. While Vatican II with its different theological approach proclaimed the significance of the laity and their baptismal call to mission, the wording in *Lumen Gentium* (n. 33) and related Vatican documents were somewhat ambiguous as to how this might happen, or what roles might occur, or how such roles might be filled (Beal, 2006).

This ambiguity provided a major problem, both in the Council and in the years preceding the proclamation of the new Code of Canon Law in 1983. Two schools of thought existed in this debate: one that there should be no suggestion of delegation to laity of governance powers; and the other that there should be a clear intent for laity to be involved in governance not associated with priestly responsibilities (Beal, 1995, pp. 18-52). This debate culminated in the wording of the 1983 Code of Canon Law in Clause 129§1 where the authority of the clergy was explained as follows:

Those who are in sacred orders are, in accordance with the provision of law, capable of the power of governance, which belongs to the Church by divine institution. This power is also the power of jurisdiction.

This was followed by Clause 129§2 where a new concept flowing from Vatican II was added: 'Lay members of Christ's faithful can cooperate in the exercise of this same power in accordance with the law'.

These revised canons left room for interpretation as to the part that laity could play in Church governance. The historical reality around this time (circa 1983) was that falling numbers meant that fewer clerics and religious were available for governance roles in many of the ministries. For some, this was a theological question rather than a legal one (Beal, 2004). Others, such as Huels (2000), put a case for lay involvement in governance from a juridical approach. In addition, Beal (1995, p 85) highlighted the value of reflecting on the Church as *communio* (i.e. a community of believers) rather than a *perfect society* which had been the model that had underpinned pre- Vatican II theology (Austin, 2011). The case was put strongly by Coriden (2000) that there was ample evidence from *Lumen Gentium* that Vatican II intended to reclaim a place for the laity in governance roles. He gave examples of lay people in significant positions in the Church as judges in tribunals, school principals, and directors of social services, noting that:

> The Canons of the Code explicitly provide for many of these offices. To pretend that these key leaders of the Church's ministry do not share in the power of governance is to perpetuate a fiction (Coriden 2000, p. 126).

Hence we have had a mixture of pragmatic, canonical-legal, and theological issues at play. Pragmatically, the question is what to do about meeting governance requirements as the number of priests, brothers and nuns continue to dwindle. Legally, the question is what is allowed under Canon Law. Theologically, the question is what should be the proper role of the laity in governance – and at a more fundamental level: *what is God's will in all of this?* While these questions remain unresolved and continue to be noted in the literature, the reality is that increasing numbers of lay people are taking on governance roles in the Public Juridic Persons (PJPs) that have been created since the proclamation of the 1983 Code of Canon Law.

Along with this phenomenon, the post Vatican II era has seen increasing numbers of Catholic lay people undertaking theological and spiritual formation for themselves. They have been encouraged to do so by their family, friends, pastors and employers in the light of their baptismal responsibilities and the need for ministry (Dixon, 2005; Hahnenberg, 2009; Lakeland, 2009; Leckey, 2006, 2009). This has been evident and important for those working at the forefront of teaching, welfare and health ministries. While those leading these ministries have had the dual priority of supporting the career development and spiritual growth of their staff, there has not been the same degree of clarity and emphasis on the capabilities and needs of those involved in canonical governance with its responsibility for mission.

There may be a number of reasons for this, but an overriding theme is that the involvement of the laity in Church governance is relatively new territory. Governance of Church ministries by lay people does not have the centuries-old traditions of the religious institutes. With increasing involvement of the laity, new understandings and pathways to governance are called for, particularly in relation to the nature of individuals' formation. One means of heeding this call is to view the preparation, induction and development of lay persons for governance roles as a three-fold task of (i) defining the elements in formation, (ii) assessing individuals' needs, and (iii) developing the programmes to meet those needs. This is becoming even more challenging given that these leadership roles are becoming more complex as demands in the ministries grow in the light of continuing technological, social, and economic change.

Much of the literature of the past twenty years has told the *story of how the change to lay involvement in canonical governance was enacted* (Bonnell, 1992; Burns, 2006; Eck and Morris, 2005a, 2005b; Ferrera, 2000; Gray, 2005; Kaiser, Tersigni, Serle, and Dover, 2007); *concerns about Catholic Identity for mission* (Arbuckle, 2006, 2007a, 2010; Gallin, 2000; Gascoigne, 1995; Gottemoeller, 1991, 1999, 2007; Hehir, 2008; Morrisey, 2001a); *what needed to be in formation programmes for canonical governors [aka 'sponsors']* (Abeles, 2008; Canales, 2008; Golden, 2006; M. K. Grant and M. Kopish, 2001; K. Homan, 2004; M. Kelly, 2007; Peters, Conroy, Lunz, Mollison, and Munley, 2003; P. Smith, 2006a); along with *sample formation programmes for canonical governors [aka sponsors]* (M. Kelly, 2007; M. Kelly and Mollison, 2005; Maltby, 2007). There has also been significant writing on the need for the *development of a theology of canonical governance [aka 'sponsorship']* (Bouchard, 2008; Casey, 1991, 2000, 2005; Downey, 2003; Grant and Vandenberg, 1998; Hester, 2000; Lynch, 1998; O'Meara, 1999; Peters, 2005; Place, 2004; Rinere, 2003; Talone, 2004, 2005); and increasingly on the *place of lay spirituality in the Church* (Bechtle, 2005; Downey, 2005; Fox, 2005a, 2010b; Fox and Bechtle, 2005; Hahnenberg, 2003; Hellwig, 2005; Pirola, 1995; Rush, 2007; Statuto, 2004). This literature reveals much about what is needed to be understood with regard to mission, Catholic identity, lay spirituality and formation for governance. The importance of an individual's personal development and formation is highlighted, especially in terms of how these relate the needs of the ministry.

Compared with their religious predecessors, lay people have come to governance roles via different pathways. In working for the mission of the Church, they bring their own life story and spirituality. Increasingly, they are being asked to be the 'sense makers' and to understand the nature and articulate the story of ministries with which they may be relatively unfamiliar (Chait et al., 2005). This can be a cause of anxiety for some. For example we are aware of people who have been invited to take governance responsibility for a health system and yet never sat beside a patient in a hospital. Similarly we know of board members who cannot articulate exactly how and why their organisation came to be labeled as 'Catholic'. This diversity of background means that the traditions and possibilities of formation for canonical governance require careful consideration. This will involve not only imagination and creativity but also an informed awareness of the signs of the times and the wisdom of the past. In short, developing new understandings and pathways to governance is a leadership challenge.

The leadership of Church ministries sits within the broader context of leadership of non-profit organizations. While these entities encompass a wide range of activities from international aid agencies to small social clubs, all are driven by the desire to bring about some good for their community. This characteristic is reflected in the descriptor *non-profit* which demonstrates that the activity is not operated to provide returns in the form of dividends for the benefit of those who have invested money in the expectation of increasing their personal income (Chait et al., 2005). Governments have recognised the difference between *for profit* and *non-profit* organizations by enacting laws which allow for a range of concessions for the latter by way of tax exemption.

While there is a range of legitimate motivations for *non-profit* status, an accepted view is that religion has been a significant motivator of non-profit activity in much of the Western world (Cleary, 2007, p. 73). Given that the focus of the religious activity is mission (i.e. proclaiming, serving and witnessing God's love in the world), there is no surprise here. Historically, the religious institutions of the 18th and 19th centuries saw needs in health and education and set out to do something about them – often in circumstances when the state or the nation did not! Over more recent times, the provision of health and education services has increasingly been accepted as the responsibility of government. This responsibilities have been fulfilled either directly through the provision of public schools and hospitals, or indirectly through funding support to non-government providers of such services. At the same time, distinctions between *for profit* and *non-profit* provision of health and education services have become blurred and contentious. Non-profit schools and hospitals are finding themselves in competition with government contractors and private providers, and are being criticised not just for the tax exemptions but also for the service and employment concessions they receive from the state. Leaders of these mission-based entities are being increasingly challenged about matters such as the medical procedures their organizations will not perform and the faith backgrounds of staff they wish to employ.

Despite the sometimes subtle and sometimes stark distinctions between *for profit* and *non-profit* agencies, the maxim of 'no margin, no mission' rings true. Certainly there is no doubt that non-profit, mission-based organizations need to exercise prudence in financial dealings. But while leading a Church organisation may have much in common with running a private sector business at least in terms of having a viable balance sheet and meeting civil law compliances, the task is much more complicated. Authentic leaders in Church ministries understand that the bottom line of profit is not their driving motivation. Rather, they recognise that the mission comes from the Church and that the organization's existence and their position of authority is a consequence of the dreams, prayers, talents and hard work of those that have gone before.

Another perspective on the leadership of Church ministries relates to the distinctions between the terms 'governance' and 'management'. Leaders are required to fulfill both roles from time to time – just as the religious did in times past. One way of distinguishing between these terms is to describe governance as a decision making process designed to transform the values of those who have a stake in the organisation into performance. Management on the other hand refers to the carrying out of these decisions, for example by allocating and mobilising the organization's resources. We define leadership as *a relational process of influence that makes a positive and meaningful difference to those working in, and served by the particular ministry*. Applying this definition, leadership is evident in both governance and management to the extent that the actions of governors and managers make a difference in the lives of those they serve.

The Church and its agencies are entering a new phase in relation to leadership and governance. In fact the expansion of such responsibilities beyond the clergy and religious raised the question as to whether these new responsibilities themselves may be seen as a ministry – the ministry of governance. This question has been discussed by a range of writers and Church authorities (Mallett, 1986; Austin, 2000; Grant, 2001b; and CHAUSA, 2006a, 2007a). We support their view that the concept of *governance as ministry* warrants further exploration, given the evolving nature of Church governance and the focus of O'Meara's (1999, p.150) definition of ministry as:

> the public activity of a baptised follower of Jesus Christ flowing from the Spirit's charism and an individual personality on behalf of the Christian community to proclaim, serve, and realise the kingdom of God.

'Professional Catholics' – New ministers in the Church

While Vatican II proclaimed the value of the secular life and spirituality of the laity and how this was to be witnessed in their day to day work life in factories and offices, subsequent years saw more lay people employed *in the Church* than ever before. These people took up roles that were either formerly filled by clergy and religious or that did not exist in previous times. For example in the decades following Vatican II, numerous parish roles have been created and filled by employed lay people including pastoral assistant, director of mission, sacramental coordinator and youth coordinator. Similarly at diocesan level, there has been a dramatic increase in the number of lay people in executive leadership roles in areas as diverse as finance and planning, personnel, mission services, spirituality and social justice (Klimoski, O'Neil, and

Schuth, 2005; Lucas, Slack, and d'Apice, 2008) . In Catholic universities, lay people hold chairs in theology, a scenario never imagined by the bishops of Vatican II.

The emergence of these new ministers in the Church has generated a deal of interest from various quarters. Some have noted that a 'professionally elite' class of Catholic lay person has been created (Pirola, 1995). These include well qualified and salaried individuals who have taken up the senior executive roles in Catholic health and education, roles that had been formerly undertaken by clerics and religious. In some cases, these roles have been filled by individuals who have previously trained, ordained and subsequently left the priesthood or by former members of religious institutes. For example, a noticeable pattern of leadership succession in Australian Catholic education over the past 40 years has been the appointment of ex-religious to diocesan directorships and other senior executive positions. This trend has, to some extent, masked the need for formation for management and governance since the individuals concerned have usually had significant spiritual formation in their younger years in novitiates and seminaries. We are now reaching the point where this generation of Catholic leaders is reaching retirement – and their replacements have had no such formative background or opportunity. In fact, many may not have ever been taught by a priest, or religious sister or brother.

In other quarters, determined efforts are being made to formalise the nature of these new roles in Church ministry. For example, the United States Conference of Catholic Bishops (USCCB) has produced a document entitled *Co-Workers in the Vineyard of the Lord* (USCCB, 2005). The document is directed toward parish based employees exercising roles as ecclesial ministers. The USCCB (2006) have subsequently described a lay person's role as an ecclesial minister to involve:

- *Authorisation* of the hierarchy to serve publicly in the local church.
- *Leadership* in a particular area of ministry.

- *Close mutual collaboration* with the pastoral ministry of bishops, priests, and deacons.
- *Preparation and formation* appropriate to the level of responsibilities that are assigned to them.

As this USCCB work and the earlier literature demonstrates, the issue of how lay people are exercising new roles in Church ministry – including responsibilities for canonical governance, have put the spotlight firmly on the nature and need for formation.

Coming to terms with formation

What do we mean when we talk about 'formation'? Especially, what do we understand as 'formation for canonical governance'? Official Church writings generally refer to formation for ministry and mission rather than to formation for governance *per se*. While Canon 375, on the role of the bishop, states that they are 'ministers of governance' (Willis, 1986, p. 160) and the power of governance is set out in the Code of Canon Law (Cns 129-144), this is not accompanied by any indication of formation for exercising such power.

In fact, the term 'formation' is itself shrouded in ambiguity. The literature commonly refers the expected outcomes from formation (Giganti, 2004; M. Kelly, 2007; Mudd, 2005; Pope John Paul II, 1988; P. Smith, 2006a) or assumes that the meaning of the term is understood (Roman Catholic Church, 1983, Cns 569-661). For example, *Pastores Dabo Vobis* on priestly formation nominates four dimensions of formation (human, spiritual, intellectual and pastoral) but does not actually define formation. Similarly, *Co-Workers in the Vineyard of the Lord* for ecclesial lay ministers nominated the same four dimensions of formation without providing a definition. While each document outlined the content for formation, neither provided a rationale nor explained what *formation* was. Perhaps the authors presumed readers already understood the meaning of the term, and that the reasons for formation were self-evident.

This gap in the literature was addressed in the doctoral research study undertaken by John Henry Thornber cfc (2012). He defines formation as:

> a reflected development on one's gifts and how the gifts contribute to the need in hand providing an holistic preparation of a person for a role – human, spiritual, intellectual, pastoral – including reflection on the experiences of their own life which might highlight some lacks in development or knowledge that are essential for meeting that need.

This definition is similar to that from Bouchard (2009, p. 40) who sees formation as:

> a transformative process, rooted in theology and spirituality, that connects us more deeply with God, creation and others. Through self-reflection it opens us to God's action so that we derive meaning from the work we do, grow in awareness of our gifts, see our work as vocation and build a communal commitment to the ministry.

These perspectives on formation provide a basis for analyzing some of the historical precedents and contemporary challenges relating to the preparation of individuals for governance roles in the Church. The significance of formation for mission and the tasks of ministry have been deeply embedded in the history of the Church. Let's now take a more detailed look at this history and the important stages in the thinking and practice of formation for priests, religious and lay people.

First with regard to priests, the Council of Trent dealt with their formation needs for Scripture study in Session 5, June 17, 1546 (Roman Catholic Church). Keogh (2008, pp. 24-33) detailed the difficulties in 18th century Ireland with the lack of priestly formation and the failure to implement the reforms of the Council of Trent. Vatican II set out the decree *Optatam Totius (Abbott, 1966f)* on priestly formation, acknowledging the debt it owed to the Council of Trent emphasised training for "the whole human being" (Confoy, 2008, p. 104). In Section 6, the bishops decreed that the following areas of priestly formation should be attended to:

> [W]atchful concern for the age of each [priest] and for his stage of progress, an inquiry should be made into the candidate's proper intention and freedom of choice, into his spiritual, moral and intellectual qualifications, into his appropriate physical and psychic health-taking into consideration also possible hereditary deficiencies. Also to be considered is the ability of the candidate to bear the priestly burdens and exercise the pastoral offices (Abbott, 1966f, p. 443).

The 1983 Code of Canon Law set out the requirements for men to become priests. It required the harmonious blending of "spiritual formation and doctrinal instruction" (Canon 244) so that the students "develop the requisite human maturity and acquire the spirit of the Gospel and a close relationship with Christ" (Canon 244). The revised Code also required that students for priesthood be educated over a period of six years in the branches of theology, philosophy, sacred Scripture and languages as well as ministerial skills in homiletics, parish administration and pastoral understanding (Cns 250-258).

The actual shape of formation envisaged by the 1983 Code was addressed by Pope John Paul II nine years later in *Pastores Dabo Vobis* (1992), which outlined a framework for priestly formation comprising of four dimensions – *human, spiritual, intellectual,* and *pastoral.* These dimensions reflected the elements required for formation in the Code of Canon Law and flowed from the Vatican II decree on priestly formation.

Our next group for consideration is the members of religious institutes and their formation for religious life. While the Canons were not as specific on the formation requirements for religious as for priests (Cns

641-661), they did require that the formation be "systematic, adapted to the capacity of the members, spiritual and apostolic, both doctrinal and practical" (Canon 660). The same canon calls for members to obtain "suitable ecclesiastical and civil degrees ... as opportunity offers".

In response to the reflections and recommendations of a Synod on Religious Life in the Church, John Paul II published the exhortation *Vita Consecrata* (1996), translated as 'The Consecrated Life'. While the scope of the document covered a range of aspects, formation was a key focus. It stated that:

> the formation of consecrated women, no less than that of men, should be adapted to modern needs and should provide sufficient time and suitable institutional opportunities for a systematic education, extending to all areas, from the theological-pastoral to the professional. Pastoral and catechetical formation, always important, is particularly relevant in view of the new evangelization, which calls for new forms of participation also on the part of women (p. 58).

Along with the need for equal emphasis to be given to the formation of consecrated women, Pope John Paul II wrote that appropriate and integral formation for religious involve human, spiritual, theological, pastoral and professional elements. Hence his framework for the formation of religious was notably similar to that used for priests in *Pastores Dabo Vobis*.

Vita Consecrata was followed by an instruction from the Congregation for Institutes of Consecrated Life and Societies of Apostolic Life (CICLSAL 2002) to encourage on-going formation for the spiritual life. In contrast to its papal precursor documents, this instruction did not include reference to the other foundational dimensions of formation. This omission is significant as it had the potential to unnecessarily limit the range of gifts and needs that individuals might bring to processes of formation.

The third group for consideration is the laity. In contrast to the previous two groups, references to the role and formation of lay persons in the Church in the Code of Canon Law are sparse. The only reference to formation of lay persons is in Canon231§1:

> Lay people who are pledged to the special service of the Church, whether permanently or for a time, have a duty to acquire the appropriate formation which their role demands, so that they may conscientiously, earnestly and diligently fulfil this role.

For priestly and religious formation, the responsibility and resourcing for members lie with the church institutions. For the laity on the other hand, the responsibility for formation is personal. Canon Law implies that lay persons should be responsible for resourcing of their formation. Furthermore, it seems to presume that lay persons understand what formation is, what is needed for whatever 'special service' they are 'pledged to'. There is a significant level of risk associated with these requirements and presumptions when considering the involvement of the laity in canonical governance. Who pays, who determines needs, who decides the content and process, and who ensures integrity of formation programmes? These are matters on which Canon Law is relatively silent.

While light on detail about formation of the laity, Canon law recognizes that lay people employed in the Church have civil rights in accordance with Catholic social tradition. This referred to in Canon 231§2 as follows:

> [Lay persons] have the right to a worthy remuneration befitting their condition, whereby, with due regard also to the provisions of the civil law, they can becomingly provide for their own needs and the needs of their families. Likewise, they have the right to have their insurance, social security and medical benefits duly safeguarded.

Some argue that the revised Code of Canon Law through making the rights and obligations of the laity more explicit (as in Canon 231§2), has provided a basis for increased participation of laypersons in the worship, witness, governance, and ministries of the church (Coriden, 2004). While this may well be the case, there are further supporting factors to consider. For example, support for involvement of the laity can be found in *Apostolicam Actuositatem* (Abbott, 1966b). In Chapter 6, Formation for the Apostolate, the seeds of a framework for formation were evident. Here the bishops set out that the apostolate required a certain human and well-rounded formation; spiritual formation; solid doctrinal instruction in theology, ethics and philosophy; and means of dealing with the reality of the temporal order of everyday life.

Further support for involvement of the laity and their formation was evident in the 1987 Synod called by Pope John Paul II. The Synod involved representatives of the Church throughout the world. In the resultant document *Christifideles Laici*, Pope John Paul II (1988) stated that formation has spiritual and apostolic purposes to help develop mature ecclesial communities and promote the maturation of faith. As such, formation programmes need to have spiritual and doctrinal dimensions, particularly Catholic social doctrine, and be personal in focus (Nicholson, 2011).

Building a framework for formation

From the range of sources and commentary on the meaning and nature formation of priests, religious and lay persons that have been covered so far, we believe that the literature on formation in *Pastores Dabo Vobis* (John Paul II, 1992) and *Co-workers in the Vineyard of the Lord* (USCCB, 2005) provides the most promising basis upon which to develop a framework for formation. Synthesising the content of these documents not only enables the ecclesial depth and significance of the writings associated priestly and lay formation to be considered, but also recognizes the need for collaboration and partnership between priests, religious and lay people as new challenges for Church ministries and new forms of governance for such ministries continue to emerge.

Both documents include the desired personal qualities for people involved in ecclesial work. *Pastores* refers to traits while *Co-Workers* refers to elements. Despite these differences in terminology, traits and elements are categorised under the same set of dimensions, i.e. human, spiritual, intellectual and pastoral. In the following sections, we describe the traits and elements related to each dimension, and how these can be used to identify the desired characteristics of individuals invited to undertake roles as governors in Church ministries.

Being 'human'

What types of people are best suited to take on governance roles in the Church? What are the desired 'human' qualities of these people – and how might they be identified and developed? These are questions relating to the human dimension of formation.

In addressing these questions, it is worth considering the purpose of formation from the viewpoints of the two documents: *Pastores Dabo Vobis* (John Paul II, 1992) on priestly formation, and *Co-Workers in the Vineyard of the Lord* (USCCB, 2005) on the formation of lay people for roles in the Church, i.e. as ecclesial ministers. For priests, formation should enable them to 'mould his human personality in such a way that it becomes a bridge and not an obstacle for others in their meeting with Jesus Christ the redeemer of humanity' (John Paul II, 1992). For lay ecclesial ministers, formation seeks to 'develop their human qualities and character, fostering a healthy and well balanced personality, for the sake of both personal growth and ministerial service' (USCCB, 2005). While these perspectives have some contrast in emphasis (for example in relation to the theological language used in *Pastores*), the message that formation is about personal development is clear. This is seen to involve the development of particular traits and elements, as shown in Table 2.1.

Table 2.1
Sample *Pastores* Traits and *Co-Workers* Elements: Human Dimension

Pastores Dabo Vobis – Traits
The priest should • love the truth; • be loyal; • have affective maturity; • respect every person; • have a sense of justice; • be genuinely compassionate; • have integrity; and • show balance in judgment and behaviour.
Co-Workers in the Vineyard of the Lord – Elements
The lay ecclesial minister should: • understand self; • relate with God and others; • demonstrate psychological and physical health; • have genuine respect and concern for others (rooted in the example of Jesus); • know their gifts and charisms; • understand family dynamics; and • learn from praise and criticism.

In comparing the desired traits and elements of priests and lay persons from the perspective of the human dimension, the following themes come through: human maturity, justice, respect for persons, compassion, and self-awareness. Let's take a closer look at these themes and their implications for formation.

First in relation to human maturity, the bishops in *Co-Workers* (USCCB, 2005) wrote of the need for ecclesial workers to develop their character and personality as a basis for ministerial service. Župarić (2010) has described the concept of human maturity as relating to one's own identity and integrity. He explained that 'maturity is a dynamic concept that includes development and the tendency toward fullness [physically and spiritually]' (p. 105). He added that this development and tendency toward fullness is never complete, nor is the process of one's maturing always perfect. In other words, there is always room for development. This understanding of human maturity takes the hopeful view that individuals are able to grow in maturity, and that formation is an important means of fostering such growth.

A second theme associated with the human dimension is having a sense of justice. This seems like a reasonable quality for people involved with governance. Nevertheless, there's a problem. This is because assessing one's (or someone else's) sense of justice has a cultural basis. Societies deem what is considered to be just. Some countries allow for capital punishment in their system of justice (Robinson, 1997); some allow for mutilation for theft (Shaykh, 2005), while other countries allow neither though are criticised by their citizens for the way immigrants are treated (Brennan, 2011). When it comes to interpreting justice in a particular context, the ways in which the cultural milieu influences the meaning of justice need to be recognised because that influences how justice is practiced in the work of the ministry. This issue about the meaning of justice *in context* is not new. While the Acts of the Apostles told of the life of the early Church and the passionate effort to help the poor, Paul's Letter to Philemon on how his friend might deal with his runaway slave, Onesimus clearly showed that Paul saw slavery as part of the justice system of the time.

Respect is a third theme that arose from consideration of the *Pastores* and *Co-Workers* documents. The rationale of respect for persons flows from a belief in their inherent dignity. To understand the significance of these ideas, we need to appreciate the way that the terminology has evolved over the centuries. The Christian concept of 'caring for the other' has a long history, and the Church has used the theological term *temple of the Holy Spirit* (1 Cor 6:19) for respecting both oneself and the other since ancient times. However the use of the terms *human dignity* and *respect for persons* is relatively recent. For example, Hursthouse (2007, p. 59) noted that the term *human dignity* can be traced the use of the term *dignity* in Kant's writings in 1785. She found that earliest formal use of the term *human dignity* in the UN Declaration of Human Rights in 1948 (2007, p. 65). Writers in Catholic social teaching had begun using the term in the mid-19th century, but in the context of the *dignity of the worker* rather than in any holistic sense (Aubert and Boileau, 2003, p. 77).

A fourth theme that emerged under the Human dimension was *compassion* and how this is expressed in acts of *charity*. Hursthouse (2007) explains that 'it is charity, not justice that requires that we stop to help the wounded stranger by the roadside'. She contends that we would be within our rights, if not to pass by, at least to do a great deal less. Thus charity, as she uses the term, is the activity of providing support for the marginalised and is therefore an expression of the compassion that one has for another. The meanings and relationships between the concepts of *compassion, charity, justice* and *mercy* are discussed in the literature. From a scriptural and theological point of view, Brueggemann (1978, p. 26) has spoken of the tension between compassion and justice. Similarly, White (2010) has dealt with the values that underpin the nature of justice and compassion and has suggested that these can shed light on the meaning of derivative terms, such as mercy and charity. These terms are seen as expressions of justice and compassion and are reflected the names of religious institutes established to act with justice and compassion, namely the Sisters of Mercy and the Sisters of Charity.

The final theme associated with the human dimension was self-awareness. Being aware of oneself, one's identity and integrity is an aspect of human maturity. O'Connell-Killen and de Beer (1994) described the process of becoming self-aware as one in which:

> [W]e enter our experience, we encounter our feelings. When we pay attention to those feelings, images arise. Considering and questioning those images may spark insight. Insight leads, if we are willing and ready, to action (pp. 21-22).

This quote highlights the link between the development of an individual's self-awareness and their process of becoming aware of new insights. For those involved in governance, these insights might involve different ways of thinking about the connections between values, decisions and actions; reflecting on needs created by a change in circumstances in the ministry operation; or fresh understandings about the meaning of the mission which the ministry serves. Formation in the human dimension should foster the emergence of insights like these.

Being 'spiritual'

What does it mean to be spiritual? McBrien (1994, p. 1019) explains that to be *spiritual* means to know, and to live according to the knowledge that there is more to life than meets the eye. Indeed, this knowledge and belief in 'something other' determines one's approach to life, or *spirituality*. For example, O'Meara (1999) defines *spirituality* as a way of seeing life, and reflected that it develops over time by:

> [L]ife's and love's preferences lead[ing] one to select, to arrange, [and] to emphasise a coherent gathering of teachings and images; That cluster, very much one's own, is a spirituality (p. 232).

This process of selection, arrangement and giving emphases comes from one's life experiences and includes both formal and informal opportunities to gather such teachings and images. Hence, formation in spirituality, or spiritual formation, occurs from reflection on the life experiences and exposure to learning which nurtures the coherent gathering of teachings and images.

These understandings of spiritual formation are evident in the two documents: *Pastores Dabo Vobis* (John Paul II, 1992) and *Co-Workers in the Vineyard of the Lord* (USCCB, 2005). Pope John Paul II (1992) when referring to the spiritual dimension of priestly formation draws on the insights of St Augustine in encouraging priests 'to have hearts that are restless until they rest in the Lord'. Similarly the bishops in *Co-Workers* explain:

> Spiritual formation [of lay ecclesial ministers] aims to arouse and animate true hunger for holiness, desire for union with the Father through Christ in the Spirit, daily growing in love of God and neighbour in life and ministry, and the practices of prayer and spirituality that foster these attitudes and dispositions (USCCB, 2005).

Both documents underscore the importance of spiritual formation as a quest for meaning and relationship with God. This is reflected in the sample traits and elements, shown in Table 2.2.

Table 2.2
Sample *Pastores* Traits and *Co-Workers* Elements: Spiritual Dimension

Pastores Dabo Vobis – Traits
The priest should • be open to transcendence, to the absolute; • live intimately united to Jesus Christ; and • be engaged in a continuing search for God.

> **Co-Workers in the Vineyard of the Lord – Elements**
>
> The lay ecclesial minister should:
> - pray and practice other forms of spirituality;
> - be in living union with Christ; and
> - engage in spiritual formation built on the word of God.

These excerpts from the *Pastores* and *Co-Workers* documents also highlight the potential depth and breadth of spiritual formation in the Christian tradition. This is reflected in McBrien's (1994) description of Christian spirituality as including the following perspectives or emphases:

- *Trinitarian* – rooted in the life of the triune God.
- *Christological* – centered on Jesus Christ.
- *Ecclesiological* – situated in the Church.
- *Pneumatological* – ever responsive to the Holy Spirit.
- *Eschatological* – oriented always to the coming of God's Reign in all its fullness at the end of human history.

In light of this listing, he notes that 'there is not, and never has been, a single Christian spirituality, nor a single Catholic spirituality' (McBrien 1994, p. 1021), a position which O'Meara (1999) affirms. This plurality of Christian spirituality reflects our earlier discussion of the various approaches to studying theology and different models of Church. Varying emphases and diversity in terminology were certainly evident in *Pastores Dabo Vobis* (John Paul II, 1992) and *Co-Workers in the Vineyard of the Lord* (USCCB, 2005). The concepts of 'transcendence', 'baptismal call', and 'vocation' deserve particular attention.

The concept of *transcendence* is described by McBrien (1994, p. 253) as 'that which is above and beyond the ordinary, the concrete, the tangible – i.e. to God'. He referred to Berger's exploration of transcendence which spoke of 'phenomena that are to be found within the domain of our "natural" reality but that appear to point beyond that reality' (Berger, 1969, pp. 65-66, cited by McBrien). Berger has identified five signals of transcendence which belong to our ordinary everyday experience. These are our propensity for order, our engagement in play, our unquenchable spirit of hope, our sense of outrage at what is thoroughly evil, and our sense of humour. These signs are part of everyday experience and yet point beyond our everyday reality.

So what has an understanding of transcendence got to do with formation for governance? Well, first we need to be aware of the signals of transcendence and the potential they have for identifying and expressing what is valued. Second when values are evident, group members are better placed to understand how they and their colleagues see the world in general, and the issues at hand. Third when this happens, better governance can result.

Another concept that is integral to the spiritual dimension of formation is *baptismal call*. This is a general call to all Christians to be engaged in the bringing about of the Kingdom of God in the world (Abbott, 1966b n. 3). There are various ways in which an individual may fulfill that call. One is by living an ordinary life and giving witness to the gospel message through their relationships with family, friends and work associates, infused with a belief in the Gospel teachings. Another is by using one's particular gifts to carry out ministries in the name of the Church (Fox, 2005b; Hagstrom, 2003; Hahnenberg, 2003, 2009). In fact, there is an expectation that in being baptised, an individual has a responsibility to engage with the Christian message of the good news of the kingdom of God. This expectation was expressed in *Lumen Gentium* (Abbott, 1966e, pp. 31, 33). Such an engagement requires not only a belief in the spiritual world, but also a willingness to be engaged with the values which have been articulated and are being lived out in the organisation which conducts the ministry in the name of the Church.

One point of contention flowing from this understanding of baptismal call is whether canonical governors of Catholic ministries need to be Catholic, or whether the baptismal responsibility allowed any Christian to undertake the role, or whether canonical governors need to be baptised Christians at all. Sweeney (2011), a canonist, is of the view that governors would be practicing members of the Catholic Church. However the Australian Catholic Bishops, Leaders of Religious Institutes and Catholic Health Australia in the recently published *Guide for Understanding the Governance of Catholic Health and Aged Care Services* (Catholic Health Australia, 2012, p. 11) were more guarded stating that 'it is *practically universally* [italics added] held by canonists that one must be a member of the Church before one can hold an office in the Church'. So the question is still on the table.

The third concept of interest emerging from the consideration of the *Pastores* and *Co-Workers* documents is *vocation*. The term 'vocation' refers to 'work individuals need to do, the inner work which will allow the consciousness of call to grow' (Fox, 2005b, p. 14). The extent to which people different people feel this need and nurture this consciousness varies. Consciousness and awareness of self has implications for ministry, and accordingly are significant elements of formation for roles in ministry. Having a vocation is different from seeking a career (Winschel, 2008). Further, awareness of one's vocation often comes 'after the fact' (Fox, 2005b). The 'fact' may be provided by planned formation input, or any other experience or insight which is formative. Either way, it is likely that such powerful experiences encourage people to engage in further formation (Hahnenberg, 2010).

Important questions arising from our consideration of the concepts of *transcendence, baptismal call* and *vocation* concern whether, and if so how engagement in the role of canonical governor is a spiritual encounter that flows from a Christian's baptismal call and expresses itself as a vocation to which individuals give themselves. The spiritual dimension of one's formation for governance roles needs to consider these questions.

Being 'Intellectual'

The third dimension of formation for canonical governance is focused on investigation and knowledge of the faith. In comparison with the *Human* dimension which centered on individual personality and character, and the *Spiritual* dimension which focused on questions of meaning and purpose in life and relationship with God, the *intellectual* dimension is concerned with the developing the knowledge base to inform and undertake governance work in ministries.

Both *Pastores Dabo Vobis* (John Paul II, 1992) on priestly formation, and *Co-Workers in the Vineyard of the Lord* (USCCB, 2005) on the formation of the laity consider the study of theology as integral to the intellectual dimension of formation. The foundations for theological study are (i) *Scripture*, which is acknowledged as containing God's revelation of God's self (Kelly, 1998) and (ii) *Tradition*, which is "the living and lived faith of the Church" (McBrien, 1994, p. 63). For the meaning of Tradition in this sense, uppercase is always used to distinguish it from 'traditions' which are "customary ways of doing things related to faith" (McBrien, p. 63).

In relation to priestly formation, a key excerpt from *Pastores* reads:

> If we expect every Christian ... to be prepared to make a defense of the faith and to account for the hope that is in us ... then all the more should candidates for the priesthood and priests have diligent care of the quality of their intellectual formation in their education and pastoral activity. For the salvation of their brothers and sisters they should seek an ever deeper knowledge of the divine mysteries (John Paul II, 1992).

The bishops in the *Co-Workers* document similarly highlight the value of intellectual formation in stating that:

> [I]ntellectual formation seeks to develop the lay ecclesial minister's understanding and appreciation of the Catholic

faith, which is rooted in God's revelation and embodied in the living tradition of the Church.

And add that:

[F]ormation for lay ecclesial ministry is a journey beyond catechesis into theological study. Theology delves into the Church's faith in a scholarly way, interpreting it according to the witness of the Scriptures and Tradition and making it understandable to the times (USCCB, 2005).

Both documents also emphasise the value of study beyond theology and the 'sacred sciences'. This point along with other sample traits and elements noted above, are summarised in Table 2.3.

Table 2.3

Sample *Pastores* Traits and *Co-Workers* Elements:
Intellectual Dimensions

Pastores Dabo Vobis – Traits
The priest should • care about the quality of their intellectual formation in their education and pastoral activity; • assent to the word of God, grow in his spiritual life, and fulfill his pastoral ministry through study of theology; and • study human sciences (e.g. sociology, psychology, education, economics, politics, and the science of social communication).

> **Co-Workers in the Vineyard of the Lord – Elements**
>
> The lay ecclesial minister should:
> - develop their understanding and appreciation of the Catholic faith;
> - study the 'sacred sciences'; and
> - draw upon other disciplines (e.g. philosophy, literature and the arts, psychology, sociology, counselling, medical ethics, culture and language studies business administration, leadership, organisational development and law).

There are four related concepts that emerge from considering what is involved in formation in the intellectual dimension, in light of the perspectives put forward in the *Pastores* and *Co-Workers* documents. These are *theological reflection*, *Word of God*, *Catholic intellectual tradition*, and *missiology*. Let's take each in turn.

In Christianity, *theological reflection* has been defined by O'Connell Killen and De Beer (1994, p. viii) as 'the discipline of exploring individual and corporate experience in conversation with the wisdom of a religious heritage'. These authors point out that one's intellectual formation assists one's faith development. Faith development is about one's relationship with God. Theological reflection is an attempt to describe this interconnectedness. The corollary is that the study of theology is not expected to be undertaken as a purely intellectual exercise, but as an engagement in faith. This long tradition in the Church was expressed by St. Augustine (354-430 CE) as 'I believe, in order to understand; and I understand, the better to believe' (Quoted in *Compendium of the Catechism of the Catholic Church*, 2008). From this viewpoint, we can readily appreciate that *theological reflection*, *self-awareness*, and *transcendence* are related concepts that need to be part of the formation for canonical governors.

Understanding the meaning of the term *Word of God* is another area of intellectual formation. The term is widely used in Jewish and Christian sacred literature. For Christians, it has two inter-related meanings. In its first sense, word of God refers to the sacred tradition and the sacred Scripture which form 'one sacred deposit' of God's revelation to people (Abbott, 1966c, *Dei Verbum* 10). In its other sense, it refers to the person of Jesus Christ, given the title with the upper case, Word of God, in whom "the history of the people continues as the history of God's words and God's works, that is, of God's revelation" (Kelly, 1998, p. 66). There is a connection between these two meanings, as Kelly points out through the Gospel accounts that 'we are conscious that the people were gradually becoming aware that in Jesus a new image of God was being revealed to them'. From this perspective, the formation of canonical governors is based on the understanding that the person 'being formed' is a believer in Jesus, has a relationship with Jesus, and is ready to have that belief and relationship nurtured. In other words, the person has 'faith' and is open to engage in deepening their faith.

The next area of interest relating to the intellectual dimension of formation covered in the *Pastores* and *Co-Workers* documents is *Catholic intellectual tradition*. In his analysis of world religions, Smart (1984) nominated seven dimensions that are common to all. Smart named the 'doctrinal and philosophical' dimension as the one relevant to Catholic intellectual tradition, describing this as a systematic formulation of religious teachings in an intellectually coherent form. The Catholic Church has a long history of systematic formulation and intellectual coherence of the basic beliefs (Lennan, 1998; McBrien, 1994). Theology itself is an example of this. It is both an intellectual discipline and an articulation of faith. The intellectual exploration and articulation inherent in theology flow from and interact with the experience of more basic dimensions including ritual, story and myth, experience and rules (Smart, 1984). On other words, the various dimensions are connected. Questions and experiences in one can lead to answers and possibilities in others.

So what principles underpin the intellectual exploration and articulation of basic beliefs in the Church? Or put another way, what exactly is *Catholic intellectual tradition*? Grassl (2009) has explored the existence of intellectual traditions with particular reference to the Catholic Church. He identified nine principles which led him to believe that a characteristic of the 'Catholic intellectual tradition' was that it gave a priority to ontology over epistemology (p. 8). Put simply, this means that 'being' has priority over 'knowing'. The modeling for this priority can be found in the Christian Scriptures where the founder, Jesus Christ, acted in healing and teaching without necessarily providing any theorising for the actions. One example is the cure of the blind man (Mk 8.22-26). Modeling is also seen in the parables, epitomised in 'The Good Samaritan' (Lk 10.25-37) which provided the story of the complete stranger and outsider helping the person in need when there was no personal or cultural expectation to do so (Arbuckle, 2007b). Similarly, it was 'after the fact' that the community of Jesus' followers used their experiences and stories to build a theory that supported such behaviour. This supports Grassl's (2009, p. 12) conclusion that Catholic intellectual tradition has practicality as essential element.

The nature of mission is a further area for consideration in the intellectual dimension of formation. Mission has been described as 'the good news in action' (Brueggemann, 2000; Schroeder, 2008). Missiology is the study of mission, or more precisely the systematic theology of mission (Bevans and Gros, 2009; Bevans and Schroeder, 2004). It is a comparatively recent theological discipline that examines the rationale and purposes of the mission of the Church (Kirk, 2000, p. 19). Schroeder (2008, p. 3) defined the mission as the "proclaiming, serving and witnessing to God's reign of love, salvation and justice". Kirk (2000, p. 21) used the phrase 'Theology of Mission' as a synonym for missiology, and has explained that:

> Theology of Mission is a disciplined study which deals with questions that arise when people of faith seek to

understand and fulfil God's purposes in the world, as these are demonstrated in the ministry of Jesus Christ. It is a critical reflection on attitudes and actions adopted by Christians in pursuit of the missionary mandate. Its task is to validate, correct and establish on better foundations the entire practice of mission.

Missiology is important because it clarifies the meaning of 'mission' in common use – for example whether this is in terms of 'the Church having a mission' or 'the mission having a Church' (Bevans and Schroder, 2011, p.16), or 'the mission of a particular ministry'.

Being 'Pastoral'

What does it mean to be 'pastoral'? In its original sense it means 'pertaining to the life of shepherds and rustics' i.e. those who live by simple manners and character. The use of the word 'pastoral' in Christian tradition comes from the image of 'carer of His flock' (John 10:11) which Jesus used to describe his role. This concept derived from the Jewish writings portraying God as the shepherd of God's people (see Psalm 23, Isaiah 40, Ezekiel 15). The contemporary meaning has evolved to describe the work of those in the Church who are caring and practical in serving others.

In reflecting on *Co-Workers in the Vineyard of the Lord* (USCCB, 2005), Fox (2010b) noted its practical orientation. This is evident in the way that the document describes the purpose of pastoral formation:

> Pastoral formation cultivates the knowledge, attitudes, and skills that directly pertain to effective functioning in the ministry setting and that also pertain to pastoral administration that supports direct ministry (USCCB, 2005).

Pastores Dabo Vobis (John Paul II, 1992) in a related way proposes that a priest's pastoral formation is central:

> The whole formation imparted to candidates for the

priesthood aims at preparing them to enter into communion with the charity of Christ the Good Shepherd. Hence their formation in its different aspects must have a fundamentally pastoral character.

The practical implications of pastoral formation are also emphasised:

> Pastoral formation develops by means of mature reflection and practical application, and it is rooted in a spirit, which is the hinge of all and the force which stimulates it and makes it develop (John Paul II, 1992).

Both *Pastores* and *Co-Workers* emphasise the communal dimensional of pastoral work. For example, John Paul II (1992) states that:

> [A]wareness of the Church as 'communion' will prepare the candidate for the priesthood to carry out his pastoral work with a community spirit, in heartfelt cooperation with the different members of the Church: priests and bishop, diocesan and religious priests, priests and lay people. Such cooperation presupposes a knowledge and appreciation of the different gifts and charisms of the diverse vocations and responsibilities which the Spirit offers and entrusts to the members of Christ's body. It demands a living and precise consciousness of one's own identity in the Church and of the identity of others.

Similarly in *Pastores*, the bishops stress the importance of working together. They state that 'the Church's pastoral ministry can be more effective if we become true collaborators' and add that:

> Listening to others with skill, understanding and compassion is essential for the lay ecclesial minister. Equally foundational is the ability to speak to others: one on one, in small groups or in large groups, with all in the Church, and with non-

Catholics and non-Christians. Lay ecclesial ministers also need to relate effectively with those whom they serve, partners (peers or those they supervise), and supervisors. Recognition and respect for different cultural styles of communication are also needed (USCCB, 2005).

The development of mindsets and capabilities that align with these understandings is an important aspect of the pastoral dimension of formation.

From the analysis above, we can say that of all dimensions, the pastoral is the one that is most 'hands on', that is most directed towards practice. This is evident in the traits and elements drawn from the *Pastores* and *Co-Workers* documents, summarised in Table 2.4.

Table 2.4

Sample *Pastores* Traits and *Co-Workers* Elements: Pastoral Dimension

Pastores Dabo Vobis – Traits
The priest should: • see all formation as fundamentally pastoral in character; • study pastoral (i.e. practical) theology; • reflect upon and practically apply their pastoral formation; • carry out pastoral service; • be aware of the Church as 'communion'; • appreciate the gifts, charisms, vocations and responsibilities of others; and • be conscious of their own identity in the Church and the identify of others.

Co-Workers in the Vineyard of the Lord – Elements
The lay ecclesial minister should: • have pastoral ministry skills – evangelization; promotion and organisation of action on behalf of justice; • have effective relationship and communication skills; • collaborate; • discern the signs of the times; • be able to discern the gifts and charisms of others; and • cultivate leadership qualities modeled on the example of Jesus.

Having listed these desired qualities of priests and lay people, the question is where do we go from here? One avenue is further reading. For example, one valuable source is *Lay Ecclesial Ministry* edited by Zeni Fox (2010b) which is a collection of writings explaining the elements required for pastoral leadership in the context of the *Co-Workers* document.

A related worthwhile endeavor is to consider how the various desired traits and elements of those invited to governance roles in the Church are related to one another, and how these qualities might be developed. Our use of the *human, spiritual, intellectual* and *pastoral* dimensions is based on the idea that governance roles involve all four areas, and that therefore effective formation methods need to address the whole person: their emotions, imagination, will, heart, and mind. It is the whole person who ministers, so the whole person is the proper subject of formation.

Formation of the Whole Person

Our exploration of *Pastores Dabo Vobis* (John Paul II, 1992) and *Co-Workers in the Vineyard of the Lord* (USCCB, 2005) indicates that formation, whether for the priesthood or lay ecclesial work requires a focus on the whole person. We also recognise that while the same dimensions were included in both documents, the content and depth expected varied considerably, depending on the roles for which people were being formed. The pastoral emphasis varies with the ministry being addressed. Nevertheless, throughout our analysis of the *Pastores* and *Co-Workers* documents, we noted a consistent emphasis on the need for each person (whether priest or lay) to develop their personal spirituality informed by the Scriptures and their understanding of theology informed by Church tradition.

Yet considering the process of formation as a 'dimension by dimension' undertaking is only part of the endeavour. For a fuller appreciation of 'the image and texture of the formation tapestry' we need to also consider how one dimension can influence another, i.e. how they weave together to form the whole person. For example, developing intellectual knowledge of Scripture and theology influences our personal spirituality and relationship with God. This in turn assists us in shaping our response to the mission for which the organisation exists and ultimately, how we exercise leadership.

Catholic ministries operate in the civil sphere as non-profit organizations (Cleary, 2007). As non-profits, these organizations operate in response to a defined mission (Sachs, 2000). It is therefore essential that leaders of Catholic, non-profit ministries understand and are committed to the mission given to the Church by its Founder, Jesus Christ – to bring about of the 'Kingdom of God' (Bevans, 2009). This mission not only requires theological reflection and the development of one's personal spirituality, but also the leadership capabilities to shape and nurture the nature of their ministry to bring it about.

We are talking about much more than high quality career development here. We are talking about deep and meaningful formation for mission. Winschel (2008) has described the difference between formation and the development of a career path by noting that 'formation begins by recognising a call and being sent' (p. 22). This view echoes the teaching of Pope John Paul II on the role of the Laity in *Christifideles Laici* (1988) that:

> The fundamental objective of the formation of the lay faithful is an ever-clearer discovery of one's vocation and the ever-greater willingness to live it so as to fulfil one's mission.

In other words leadership for mission requires self-awareness, personal commitment to the mission,. and the capacity and willingness to articulate and decide how the ministry serves the mission to best effect. Senge (1990) has described these types of leaders as *designers*, *stewards* and *teachers*. Effective leaders for mission exhibit these different qualities at different times, in different contexts.

The point of formation is to provide support to those that are called to leadership in Church ministries. Those in governance roles exercise a particular leadership responsibility – to ensure the integrity, responsiveness and development of the ministry for the mission. The process of formation is designed to assist in the development of such leaders. In circumstances where increasing numbers of lay people are being invited to take on governance roles in the Church, the nature of formation is more demanding. Changing times and the diversity of background of these 'new professionals' in the Church requires fresh and creative approaches to the human, spiritual, intellectual and pastoral dimensions of their formation.

In this chapter we have traced the background in Canon Law regarding the role of the laity and made the case for new understandings and pathways to governance in the Church. A key consideration is the meaning of the term *formation* and what this involves when it applied to the preparation and development of lay people for governance roles. Here, the two Church documents, *Pastores Dabo Vobis* (John Paul II, 1992) and *Co-Workers in the Vineyard of the Lord* (USCCB, 2005), provided an authoritative base for examining the nature of formation from the priestly and lay perspectives, respectively. This combination of perspectives highlights the value of building a framework for formation based upon human, spiritual, intellectual and pastoral dimensions. Importantly we see the combination and relationships between these dimensions as being integral to the formation of the 'whole person'. When viewed in this light, we believe that formation can assist those called to governance roles to serve the mission and lead the ministry in ways that life giving to them, to those they serve, and to the Church and society at large.

3
Identifying Formation Needs

Formation to undertake a responsibility is important. In their *Co-Workers in the Vineyard of the Lord* document on formation of the laity, the bishops of the United States of America quoted Pope John Paul II on the need and responsibility of the Church, and of the individual, for formation (USCCB, p. 33):

> To set high standards [for formation] means both to provide a thorough basic training and to keep it constantly updated. This is a fundamental duty, in order to ensure qualified personnel for the Church's mission.

These words, while spoken for catechists (i.e. men and women fulfilling a broad range of pastoral duties in mission lands), apply as well to the lay ecclesial ministers in any setting, including canonical governors. Moreover, this exhortation by Pope John Paul II raises the question: *what exactly are the formation needs for people with responsibility for canonical governance of the ministries in the Catholic Church?* To answer this question it is worth recapping what we mean by *formation*, and why it is important for those who have governance responsibilities for Church ministries.

Formation is a process of preparation and ongoing reflection and development for the purpose of ensuring that individuals are appropriately self-aware and understand the meaning of their ministry at a depth that is beyond that of 'a worker doing a job'. We therefore define formation as:

> a reflected development on one's gifts and how the gifts contribute to the need in hand providing an holistic

preparation of a person for a role – human, spiritual, intellectual, pastoral – including reflection on the experiences of their own life which might highlight some lacks in development or knowledge that are essential for meeting that need (Thornber, 2012).

In other words, formation is beyond training or professional education. It involves engagement of the heart and soul of a person, their personality, their spirit, the intellect, and their concern and service for others. That is why it is important for those with canonical governance responsibilities. Their role is to lead people to God through the strategic decisions they make for their ministry. This type of leadership means being true to the mission and demands more than training in the knowledge and skills of a trade or a profession.

In this chapter we will explain our approach to identifying formation needs. This is based on the research design developed by Thornber (2012) in his doctoral research. The research design involved a three part reflective process:

- Mapping the suggested traits of canonical governors.
- Surveying the desirability and existing evidence of those traits.
- Interpreting (via interviews) the relationship between what is desired and what exists as a basis for determining the types and levels of need for formation.

These three components constituted a means whereby those whose needs were being identified and those who were doing the identifying were related so that the 'findings' were created as the investigation proceeded. In practical terms, this meant that the types of traits, the desirability and evidence of those traits, and the determination of needs for formation were analyzed and reflected upon at each stage of the process. Hence the Thornber study had a constructivist flavour where, as Cleary (2007, p.104) explains:

[R]ealities are understood to be in the form of multiple, intangible mental constructions, socially and experientially based, local and specific in nature and dependent for their form and content on the individual persons or groups holding the constructions.

The nature of these multiple and emerging realities was borne out in the research in several ways. First, the mapping of traits and the construction of the survey involved an Expert Advisory Group with expertise in Canon Law, theology and related disciplines. Each member considered the source documents and the related literature from their individual perspective and experience of canonical governance and formation. The final version of the survey was therefore a synthesis of the views, reflections and preferences of the members of this group. Second, each survey respondent rated the desirability and the evidence of trait in light of their experience. While patterns of responses emerged, the contexts from which those responses were drawn varied considerably. Third, the interviewees in reflecting on the survey data gained insights that both confirmed and challenged their previous understandings about traits of canonical governors and their needs for formation. Taken together, these three features highlight the value of grounding approaches for identifying formation needs on constructivist principles, where the types of traits, the desirability and evidence of those traits and determination of need are validated at each stage of the process. The practical implication is that the identification of formation needs should be customised for each situation. The type and significance of needs and the nature of formation to meet those needs always depends on the people involved, their aspirations and talents, the nature of their governance body and its particular traditions and challenges. Our view is that the research design of the Thornber study provides a useful basis upon which others can plan and develop their approach to identifying formation needs in light of the particular context of their ministry and Church organization.

Researching needs for formation

The research questions underpinning the Thornber study (2012) were:

- What are the *formation needs* of canonical governors in the existing and emerging forms of Church governance.
- What is an appropriate *formation framework* for canonical governors for identifying and addressing these needs.

The study set out to chart new territory in the governance of Church ministries in two important ways. First, it drew on Church documents and related literature to develop a definition of *formation* that could take account of the increasing involvement of lay people in the governance of Church ministries. Second, it used authoritative documents on formation – *Pastores Dabo Vobis* (John Paul II, 1992) on priestly formation and *Co-Workers in the Vineyard of the Lord* (USCCB, 2005) on the formation of the laity – to draft a series of traits classified in terms of one of four dimensions (human, spiritual, intellectual and pastoral) that was deemed desirable for canonical governors to possess. These traits were subsequently piloted with an Expert Advisory Group and refined into a survey. This survey gauged the opinions of respondents who were knowledgeable about Church governance and formation about the desirable traits of canonical governors and the extent to which they perceived those traits to be currently in evidence. Researching the differences between the *desired* and the *perceived* levels of various traits provided an indication of the type and level of potential need for formation. Various statistical techniques were employed to analyse the survey responses, including t-tests and factor analysis. The survey data were further interpreted by members of the Expert Advisory Group through a series of *one-on-one* interviews.

The research design for the Thornber study involved a range of participants and a variety of data collection and analysis strategies. These are summarised in Table 3.1. A combination of quantitative and qualitative methods was used for data gathering for the research. The survey provided quantitative data which were used as a basis for conducting follow-up semi-structured interviews. In a qualitative sense, the intent of the research was to develop a deeper understanding of the central phenomenon of *formation for canonical governance*. This involved selecting people that could best help the researcher to understand this phenomenon, through a technique known as *purposeful sampling* (Creswell, 2008).

Table 3.1
Researching Needs for Formation:
Data Collection, Participants and Data Analysis

Data Collection	Participants	Data Analysis
Design and piloting of survey	Expert Advisory Group with expertise in governance and survey design	Analysis of Expert Advisory Group responses – collation and coding
Distribution of survey	Respondents with interest and experience in governance (from Australia, North America, Ireland)	Analysis of survey responses – frequency counts, t-tests and factor analysis
Design and conduct of semi-structured one-on-one interviews, in *face-to-face* and *telephone* mode	Interviewees with interest and experience in governance (from Australia and United States of America)	Analysis of interview responses – collation and coding

The design of the survey enabled data to be gathered in the light of the existing language and frameworks used in church documents, the key ones being *Pastores Dabo Vobis* (John Paul II, 1992) and *Co-Workers in the Vineyard of the Lord* (USCCB, 2005). The introductory section of the survey was used to collect demographic information about the respondents' background and experience in governance, theology, formation, Canon Law, ministry and spirituality as well as the country from which their experience was based. This was followed by a sequence of sections covering each of the four dimensions: human (12 items), spiritual (10 items), intellectual (11 items) and pastoral (10 items). The individual items relating to each of these dimensions, together with the sources for each item, are shown in Tables 3.2 to 3.5.

The traits relating to the human dimension focused on the personality and character of people invited to take on governance roles. Aspects of personal maturity such as integrity, balanced judgment and behaviour, sense of justice, compassion, concern and respect for others were highlighted, along with an appropriate degree of self-knowledge evidenced by an awareness of one's gifts, and the ability to learn from criticism and praise. In other words, these traits were designed to investigate the type of personal qualities that canonical governors should have to perform effectively in the role.

Table 3.2
Traits of Canonical Governors – Human Dimension

Canonical governors	Sources
are people of integrity	Pope John Paul II, 1992, p. 26; USCCB, 2005, p. 36
exhibit balance in judgement	Pope John Paul II, 1992, p. 33, 43; USCCB, 2005, p. 36
possess a deep sense of justice	Pope John Paul II, 1992, p. 43; USCCB, 2005, p. 37
are genuinely compassionate	Pope John Paul II, 1992, p. 43
show a genuine concern for others	Pope John Paul II, 1992, p. 43; USCCB, 2005, p. 37
possess well-developed personal maturity	Pope John Paul II, 1992, p. 43; USCCB, 2005, p. 36
demonstrate self-knowledge	USCCB, 2005, p. 36
respect every person	Pope John Paul II, 1992, p. 43; USCCB, 2005, pp. 37, 60
are aware of their gifts	USCCB, 2005, pp. 36, 48
demonstrate an ability to learn from praise	USCCB, 2005, p. 37
exhibit balance in behaviour	Pope John Paul II, 1992, pp. 33, 43; USCCB, 2005, p. 60
demonstrate an ability to learn from criticism	USCCB, 2005, p. 37

Next, the traits listed under the spiritual dimension were concerned with the canonical governors' understanding and engagement with the deeper purposes and foundations of the role. This included understanding and appreciation of one's baptismal call and vocation, and one's ministry as working for the mission. The spiritual dimension also involves one's openness to transcendence and relationship with God, one's preparedness to publically identify with the ecclesial community, and one's prayer life and practice of other forms of spirituality.

Table 3.3
Traits of Canonical Governors – Spiritual Dimension

Canonical governors	Sources
understand their baptismal call to mission	Downey, 2003; Fox, 2003; Hagstrom, 2003; Pope John Paul II, 1988; 1992, p.17; Rinere, 2003; USCCB, 2005, pp. 12, 48, 49
have a sense of vocation to their role	Hagstrom, 2003; Hahnenberg, 2003; USCCB, 2005, p. 12; Winschel, 2008
are aware that spiritual formation requires individuals to be open to the transcendent	McTernan, 2005; Pope John Paul II, 1988, p. 16; 1992, p. 45; USCCB, 2005, p. 7
view their role as a ministry of governance	Austin, 2000; Cunningham, 1986; Hagstrom, 1996; Huels, 1986, 2000; Morrisey, 2007c; Willis, 1986
understand that spiritual formation is about living intimately united to the Word of God	Casey, 1991; MacLennan and Marr, 2008; Pope John Paul II, 1992; Thornhill, 2007; USCCB, 2005

are committed to the mission of the Church	Arbuckle, 2000, 2005; Grant, 2001a; Hahnenberg, 2003; K. Homan, 2004; Hume, 1999; G. Kelly, 2007; Lucas, 2007; Place, 2004; Pope John Paul II, 1992, p. 32; USCCB, 2005, p. 19; Yanofchick, 2007a
are aware that spiritual formation aims for a daily growing in love of God and neighbour.	Casey, 1991; Pope John Paul II, 1992, p. 45; USCCB, 2005, p. 38
understand that they are a bridge for people to Christ	Gottemoeller, 2007; Pope John Paul II, 1992, p. 43
enjoy a public identification with the Catholic ecclesial community expressed in a variety of ways	Morrisey, 2002; Roman Catholic Church, 1983, Canon116 (1), pp. 149, 204, 298, 1282
pray and practice other forms of spirituality that foster the attitudes and dispositions (listed above)	Pope John Paul II, 1992, pp. 33, 48; USCCB, 2005, p. 59

The intellectual dimension is concerned with the knowledge and understanding that canonical governors have about the Catholic faith. The meaning of revelation, appreciation of the nature and links between Scripture and Tradition, appropriate background in study of mission, of the Church as an organisation, and of Canon Law, along with knowledge of Catholic social teaching and the Catechism of the Catholic Church are the important areas for consideration under this dimension.

Table 3.4
Traits of Canonical Governors – Intellectual Dimension

Canonical governors	Sources
understand that the Catholic Faith is rooted in God's revelation	Pope John Paul II, 1992, p. 53; USCCB, 2005, p. 42
understand that the Catholic Faith is embodied in the living tradition of the Church	Pope John Paul II, 1992, p. 54; USCCB, 2005, p. 42
are aware that formation for lay ecclesial ministry is a journey beyond catechesis into theological reflection	Hahnenberg, 2003; USCCB, 2005
have some background in missiology	Pope John Paul II, 1992, p. 54
have some background in ecclesiology	Pope John Paul II, 1992, p. 12; USCCB, 2005, p. 46
have some background in Canon Law	Abeles, 2008; P. Smith, 2006b; USCCB, 2005
can articulate the missiology which underpins the operation of the ministry	USCCB, 2005
use theology to help understand the needs of the time in the light of Scripture and Tradition	Pope John Paul II, 1992, p. 26; USCCB, 2005, p. 47
have a sound knowledge of Catholic social teaching	Pope John Paul II, 1992, p. 12; USCCB 2005, p. 52
have a sound knowledge of the *Catechism of the Catholic Church*	USCCB, 2005, p. 43
seek to develop their appreciation of the Catholic faith through intellectual formation	Pope John Paul II, 1992, p. 53; USCCB, 2005, p. 42

The operational or practical side of Church governance is the focus of the pastoral dimension. Canonical governors who work effectively in this dimension understand the ministry and their responsibility for its ongoing Catholic identity. They use these understandings in their dealings with bishops and others in the Church, in their day-to-day decision making about organizational priorities, structures and processes, and in their role in selecting and forming future canonical governors. In these ways, they work to inform and inspire a shared communal sense of purpose and vision, and therefore play a vital role in sustaining the mission and identity of their Church ministry.

Table 3.5

Traits of Canonical Governors – Pastoral Dimension

Canonical governors	Sources
understand the ministry they lead	Hahnenberg, 2003; Morrisey, 2007a, 2007c
understand their responsibility for the ongoing Catholic identity of the ministry	Arbuckle, 2006, 2007a; Casey, 2000; Clifton and McEnroe, 1994; Curran, 1997; Hehir, 2008; Morrisey, 2007c
work together in the ministry of leadership to discern the signs of the times for the mission of the Church	Pope John Paul II, 1992, p. 26; USCCB, 2005, p. 47
have an appropriate way of calling those leading the operation of the ministry to account	CHAUSA, 2009; Lakeland, 2004; Zagano, 2007
understand the responsibilities of the local bishop for the coordination of ministerial services in the diocese	Cusack, 2007, 2008; Euart, 2005; USCCB, 2005, pp. 12, 52
use mission-based criteria in forming future governors	CHAUSA, 2006a, 2007a, 2009; Gottemoeller, 2007; Stanley, 2007; Yanofchick, 2007a, 2007b

understand organisational systems and dynamics	Pope John Paul II, 1992, p. 66; USCCB, 2005, pp. 48, 49
understand that they have a responsibility for the spiritual life of their ministry	Casey, 1991; USCCB, 2005, pp. 14, 51
inspire communal purpose and vision	Downey, 2005; Homan et al., 2003
use mission-based criteria in selecting future governors	CHAUSA, 2006a, 2007a, 2009; Gottemoeller, 2007; Stanley, 2007; Statuto, 2004; Weisenbeck, 2007; Yanofchick, 2007a, 2007b

We believe that the traits listed under the various human, spiritual, intellectual and pastoral dimensions in Tables 3.2 to 3.5 can provide a useful means for investigating the formation needs of canonical governors. For example, the individual traits may be used to initiate discussion among those wishing to identify formation needs – *What do the traits mean? Why are they desirable? And, how are they evidenced?* Once agreed, the traits considered to be important can be recast in the form of a survey for selected stakeholders and respondents. This is what we did. Our approach was to invite respondents to rate the desirability of various traits and then to indicate the extent to which they found these traits to be evidenced by those in canonical governance roles.

Survey respondents were invited to indicate their level of agreement in regard to desired traits of canonical governors by choosing one of the following options: *Strongly Agree – Agree – Disagree – Strongly Disagree* (with a further option of *No Answer*). They indicated the extent to which they perceived these traits to be evident by using the following rating scale: *Very High – High – Fair – Low* with further options of *Unable to Judge* and *No Answer*. A copy of the survey can be found Appendix 1.

In the Thornber study, it was decided to distribute the survey online. The particular software used for the online survey was LimeSurvey

(2010) which is licensed to Australian Catholic University. There are several advantages to online surveys, including *cost effectiveness*, since the cost per response decreases as sample size increases (Andrews, Nonnecke, and Preece, 2003); *efficiency*, results can be the same as postal survey content results with the advantages of speedy distribution and response cycles (Andrews et al., 2003); *accessibility*, especially where there is geographical spread of respondents combined with a limited field of potential participants because of the expertise expected; *snowball sampling*, where the researcher asks respondents to recommend other individuals to participate in the study (Creswell, 2008). This technique was used in the Thornber study not only to increase the number of respondents, but also to more deeply engage the respondents in the research process, through encouraging them to email invitations to knowledgeable and interested colleagues to respond to the survey. This had the effect of building trust among the researcher and the respondents as well as increasing the response rate. Throughout the survey process, it was important to ensure that the distribution procedures did not to offend or intrude inappropriately, and to assure respondents about the purpose of the research and the credibility of the researchers (Andrews et al., 2003). Each of these features of survey design and distribution assisted in the development of questions to be asked in the next stage of data collection, i.e. the follow-up interviews.

These interviews were semi-structured and conducted one-on-one. One advantage of interviewing in this way was that it allowed the interviewees to create the options for responding (Creswell, 2008), sometimes providing opportunity for clarification of the question being asked, at other times the prospect for reflecting upon and extending their response. This was important as the Thornber study participants came from a range of backgrounds, including theology, spirituality, executive management, governance, Canon Law, civil law and human resources. Their perspectives highlighted different emphases in the nature of formation and formation needs for canonical governance. Another advantage of interviewing was that it allowed for the meanings of key terms and concepts to be explained and clarified. This helped in developing shared understanding about the substance of each interview question.

On the other hand, we need to be mindful that interviews can have pitfalls. For example, Creswell (2008, p. 226) has noted the problem of an interviewer filtering an interviewee's responses, selectively omitting views that do not support the claims of the research. To address this concern, the Thornber study interviewees were provided with a transcript of their interview to ensure that they could see that they had been reported correctly. They were then able to make any changes and clarifications they thought necessary. Another danger in interviewing is that the interviewees give the answer which they think the interviewers want to hear. The Thornber study addressed this concern by the interviewer making it clear to interviewees that there were 'no right answers' and that he had no preconceived or predetermined position on the question or issue under discussion.

While these potential pitfalls were recognised, the interviews in the Thornber study were conducted to maximise the validity of the interviewee responses. All of those interviewed had recognised expertise in and involvement with existing or planned Public Juridic Persons (PJPs). Many had published on aspects of the topic and the works of some have been cited in this book. Often their writings outlined their experience in the development of forms of canonical governance for PJPs with which they had been associated over periods of up to 20 years. In short, they were experts in the fields of Canon Law, theology, spirituality, governance and formation or leaders of existing PJPs, and many had been involved in developing formation programmemes and facilitating their provision to existing and potential canonical governors.

The purpose of the interview was two-fold: to validate the definition of formation, and to seek comments and insights about patterns in the survey data. Therefore the interview was conducted in two parts.

Part 1. Consider the following definition of formation:

> a reflected development on one's gifts and how they contribute to the need in hand providing an holistic preparation of a person for a role – human, spiritual, intellectual, pastoral – including reflection on the experiences of their own life which might highlight some lacks in development or knowledge that are essential for that need.

Do you think this definition is reasonable for researching the formation needs of those invited to undertake roles in canonical governance? What aspects, if any, require clarification or amendment?

Part 2. Consider the following survey responses relating to each dimension:

Dimension of formation	Items related to
Human	sense of justice, compassion, respect for every person
Spiritual	baptismal call, vocation, openness to transcendence, living united to the Word of God, formation as growing in love of God and neighbour, enjoyment of public identification with the Catholic ecclesial community
Intellectual	awareness of formation as a journey beyond catechesis into theological reflection, missiology, ecclesiology, theology, Scripture and Tradition, appreciation of Catholic Faith through formation
Pastoral	discerning the signs of the times, calling those leading the ministry to account, responsibilities of the local bishop, responsibility for the spiritual life of the ministry

Given the distribution of survey responses for each item listed above – what issues, if any, strike you as significant in relation to the desirability of the trait and its evidence in practice? What do you think are the implications for formation for canonical governance in light of these responses?

Figure 3.1 Outline of the Interview Schedule

An outline of the interview schedule listing the questions and related information is presented in Figure 3.1.

First, interviewees were invited to consider the following definition for formation:

> a reflected development on one's gifts and how they contribute to the need in hand providing an holistic preparation of a person for a role – human, spiritual, intellectual, pastoral – including reflection on the experiences of their own life which might highlight some lacks in development or knowledge that are essential for that need.

This definition was formulated on the basis of available literature – very little of which provided explicit reference to what 'formation' actually meant. Interviewees were invited to reflect and respond on the reasonableness of the wording of the proposed definition.

In the second part of the interview, interviewees were asked to comment on patterns in the survey responses. They were provided in advance, with a selection of the survey data together with a summary of the responses to all 43 survey items. The selection of data was made as it was considered that it was not possible to elicit responses in a single interview to all survey items within an appropriate timeframe. Instead, items were chosen on the basis of their face validity as areas and issues for further clarification and interpretation. For example, the human dimension questions focused human qualities – justice, compassion and respect. The spiritual dimension included discussion about the nature of baptismal call, vocation, elements of spiritual formation and identification with Church. Issues considered relating to the intellectual dimension included formal elements in the study of theology, while questions about the pastoral dimension focused on the nature of ministry, mission, governance and Catholic identity.

Finding Meaning – Analysis of the Data

The online survey data was collated by the LimeSurvey Programme and provided the data which was exported to spreadsheets where it was statistically analysed. The data was tested for statistical significance using the t-test (Field, 2000, pp. 239-241) and subjected to Factor Analysis to seek possible relationships (Field, 2000, Chp 11). Cronbach's alpha coefficient was calculated to provide evidence of the reliability of the survey data.

Analysis of the interview data involved systematically searching and arranging the interview transcripts, related field notes and other collected materials. As Bogdan and Biklen (2007, p. 159) explain:

> Data analysis involves working with the data, organising them, breaking them into manageable units. Coding them, synthesising them, and searching for patterns.

In the Thornber study, this entailed taking the raw data and seeking to elicit the key concepts and ideas which might be contained in them in order to shed light on the research questions (Lichtman, 2006). The interviews were audio recorded and transcribed. Coding was done and a schema was created for grouping the data using NVivo software (*NVivo 8 Fundamentals*, 2008). Themes emerging from this coding were based on groupings from the factor analysis of the survey data.

Are the findings verifiable and ethical?

Verification is the provision of evidence that the findings are valid and reliable from the viewpoint of the research method used and the interpretations and claims that follow (Bush, 2007). Validity in the Thornber study relied on the quality of the items in the survey and the questions and conduct of the interviews. The fact that informants involved in the research had expertise in the field provided a presumption of validity, in that, if the questions were initially poorly phrased, the researcher would expect to have any shortcomings pointed out very quickly by the interviewees. The validity of the data in the survey was tested via factor analysis.

In the Thornber study, reliability referred to the question: Would similar survey and interviewee responses be obtained by different researchers with the same level of expertise on different occasions? Given the newness of the field, it is possible that the interviewees' views on questions and issues associated with the Thornber research might change over time. For example, Arbuckle (1993, 1995, 2000, 2007a) has written over the last 20 years of the changes in the Church and their implications, particularly for health care and in the light of an understanding of the mission of the Church. Thus different findings at a future time should not be taken to imply that the results of Thornber research are not reliable. In fact, reliability in the Thornber study was strengthened by using Cronbach's alpha coefficient to test the survey data, and by providing ample opportunity for interviewees to change their responses in the light of their further reflection, including reviewing a transcript of their interview and the interpretations made with a right to correct any possible misunderstandings in their responses.

The ethical issues associated with identifying formation also need to be carefully considered. Deliberate efforts were made in the Thornber study to minimise the likelihood of harm to participants, to protect their privacy and to maintain confidentiality (Punch, cited in Berg, 2004, p. 43). Approval of the ACU Human Research Ethics Committee was gained before the research commenced. Letters were emailed to prospective participants for the online survey, outlining the research and its purpose, and inviting them to participate in an online questionnaire survey (see Appendix 2). They were assured of the confidentiality of their responses. Letters were sent to prospective interviewees, inviting them to participate in a semi-structured, face-to-face or telephone interview of not more than one hour duration (see Appendix 3). Their letters similarly outlined the research and its purpose, assuring them of anonymity and informing them of their right to withdraw from the research at any time. In light of this planning, no situations of a conflict of interest were envisioned or arose during the study. The data were stored in accordance with Australian Catholic University guidelines on data storage.

In this chapter, we have outlined the research design used in the Thornber study to identify formation needs. The methods that were used to design the online survey and the interview schedule have been described, along with the steps taken to ensure validity and reliability of findings. Our purpose was to explain the approach to identifying formation used in Thornber's PhD research, and thereby provide guidance for others interested in conducting similar investigations. The significance of the Thornber study, as noted by the examiners, is that it addressed important issues and challenges involved with the increased roles and responsibilities for lay women and men in today's Church. Both examiners commended the use of the source documents (Pope John Paul II, 1992; USCCB, 2005) as a foundation for desired traits. In fact, one examiner explained that to her knowledge:

> [m]y initial, and sustained, view relates to the cultural authenticity of the [Thornber] research. That is, within the arena of Catholic education leadership it holds a critical place because of its timing, and its attentiveness to foundational sources centred in ecclesial, organisational and formational literature. Clearly, an argument for the nature and rationale for formation in the area of canonical governance is expanded sequentially and powerfully.

The approach taken to identifying formation need explained in this chapter yielded some interesting results! These are examined in detail in the following chapters.

4
Mature and Self-Aware Canonical Governors: The Human Dimension

What types of people are canonical governors? What personal attributes do they have that help them perform well in the role? These questions focus on the *humanity* (or human dimension) of those in governance roles. They are concerned with the character of the people involved, their maturity and their knowledge of themselves. In this chapter, we report findings from Thornber study (2012) relating to the desired and existing traits of canonical governors relating to this human dimension of their work.

The 'Human' Traits of Canonical Governors

The importance of the human qualities and character of those called to governance roles in the Church was evident in *Pastores Dabo Vobis* (Pope John Paul II, 1992) and *Co-Workers in the Vineyard of the Lord* (USCCB, 2005). For example, in the *Co-Workers* document (USCCB, 2005) the American bishops explained that the goal of formation was to develop the lay ecclesial ministers' human qualities and character and to foster a healthy and well-balanced personality for the sake of both personal growth and ministerial service.

The significance given to the human dimension in these documents was reflected in the responses to the survey, as shown in Table 4.1. The desirability of human traits was emphasised with over 90 per cent of respondents agreeing or strongly agreeing with all but one of the items listed under this dimension. The exception was the item: *Canonical governors demonstrate an ability to learn from praise*. Thirteen per cent (13 per cent) of respondents believe that this was not a desirable trait for canonical governors. It could be that these respondents simply regard praise as recognition of a job well done rather than something from which to learn.

Given the desirability of most of these traits, it is interesting to note the relative proportion of respondents who regarded them to be evident to only a fair degree or less. While there appears to be a general consensus that canonical governors are people of integrity and are aware of their 'gifts', namely, the particular qualities and attributes that they bring to the role, the perceived existence of other traits was not so pronounced. In fact almost half of the respondents indicated that the canonical governors with whom they were familiar showed balance in their behaviour and an ability to learn from criticism to only a fair extent at best. Other areas where human traits were more modestly evident included canonical governors' level of personal maturity, self-knowledge, respect for every person, and ability to learn from praise.

Table 4.1

Desired and Existing Traits of Canonical Governors – Human Dimension (N=92)

Canonical governors	This trait is desirable (%)					The extent to which this trait exists (%)				
are people of integrity	88	10	1	-	1	41	43	10	-	6
exhibit balance in judgment	66	32	1	-	1	12	61	18	2	7
possess a deep sense of justice	69	29	-	-	2	20	46	25	2	7
are genuinely compassionate	57	38	3	-	1	20	47	20	2	11

	Strongly Agree	Agree	Disagree	Strongly Disagree	No Answer	Very High	High	Fair	Low	Unable to Judge/No Answer
show a genuine concern for others	61	36	1	-	2	20	55	20	-	5
possess well-developed personal maturity	67	31	1	-	1	12	52	29	1	6
demonstrate self-knowledge	48	45	4	-	3	5	41	31	4	19
respect every person	63	31	4	-	2	14	45	28	4	9
are aware of their gifts	29	62	7	-	2	13	70	11	2	4
demonstrate an ability to learn from praise	13	70	11	2	4	2	39	32	4	23
exhibit balance in behaviour	41	53	1	-	4	2	34	40	8	16
demonstrate an ability to learn from criticism	33	60	2	1	4	2	34	40	8	16

One further point of interest is the proportion of respondents who were unable or did not answer particular items. For example, it appears that respondents were less confident about assessing the extent to which canonical governors were compassionate, demonstrated self-knowledge, learnt from praise as well as criticism, and exhibited balance in behaviour. In some cases, this may be due to the item being difficult to answer; for example how does somebody estimate another's level of self-knowledge? In other cases, it may have been because the respondents perceived that they only saw canonical governors in certain contexts and were unwilling to generalize.

The patterns in the survey responses, shown in Table 4.1 are a starting point for considering the formation needs of canonical governors. While the existence of a discrepancy between what is desired and what exists does not necessarily indicate a need, it can be used as a basis for discussion. The aim of the interviews was to gather insights from those experienced in the field of formation for canonical governance about the meanings and patterns in the survey responses. Two themes relating to the human dimension emerged from the factor analysis. These were *human maturity* and *self-awareness*.

Human Maturity and Canonical Governors

The theme of human maturity is associated with the idea that canonical governors need to be people of integrity. Such integrity is evidenced by a deep sense of justice, genuine compassion and respect for every person.

Having a deep sense of justice. There was strong agreement among survey respondents that canonical governors need to have a sense of justice (see Table 4.1). However over a quarter of the respondents considered this trait to be evident to only a fair degree or less. Interviewees had a range of reactions to these survey results. Some were encouraged by the finding that the majority (65 per cent) of survey respondents thought that canonical governors had a high to very high sense of justice, as one interviewee explained:

> What I am happy to see is that canonical governors [do] possess a deep sense of justice. (Interviewee D)

Another interviewee commented on the desirability of this trait:

> What we are about in Catholic healthcare is being able to provide just and equitable services to those most in need so I think having a deep a sense of justice would be certainly a desired trait for someone who served at that level. (Interviewee Z)

Other interviewees explained that they would have expected more similarity in survey responses between the desired and existing traits of canonical governors. Comments included the following:

> Well the desired traits didn't surprise me in terms of the higher percentages, but the response [on existing traits] I have to admit did surprise me a little bit. It gave me pause to think. (Interviewee N)

> I am not dismayed either because sense of justice still has a fairly high standing at 65 per cent. That is probably not bad in reality; though not as high as you might like. (Interviewee A)

While cautious in expressing surprise or concern about the extent to which this trait is evidenced, interviewees supported the idea that a deep sense of justice was a desirable trait. They also agreed that formation was needed to bridge the gap between what was desired and what was currently perceived as the reality of this trait.

One intriguing finding emerging from the interviews was the way that interviewees interpreted the concept of justice and how its meaning is shaped by culture and politics. Several of the interviewees in the US for example pondered the meaning and importance of canonical governors having a sense of justice, and what it meant to have a sense of justice. At the time of the interviews, US President Barack Obama was working to have a Bill passed which would provide health care cover for some 30 million citizens who currently had no cover. The justice issue being debated was whether health care should be a social right or a paid-for service (Keehan, 2009a, 2009b). This situation underlined the point that the interpretation and practice of justice is contingent on the culture of a society. There is no single and agreed definition of justice that can be applied in every situation. The following comments illustrate this point:

> *The first issue is do we agree about the definition of justice?* (Interviewee H)
>
> *I do not know how fully they understand the meaning of justice.* (Interviewee X)

Some interviewees reflected on what they saw as a developing sense of justice over recent times:

> *Well I wonder whether if you had done this study forty years ago that 'deep sense of justice' would have been recognised as being important. I also wonder whether, for the responders, the greater awareness that we now have of the centrality of justice causes them to look for that in others.* (Interviewee L)

Another interviewee reflected on changing understandings of justice, and the challenge of working with people who have different views:

> *The legislation [for American healthcare reform] does reflect at least some change in the national consciousness that health care is a right. [Though] we are still dealing with people who think it is a consumer good and if you have money you can pay for it.* (Interviewee H)

Related to this point, some interviewees were critical of the understanding and practice of justice of some canonical governors yet questioned whether they should be regarded as 'unjust'. For example:

> *We have a number of board members in our hospitals who I think are very good people, very dedicated to the ministry but they were very opposed to healthcare reform in this country. Their views are based on a certain sense of the economy and so forth, but would I say that they are unjust?* (Interviewee X)

This interviewee went on to explain that:

> *There might be kind of a naïveté where they would say 'I am a just person' without fully understanding what the tradition is.* (Interviewee X)

Interviewees' reflections about justice were centered on the needs of particular ministries as those in charge grappled with the tension of serving the mission with finite resources. This meant that decisions and choices had to be made. These decisions saw lower priority given to some needs and higher priority given to others. Interviewees felt that this could lead to the perception that the canonical governors of the ministry were unjust. Interviewees who were or had been members of PJPs were particularly passionate about this. They spoke of their experience about the difficulties of providing quality service in the light of the mission with limited resources. Their concern was that those not involved in the decision making might perceive that their decisions as unjust. For example:

> *When some of those issues are brought to bear [that would indicate] whether or not they [i.e. the governors] have a deep sense of justice, whoever is not around that table will not really know.* (Interviewee Z)

The comments and concerns raise questions about who is entitled to judge whether someone is acting justly, and on what criteria should such judgments be made. The following reflection illustrates the potential ambiguity and uncertainty around decisions involving the exercise of justice:

> *It depends on perspective. But I would sort of defend the position that was taken and the way we went about coming to a decision. These things were very high in our minds. But there could be a perception that certain people perhaps, in making that decision, were not treated justly.* (Interviewee I)

Diverse cultural understandings about the meaning of justice and varied perceptions, knowledge and involvement in decision making processes highlight the value and need for formation in this area of canonical governance. The survey responses and interviewee reflections indicate that people have varied understandings of justice and what it means to act justly. Formation in this area might usefully focus on the nature and application of Catholic social teaching to the dilemmas faced by canonical governors. The aim would be to develop a more informed and shared understanding of the meaning and dynamics of acting with justice.

Being genuinely compassionate. Another desirable human trait of canonical governors identified through the survey responses and validated by the interviewees was showing genuine compassion in their decision making. Over 95 per cent of survey respondents agreed the being compassionate was a desirable quality and over 66 per cent indicated that they perceived the existence of this quality in canonical governors to a high (47 per cent) or very high (20 per cent) extent. On the other hand, around 20 per cent of respondents felt that the canonical governors with whom they were familiar were genuinely compassionate to a fair degree.

Several interviewees grappled with what was meant by 'being genuinely compassionate', as illustrated by the following comments:

> *Compassion is not 'bleeding heart' stuff.* (Interviewee R)
>
> *With some [canonical governors] there is not a whole lot of room for what I would call sympathy – as opposed to compassion.* (Interviewee D)
>
> *I think we struggle to really understand things like compassion. It is not unmitigated kindness at all costs and it can often appear in that guise, which is counterproductive.* (Interviewee A)

Another reflected on how the trait of compassion had been part of the canonical governors' decision making, and how this may, or may not be recognised by those affected by the decisions. Seen in this light, it is important that board members be able to explain their decisions and the way that they came about making those decisions:

> I know we are dealing with perceptions and maybe I could be defensive but I can understand people's perceptions. You are in it, you make your decisions. and there may be some people who may consider themselves treated unjustly or without compassion. (Interviewee I)

These responses indicate that people need to be clear about the meaning of compassion, and be able to recognise and explain how it works in practice (Catholic Health World, 2011b). Compassion is a virtue and can be in tension with the capacity (as opposed to the willingness) of an individual or organisation to provide the resources required (White, 1996).

A related issue in assessing the degree of compassion evident in governance is the extent to which an organisation's culture (and its manifestations in hierarchical authority and bureaucratic processes) support or inhibit the exercise of compassion. Authoritarianism and bureaucratic inertia are frequently sources of tension in human service organisations devoted to the health, welfare and education of individuals, especially those in most need, as evidenced by the following reflection:

> It seems to me that people who are drawn to [healthcare] would be strong in compassion when they come in at the beginning levels. But does it get bred out of them as they rise to a position of leadership, or is it just the perception? Perceptions are important. (Interviewee L)

There are several implications for formation when it comes to the issue of compassion. First, canonical governors need to be able to articulate what compassion means and how it is enacted in the ministry. Second, they need to be aware of the factors which sometimes make the 'face of compassion' in the ministry difficult to see. Third, they need the capability to confront and remedy those instances where the delivery of services is comprised by a 'cult of efficiency' (Stein, 2002) and a corresponding neglect of the individuals and communities that the ministry is supposed to serve.

Respecting every person. Another trait that was considered important was *having respect for every person*. Over 93 per cent of survey respondents agreed that this trait was desirable. Yet following a similar pattern to the previous two traits, there was some discrepancy between the level of agreement about desirability of canonical governors being respectful of every person and the extent to which such respect was evidenced in practice. In fact when the interviewees compared the survey responses with the items relating to justice and compassion, some were struck by the relatively low ratings given to the practice of respect for others. For example:

> *It was interesting to me that the question about wanting someone who respects every person was ranked the lowest of these three [traits]. Somehow respect for persons seems to be the basis for justice and compassion and so it should be highest rather than lowest.* (Interviewee P)

This concern was echoed by other interviewees:

> *I would have expected higher level responses because compassion, respect, [and] the dignity of the person is the core from which everything else flows. If it is not very high then that is surprising.* (Interviewee J)

> *I was surprised. I mean, thirty per cent of respondents giving a rating of fair to low for respecting every person is a concern. I do not know how you would probe why that is said, but it surprised me.* (Interviewee L)

Respect for others is seen as a fundamental aspect of governance. For example, one interviewee commented that:

> *[At meetings] you take respect for granted. That is something the participants owe one another.* (Interviewee V)

Another said:

> *When you start looking at Catholic social teaching and the dignity of each person — that is what we are grounded upon!* (Interviewee Z)

These responses strongly support the view that canonical governors need to show respect for every person. However, as with the items relating to 'sense of justice' and 'compassion', there was little articulation of what the interviewees meant by respect. This may provide a focus for formation: what does it mean to have respect for the person that one serves and works with.

The trait of respect for others flows from Catholic social teaching principle of the dignity of the human person (Aubert and Boileau, 2003) and should therefore be fundamental to the exercise of ministry. The aims of formation in this context are that canonical governors develop and demonstrate 'respect for every person', understand the rationale of this trait in the light of Catholic social teaching, and be able to articulate it to those involved in and served by the ministry.

Other insights from interviewees on the maturity of canonical governors extended beyond the consideration of individual traits relating to justice, compassion and respect to seeing these traits in relation to one another. The interviewees did not see the traits relating to human maturity in stand-alone terms. Their view was that justice, compassion and respect are important requirements and that people would not be considered for roles in canonical governance if these traits were absent. For example, one interviewee explained that:

> *They are human qualities, and they [justice, compassion, respect] are very much Gospel [values]* (Interviewee D)

Another interviewee stated that:

> *We do not name justice, compassion and respect but we would never choose someone who did not have those because they are special requirements of the Church.* (Interviewee E)

Others spoke of the value of articulating these traits to develop shared understanding about the purpose and process of their endeavours. For example:

> *As canonical governors, we have considered justice, compassion and respect in our discernment process for the benefit of the mission and the organisation.* (Interviewee I)

Interviewees also explained that sometimes these traits may come into conflict. One example is the tension between compassion and justice. This tension can arise when decisions need to be made about the allocation of finite resources in circumstances where all needs cannot be met. It may seem that there is a lack of compassion, for example, when the organisation makes decisions about long-term survival at the expense of the needs of a particular group. In these situations, it could be argued that such a decision was just because it was based on the needs for survival of the ministry. Alternatively it may be seen as unjust because it neglects the needs of those most at risk.

The interplay of the human traits of acting justly, being compassionate and having respect for others with the issues and contexts faced by those in governance roles is complex. Canonical governors require the human maturity to deal with such complexity. In short, they need to be people who are well-rounded. The following statements by interviewees indicate the tension and need for clarity in decision making about complex issues:

> *I believe that there is justice, compassion and respect but there have been occasions when certain decisions have had to be made for the good of the mission, if you like, and I can understand an outsider's perception that perhaps there has not been justice exercised.* (Interviewee I)

These responses indicate the complexity of issues facing canonical governors and support our view that they need to be people who have the maturity to act with integrity when dealing with these issues. Integrity in this sense has to do with our capability to understand and live out our values through acting justly, being compassionate and showing respect for others – and appreciating the connections between these traits.

Formation has an important place in developing these traits. Interviewees highlighted the need for canonical governors to learn to make decisions appropriate to the values of their ministry. The interviewees' grappling with the meanings and practice of justice, compassion and respect, indicate the necessity for formation experiences that help canonical governors develop, articulate and enact the values that underpin their ministry. This was best summed up in the observation of one interviewee:

Maybe it means that we acknowledge we still have a way to go, that we are being realistic about it. (Interviewee A)

This viewpoint was typical of how interviewees spoke about the focus, content and need for formation. They expressed confidence that such needs can be met, believing that people can be encouraged and guided to a fuller understanding and realisation of personal maturity. Their views align well with Župarić's (2010) claim that maturity is a dynamic concept.

Self-Awareness and Canonical Governors

A second theme to emerge from the factor analysis was *self-awareness*. This theme is associated with canonical governors being aware of their 'gifts' and to be open to the possibility that through formation, their individual talents and other attributes (and their awareness of them) may deepen and grow. The trait of canonical governors being aware of their gifts was strongly supported. Over 90 per cent of survey respondents agreed that this was a desirable trait, and more than 80 per cent of respondents indicated that the trait was evidenced to a high degree or more (see Table 4.1). From these results, it appears that canonical governors have a strong sense of the personal talents that they bring to the role – at least in the minds of those who work with them.

Awareness of a person's particular talents and other attributes, and how these have been shaped by their experiences constitutes an important starting point for formation. In fact interviewees spoke of the value of commencing formation from the experience of the person. For example, one interviewee with experience in running formation programmes explained their approach of gathering information about participants beforehand and using it as a basis for developing the content and the processes of the programme.

> We clearly try to use that information to raise a person's awareness of the gifts that they bring to this ministry and how they contribute to that need. We definitely try to connect formation experience with their personal experience. (Interviewee X)

Related to this, several interviewees emphasised the value of deliberately reflecting on your own talents and needs as a basis for further development, for example:

> Yes, there is only one way to find out what else you need, [that is] by bringing together all your own gifts and reflecting on them and how in fact you can apply them to the work to be done. Then you find out that you may have some strong gifts in one area and be sadly lacking in another. (Interviewee J)

Another interviewee explained their formation experience for the role of canonical governor in these terms:

> The personal reflection made me consider all the elements that made a difference in my spiritual life. It helped me question the knowledge that I have – and what I would like to have. It [was] a very personal thing. (Interviewee I)

Other interviewees spoke of the connection between developing an awareness of the gifts that a person brings to the role and their understanding and recognition of their spirituality. For some, this can involve issues of faith and theology, as one interviewee suggested:

> We need to have more of an understanding [of the] connection between

baptism and mission. So that just reaffirms for me that there is more that should be done there. (Interviewee Z)

For others, the deepening of one's level of self-awareness can be understood as a consequence of their experience as canonical governors and their formation based on that experience, as one interviewee described:

I gradually grew into doing what I now do. It was not by accident. It was by choice. (Interviewee A)

Self-awareness, especially awareness of one's gifts, is a necessary element of formation for canonical governance. Practically, this is demonstrated through formation programmes that recognise and respect each participant's experience and the gifts that they bring to the role.

The Human Dimension of Canonical Governance

Those charged with the responsibility under Canon Law for maintaining a ministry of the Church need to be mature and self-aware human beings with the capacity to discern the needs of those serving and served by the ministry in complex and changing times.

In this chapter, we have explored the nature and issues surrounding the factors of human maturity and self-awareness related to the human dimension of canonical governance. Having a deep sense of justice, being compassionate and respecting every person were identified as highly valuable traits, though in the minds of some survey respondents and interviewees these traits were not always evident to the level desired. One complicating feature in analyzing differences between *what is desired* and *what is evidenced* is the meaning that individuals place on terms like justice, compassion and respect. It became clear from the interviewee reflections that these terms can have different meanings depending on the context and the perspective from which one views the decision making process.

In a world of finite resources, the exercise of justice, compassion and respect can sometimes be in tension. A decision that may seem just to some people may be regarded as unjust to others because they are not aware of all the facts, or all the needs. Sometimes it can appear that important values have been ignored when in fact they have not. Such circumstances make life difficult for canonical governors. Justice, compassion and respect are essential concepts with which canonical governors are required to grapple. Doing so requires human maturity and self-awareness (Hester, 2000; Talone, 2004, 2005). Self-awareness and specifically awareness of one's gifts is both a resource for tackling complex governance issues as well as a potential window into the spiritual dimension of one's work.

The implication from the findings presented in this chapter on the human dimension of canonical governance is that formation is fundamental. Effective formation can develop the 'person' of the canonical governor. It cultivates the ways participants learn from praise and criticism; their understanding and practice of justice, compassion and respect; and their knowledge of themselves and their needs. In short, it helps those in governance roles to grow in maturity and self-awareness and thereby make better decisions.

5
Called and Committed Canonical Governors: The Spiritual Dimension

The spiritual dimension of formation for canonical governance is concerned with how people engage with the transcendent (i.e. beyond the limits of experience) as well as the immanent (existing within and all in things). This means recognising that the mission in all human forms, that is, those working in health, education and social welfare ministries, draws its meaning from the belief in a creator God who intended good for the world (McBrien, 1994). Brueggemann (2007) reflected on this engagement with a personal deity as both transcendent and immanent in the text of Deuteronomy 10:17-18:

> For the Lord your God, is the God of gods and the Lord of lords, the great God, mighty and awesome, who has no favourites and accepts no bribes; who executes justice for the orphan and the widow, and who befriends the alien, feeding and clothing him.

He described its implications as expressing 'God's grand sovereignty and God's compassionate neighbourliness' (p. 56). Canonical governors are invited to engage with God recognising both of these elements. Once the invitation is accepted, this requires their involvement in faith and action, or faith and good works as described by the Letter of St. James (2:14-17):

> What good is it, my brothers, if someone says he has faith but does not have works? Can that faith save him? If a brother or a sister has nothing to wear and has no food for

the day and one of you says to them 'Go in peace, keep warm, and eat well' but you do not give them the necessities of the body, what good is it? So also faith of itself, if it does not have works, is dead.

And so, the role of canonical governors goes beyond that of ordinary corporate governors. While both are concerned with the quality of service and the culture and sustainability of the organisation, they differ in one critical respect. Canonical governors acknowledge and engage with the spiritual aspects of their role and work – and do so in the light of Canon Law. In this chapter we explore this distinctive spiritual dimension and describe the ways and extent to which those in canonical governance are called and committed to their roles.

The 'Spiritual' Traits of Canonical Governors

Spirituality means to live with a belief that there is more to life than is physically observable, and that there is a reality beyond human that is regarded as transcendent. Christian spirituality as informed by the Jewish and Christian Scriptures is often termed "the Word of God". The other source is the Christian tradition which is the teaching of the Church that arises from the long, reflected living experience of the Church and its members and tested against the Scriptures (G. Kelly, 1998).

The Thornber study (2012) examined the meaning and various elements of spirituality that were highlighted in the ecclesial literature, particularly in *Pastores Dabo Vobis* (Pope John Paul II, 1992) and *Co-Workers in the Vineyard of the Lord* (USCCB, 2005). These documents refer to spirituality in terms of how those working in Church ministries understand and experience their baptismal call and sense of vocation to their role; how they see their governance role as a public ministry of the Church; and how they view prayer and other types of spiritual formation.

A series of traits based around the themes evident in the literature (Pope John Paul II, 1992; USCCB; 2005) were developed as survey items.

Survey respondents were invited to express the extent to which they agreed that each trait was desirable, and then indicate the level to which they perceived that those currently in governance roles exhibited those traits. The differences between desired and existing traits in the spiritual dimension are shown in Table 5.1.

There were high levels of agreement among survey respondents that canonical governors need to understand their baptismal call, have a sense of vocation, see their role as a ministry, and appreciate the nature and significance of spiritual formation as an important supporting element for their work. Respondents were less supportive of the idea that canonical governors need to *understand that they are a bridge for people to Christ* or *enjoy a public identification with the Catholic ecclesial community* with 17 per cent and 13 per cent respectively disagreeing that these were desirable traits. Subsequent interviews indicated these results may have been due to respondents regarding the language of the former item as being somewhat obscure and difficult to assess, and the notion of 'enjoyment' in the latter item as not really capturing the sense that canonical governors should have with respect to their identification with the Catholic ecclesial community – especially in times of controversy and challenge.

Table 5.1

Desired and Existing Traits of Canonical Governors – Spiritual Dimension (N=92)

Canonical governors	This trait is desirable (%)					The extent to which this trait exists (%)				
understand their baptismal call to mission	71	25	3	-	1	23	40	22	9	6
have a sense of vocation to their role	59	38	1	-	2	20	42	24	8	6

are aware that spiritual formation requires individuals to be open to the transcendent	61	32	3	-	4	17	34	26	7	16
view their role as a ministry of governance	66	30	3	-	1	25	41	23	8	3
understand that spiritual formation is about living intimately united to the Word of God	46	43	8	-	3	10	35	32	10	13
are committed to the mission of the Church	71	26	1	1	1	32	36	24	3	5
are aware that spiritual formation aims for a daily growing in love of God and neighbour	47	48	3	-	2	12	38	32	4	14
understand that they are a bridge for people to Christ	23	50	17	3	7	1	24	41	16	17

enjoy a public identification with the Catholic ecclesial community expressed in a variety of ways	46	39	13	-	2	14	31	30	16	9
pray and practice other forms of spirituality that foster the attitudes and dispositions (listed above)	54	37	6	-	3	16	32	30	13	9
	Strongly Agree	Agree	Disagree	Strongly Disagree	No Answer	Very High	High	Fair	Low	Unable to Judge/No Answer

While there was general agreement on the desirability of most of the traits relating to the spiritual dimension, the survey respondents' perceptions of the actual existence of those traits were more varied. Between 20 per cent and 30 per cent of respondents indicated that most traits were evident to only a fair extent. For some items – for example those relating to the understanding and practice of spiritual formation, the existence of such traits was even more modest. The incidence of responses in the 'fair' to 'low' categories, as shown in Table 5.1 provided a basis for discussion at follow-up interviews.

The factor analysis of the survey responses to items associated with the spiritual dimension identified *Sense of Call and Vocation* and *Call to Spirituality* as two themes underpinning the work of canonical governors. In the following sections, we explore these themes by considering the survey responses and the reflections of the interviewees on those responses.

Sense of Call and Vocation

What does it mean to say someone is 'called' to a role? Why do some people regard their work as a vocation and others do not? These are questions that go to the heart of the spiritual dimension of canonical governance. In the Catholic Church, the concepts of baptismal call and sense of vocation have been expressed in the long tradition of social teaching linking God and neighbour (CHAUSA, 2007b; Conway, 2003; Cornish, 1993; McClellan and Dominguez, 2006).

Baptismal Call. For Catholics and other Christians, the sacrament of baptism is a call to live according to the teachings of Jesus Christ. The nature of this 'baptismal call' has been described as requiring a deeper level of understanding and commitment than what might be the case for people who feel drawn to a particular job or profession in a secular sense (Hahnenberg, 2003). For this reason, having an understanding of one's baptismal call is considered by many to be fundamental. The desirability of the trait that they *understand their baptismal call as a call to mission* was rated very strongly by survey respondents with over 95 per cent expressing agreement. However, the perception that such understanding was in evidence was rated as *very high* by only 17 per cent of respondents and as High by 34 per cent, giving a combined figure of 51 per cent. Interviewees expressed a range of concerns and opinions about why this might be the case. One interviewee was particularly critical:

> *You only have 17 per cent of respondents saying that canonical governors have a very high degree of understanding of their baptismal call, right? You should have 100 per cent! If a canonical governor*

> *does not understand their baptismal call to mission how can they be a canonical governor?* (Interviewee F)

In contrast, other interviewees saw the survey responses as meeting their expectations, at least in terms of what is desired. For example:

> *I'm not surprised that the ideal is there. It is an admirable ideal that canonical governors actually understand their baptismal call to mission.* (Interviewee D)

On the other hand when asked about existing levels of understanding, several interviewees raised the issue of how 'baptismal call' is understood and practiced by canonical governors, noting that the term is not part of the general vocabulary of most people. For example, one interviewee said:

> *I'm not sure that the governors that I know would be able to articulate that as a quality themselves, yet they probably live it without consciously putting it in those terms.* (Interviewee H)

Another interviewee explained that:

> *Lots of card-carrying Catholics do not talk in that sort of language.* (Interviewee D)

Interviewees were generally of the view that canonical governors, while they may not understand the term 'baptismal call' were nevertheless committed to following Jesus Christ and to their involvement in the mission of bringing the good news. For example:

> *I think they live as authentic Christians who are following Jesus and the Gospel to the best of their ability, but they don't define it in terms of a baptismal call to mission.* (Interviewee D)

Similarly another interviewee noted:

> *They may feel called to service but they may not identify it as an expression of their baptismal call.* (Interviewee H)

This apparent lack of understanding (at least in terms of recognising the concept of 'baptismal call') led some interviewees to reflect on the nature of formation programmes and in particular that:

> *The key to formation is emphasising the call to service and holiness through our baptism.* (Interviewee H)

This point was similarly emphasised as follows:

> *There needs to be more work done helping people to understand that [in] this role of canonical governance [or] any ministry connected to our baptismal call, we need to [do more] in helping people understand that connection between baptism and mission. That just reaffirms for me that there is more that should be done there.* (Interviewee Z)

Several interviewees reasoned that part of the problem of why the understanding of the baptismal call was regarded as important, but was not being seen in action related to the task of the Catholic Church in educating its people in the language of Vatican II. For example:

> *Thinking about our folks understanding their baptismal call to mission, I would have answered that very much in the context of how that appreciation from the Second Vatican Council is still taking root in people.* (Interviewee H)

Others argued that the problem is due to a lack of theological education about baptism and mission:

> *A baptismal call to mission is a serious and challenging concept that requires serious action. Baptism is not one of the sacraments that people have had a good theological grounding in. Canonical governors need some formation in sacramental theology particularly around the sacrament of baptism.* (Interviewee D)

Interviewees stressed the importance of those in governance roles understanding the nature of their baptismal call (as expressed in the documents of Vatican II) and its significance for their own spiritual development and the spiritual life of the ministry for which they are responsible. Such sentiments are certainly reasonable when it comes to the formation of those who are baptised Catholics. Just because someone is baptised, this does not mean that they understand or heed their baptismal call. Seen in this light, formation can serve to explain and remind people of their baptismal call (even though most may have been baptised as babies or young children).

But what about the situation where those in canonical governance roles are not baptised members of the Catholic Church? The debate about whether canonical governors needed to be members of the Catholic Church has surfaced in recent literature (Catholic Health Australia, 2011; Sweeney, 2011). The issue was raised by interviewees in expressing their concern about recently established PJPs allowing the appointment of people as canonical governors who were not members of the Catholic Church. They spoke of the confusion being created by this move, especially given that the ministries existed as a response to the baptismal call in the first place! They saw the understanding of this baptismal call as central. For example:

> *I do not think you can legitimately accept a governance position unless you have an openly expressed faith. I think it is such a contradiction.* (Interviewee A)

Another interviewee expressed concern at actions taken by the Church in appointing non-Catholics in these terms:

> *I have been amazed that the Vatican has approved some PJPs here and apparently allowed them to have non-Catholics as members on them. That is totally astonishing to me and it leads me to think that they just do not understand what is happening here.* (Interviewee X)

In a similar vein, another stated:

> *We have now a number of PJPs who do not require their members to*

be Catholic. I think if that is the case I think when we talk about a 'baptismal call to mission', I am not sure to what extent that makes up part of their understanding of their own faith tradition. (Interviewee J)

The consequent challenge for canonical governors to straddle religious traditions was recognised by several interviewees. For example:

I cannot exercise that kind of responsibility for a tradition I do not belong to. (Interviewee X)

I think it would be hard for a non-Christian. The reality is that if the organisations are correctly structured the people that are going to make appointments of canonical governors will be looking for people with particular characteristics; and they are characteristics that would relate to someone who can participate in that aspect of the Church and its ministry in the full sense of the word. (Interviewee C)

The issue of whether the baptismal call to serve the mission can be exercised by someone who is not baptised is a complex one. On the one hand, one can argue that if you are not baptised, it is simply not possible to respond to a 'baptismal call'. On the other hand, it is important to consider how and why those who are baptised (or not) are called to serve in the first place. One does not have to be Catholic or Christian (or a member of any other religious tradition) to experience a sense of 'being called'. Indeed, one can be a baptised Catholic and not experience any sense of being called whatsoever. Hence we have an ethical tension here. Do we exclude good people because they are not Catholics? Or do we include Catholics simply on the basis of their baptismal certificate? Answers to these questions require more than a cursory response. In fact the Catholic Church at its best is a broad and inclusive entity, as one interviewee explained:

My view is that every person participates at their own level within the church and it is possible for a person who is not Catholic to demonstrate an active promotion of the Catholicity and the spiritual ministry of the healthcare facility. (Interviewee C)

Whether baptised or not, canonical governors require an understanding of the significance of baptismal call. For those who are not baptised, formation can provide a basis to consider the reasons why they are attracted to the role of canonical governor. For those who are baptised, formation might similarly provide them with the rationale for undertaking the role to which they have been called. A commitment to, understanding of, and engagement with the baptismal call and mission of the Catholic Church are important criteria to be considered for canonical governance. How members of other faith traditions may exhibit their understanding of such features is clearly an area of uncertainty and in need of further investigation.

Baptismal call is a general call to all Christians (Abbott, 1966b, n. 3) to be engaged in the bringing about of the kingdom of God in the world. Interviewees indicated that the Vatican Council call for responsibility for all Christians to be involved in the spreading of the good news of the kingdom of God had not been appropriately part of the education in faith for the laity in the decades following the Council. The past decade has seen greater exposure of the topic of baptismal call in the literature (Dunn, 1995; Leckey, 2006, 2009; Morrisey, 2007b, 2011; O'Meara, 1999; Ranson, 2010; Schuth, 1999; Wood, 2003) and efforts to promote the understanding of the baptismal responsibility.

Another area for development in the formation for canonical governors is an understanding of the relationship between the baptismal call and 'the mission'. Mission is referred to by Schroeder (2008, p. 3) as the 'proclaiming, serving, and witnessing to God's reign of love, salvation, and justice'. The relationship between baptism and mission is important because baptism is the entry into the mystery of Church and the pilgrim Church, as expressed in *Gaudium et Spes* (2), is missionary by its very nature (Abbott, 1966d). Survey results and interviewee reflections strongly supported the desirability of canonical governors understanding the link between baptismal call and mission. However, interviewees were not surprised at survey responses that indicated varied levels of understanding about baptismal call and mission. They reasoned that the language is not in common use among lay people, and that in fact lay people may be living their lives doing good works because of their faith, but not express it in the language of 'baptism for mission'. The implication for formation is that canonical governors need a level of comfort with the language when linking it to their lived experience.

Sense of Vocation. The feeling of being 'called' to do a particular type of work is sometimes referred to as having a sense of vocation and has been widely explored in the literature for ecclesial workers (Fox, 2005a, 2005b, 2010b; Gaillardetz, 2010; Lakeland, 2009; McCord, 2010; United States Conference of Catholic Bishops, 2005; Winschel, 2008). In that respect, vocation has a similar meaning to baptismal call (especially one feels that it is God doing the calling!)

The desirability of canonical governors having a sense of vocation to the role was also strongly supported by survey respondents (see Table 5.1). While most respondents (62 per cent) considered that canonical governors had a *high* to *very high* sense of vocation, more than 30 per cent of respondents indicated that they felt that canonical governors had only a *fair* to *low* sense of vocation to their role. Several interviewees expressed concern about these figures, arguing that canonical governance is more than ordinary work and therefore required, as one interview put it:

> *A sense of vocation to the role; that is what canonical governance is. It is not a job. It is not being on a board. It is the vocation of leading Church mission.* (Interviewee F)

In a similar vein others spoke directly of their vocation to the ministry of governance, highlighting the connection between their leadership responsibilities and their acceptance of the invitation to work for the Church.

> *Is being a canonical governor part of one's vocation? Yes, without a doubt. It is an invitation offered by a congregation and it is the response of people saying 'yes, this is how I can express my gifts in a*

way that are true to me and this is how I can express part of the love of my life'. (Interviewee D)

The meaning of the term 'vocation' proved a little problematic for some. For example:

When you are talking about lay people having a sense of vocation to a role, I suppose the question that I would ask is 'define vocation'. Speaking personally it is not something I ever felt was a vocation because I do not understand what that word means for me. (Interviewee A)

Other interviewees volunteered what a definition of vocation might be:

Vocation means being united to the Word of God. I think it is just a question of lay people seeing that this is a much more serious commitment and a deeper reality than maybe they were aware. (Interviewee X)

Vocation is a choice we each make to live the Gospel in a loving and creative way. It is about how I best express the love in my heart in an integrated and authentic way, in a way that keeps me integrated and is credible to people out there. (Interviewee D)

One of the issues around the meaning of 'vocation' is that it has come to be associated exclusively with ordained ministry or religious life. Sample quotes included:

We have, for so many years, narrowed the concept of vocation so that our lay colleagues might not tend to see this [canonical governance] as a vocation. (Interviewee J)

I think there is a belief out there in the Catholic population that vocations are about priesthood and religious life. (Interviewee D)

Sense of vocation has been [generally associated with] people who are either ordained or vowed and not to any one in any other walk of life. (Interviewee Z)

Alternatively, interviewees recognised that there is a growing awareness in the literature (Casey, 2010; Hahnenberg, 2010) that vocation is a call to a particular ministry; and that therefore formation processes and programmes have an important part to play in developing one's sense of vocation, as one interviewee proposed:

> *This is another area that is worth pursuing in the formation of governors because the notion of vocation is very poorly understood.* (Interviewee D)

The need for appropriate formation around the nature and sense of vocation was highlighted by other several interviewees. For example, one spoke of the impact of introducing people to the concept of vocation:

> *When you tell them it is a 'vocation' to the ministry of sponsorship [i.e. canonical governance], sometimes that amazes them. They say 'well I do not know if I could do that' because of their understanding of the word – vocation.* (Interviewee J)

Another indicated that vocation is a learned response that can be developed through formation.

> *Vocation to the role is a learned response that might not be there depending upon what formation people have been exposed to. People [need to] be helped to see the vocation that is there.* (Interviewee L)

Other interviewees spoke about growth in a person's awareness of vocation through their actual experience in the role:

> *I think sometimes they get involved in the experience then they realise that it is a call.* (Interviewee R)
>
> *Did I hear a voice calling in the night? No. I gradually grew into doing what I now do. It was not by accident, it was by choice* (Interviewee A)
>
> *One member said on leaving after a number of years: 'In retrospect I was called to it, but at the time I did it because I thought it was an important thing to do'.* (Interviewee E)

This developing sense of vocation was a recurrent theme for many interviewees. In fact, some described it in terms of providence:

In my role I have a strong sense that – call it 'providence' or whatever else, opportunities have come my way to do certain things and use some of the skills that I have at different times. The way this particular canonical governance opportunity arose as well, it is there, there is a certain amount of providence in it, so you kind of take it. (Interviewee I)

Another interviewee spoke in similar spiritual terms of the redemptive experience of a colleague being invited to be a canonical governor:

One member said 'I accept this invitation and this offer with joy because this is a redemptive experience for me'. She is the only one that said that but I think the others may have felt it. (Interviewee E)

These comments highlight that the realisation of one's vocation can be a life changing experience with long term implications, as one interviewee put it:

If this is a vocation then you are in it for the long haul. (Interviewee T)

On the other hand, some interviewees reported that engagement in formation processes does not always lead to the realisation of vocation:

One of them in particular would have said at the end 'I am not a theologian. I never planned to be a theologian. I have contributed nothing theologically to this organisation at all. My profession is medicine and my contribution has been that.' And brilliant he was. We could not have done without him. So at the beginning and the end [there was] no sense of vocation, no sense of redemption, no sense of formation. But we held him. (Interviewee E)

This anecdote raises some interesting questions. Why did this person seem to regard their experience with the vocational aspects of their role as being essentially about learning *theology*? Did the interviewee in fact regard this medical professional as having a vocation? In what sense could his work be regarded as a vocation? In what sense could it not? And, does it matter?

From one perspective the answer is no, it does not matter. Presumably the person is a good person, knowledgeable and a willing contributor to decision making. Saying that he or she has or does not have a 'vocation' is neither here nor there. From another perspective is does matter. For someone to understand that they have been called by God is for them to give their work a deeper meaning. It was the Blues Brothers who announced that they were 'on a mission from God'. Now as the movie goes, Jake and Elwood Blues were certainly not theologians, or even medical practitioners. They were struggling musicians with a colourful and sometimes shady past. One could well contend that their sense of vocation indeed helped them to 'get the band back together' in order to raise the funds to save the orphanage on behalf of the Sister they affectionately referred to as 'The Penguin' – or one might not!

Notwithstanding the lessons might be learned from the 'Blues Brothers' movie, the reflections of the interviewees indicate a growing awareness that working on boards of Catholic ministries involves more than a career move. But such awareness usually does not happen over night, as one interviewee put it:

> *I think in some cases it might be happening but I don't know that it is always across the board. I think that it is something that we need to continue to work towards and articulate. The recognition of the vocational part of this can come later.* (Interviewee R)

The survey and interview responses from the Thornber study (2012) support the view that the concept of vocation is significant for canonical governors and stress the point that the term 'vocation' needs to be recovered from the narrow use of the past which confined it to vocation to priesthood or religious life (Casey, 2010; Fox, 2005b; Talone,

2009). Rather, 'vocation' should be understood as 'the work God calls one to' (Fox, 2005b, p. 13; see also Hahnenberg, 2003, p. 134). Such a view would help to reclaim the broader understanding of vocation and lead to more realistic involvement of lay people being formed for the ministry of canonical governance as a calling in the Church.

The survey responses and the interviewee reflections also indicate that formation is needed in this aspect of the role. What is more, because one's sense of vocation has a lifelong influence, the nature and opportunity for formation is something that needs to evolve over time. This thinking is in contrast to those approaches that resemble 'one-off inoculations' that are given early, and then recurrently (perhaps) during the tenure of canonical governors.

Call to Spirituality

Appreciating the existence of 'something other', wishing to deepen one's relationship with God, and feeling that sense of invitation and connection between one's work and life and God's will are aspects of the spiritual dimension of the role of canonical governors. These aspects were identified through by the factor analysis of responses to the spiritual dimension items. Each of the items was concerned in some way with the notion of spiritual formation and how such formation can assist individuals in being open to the transcendent, living intimately with the Word of God, growing in love of God, and praying and practicing other forms of spirituality. The theme chosen to describe the general meaning and thrust of these aspects was call to spirituality. Let's take a look at this theme by considering the survey responses and interviewee reflections relating to each of its aspects.

Being open to the transcendent. The desirability of canonical governors understanding that spiritual formation requires individuals to be open to the transcendent was rated highly by survey respondents with 93 per cent expressing agreement. However, respondent perceptions about the extent to which the understanding was evident were more varied with 17 per cent rating *very high*; 34 per cent rating *high*; 26 per cent rating *fair*; 7 per cent rating *low*; and 16 per cent rating as *unable to judge* or providing *no answer*.

Interviewees reflected on the meaning of transcendence, the connection between involvement with the transcendent and the development of the spiritual life, and the awareness that while the transcendent speaks of the *world beyond*, the engagement with it involves deepening reflection within a person. The following quotes illustrate this.

> *As Christians, a relationship with God, with the divine, with the transcendent, with Jesus is important to us all. Particularly as Christians, relationship with Jesus is an essential and that happens over a whole lifetime.* (Interviewee D)

> *Yes, I think being open to the transcendent is significant but it is a very personal experience and I think the way that people experience it is essentially different as people are different. But to be open to it, yes I do.* (Interviewee A)

Another commented:

> *Certainly I think that this awareness for individuals to be open to the transcendent is very much uppermost in their minds — in my PJP formation work that is quite obvious. The participants are eager to learn.* (Interviewee J)

Language was a concern for those interviewees who had not come across the word 'transcendent' before. In light of this the interviewer provided the following explanation, drawn from McBrien (1994) to those with such concerns:

> *Church documents refer to the 'transcendence of God' and the 'immanence of God'; the God within and the God without; the Jesus of the Trinity and the Jesus of the cross. So 'being open to the transcendent' means being open to see that there is more beyond us or*

more than what reason alone might provide us.

This explanation seemed to tap into interviewees' understandings and experiences, and so provided a useful basis for further discussion. For example, one interviewee proposed that the term 'interiority' was closely aligned with the concept of 'transcendence'. By way of explanation, Rivera (2011) in examining the writings of Michel Henry argues that human life is a form of divine energy that manifests itself within the human sphere of 'interiority'. He defines interiority as 'auto-affective feelings irreducible to scientific study, objectification, or physical appearance within the world'! Given this explanation, there is no doubting that we are entering complex metaphysical territory when we consider what is involved in spiritual formation. This raises the question of whether the level of formation for most Catholics is adequate for understanding of the concept of transcendence. For example as one interviewee stated:

> *I think that the average Catholic still struggles with the idea of heaven being up in the sky, the old man with the beard and the young man and the dove. They do not get past that.* (Interviewee G)

Added to this was the view that while the concept of transcendence was important, it was not typically used by people in the role of canonical governance. Some interviewees explained that they therefore tended to avoid using such 'churchy' language when they were running formation programmes. Instead, as one interviewee explained:

> *We would call it the awareness of the presence of God within us.* (Interviewee J)

Another spoke of the difficulty in grasping the concept of transcendence:

> *I guess I am not sure what transcendence means. I don't know if I have a judgment about that. Again it may be language. How do we connect the seen and the unseen?* (Interviewee H)

Given the high levels of agreement about the desirability of canonical governors being aware that spiritual formation requires individuals to be open to the transcendent, one implication is that meaning of transcendence be a topic for discussion in formation programmes. This would have the effect of not only making explicit the value of the spiritual dimension of canonical governance, but would also provide a basis for individuals to consider the ways and extent to which they are open to that which is beyond their everyday senses and experience.

Living united the Word of God. Another aspect of the 'call to spirituality' theme concerned canonical governors' understanding of the meaning and significance of the term, Word of God and how spiritual formation helps in fostering such understanding Three traits related to this aspect were investigated in the survey. These related to understanding that spiritual formation involved: being united with the Word of God; growing in love of God and neighbour; and prayer as a means of fostering relevant attitudes and dispositions.

Approximately 90 per cent of survey respondents agreed that the following understandings about spiritual formation were desirable:

- Canonical governors understand that spiritual formation is about living intimately united with the Word of God
- Canonical governors are aware that spiritual formation aims for a daily growing in love of God and neighbour
- Canonical governors are aware that spiritual formation involves the practices of prayer and spirituality that foster these (above) attitudes and dispositions.

In contrast, a significant proportion of respondents indicated that they believed that canonical governors exhibited these traits to only a fair extent or less [From Table 5.1, the proportion for (a) was 42 per cent; for (b) – 36 per cent, and for (c) – 43 per cent].

The links between these traits were readily appreciated by the interviewees. Their views supported contentions in the literature about the relationships between engagement with the Word of God, love of neighbour, and the practice of prayer as elements of an individual's spiritual formation (G. Kelly, 1998; O'Connell Killen and De Beer, 1994).

While the interviewees were conscious of the relationships between these traits, they did express some concern about the differences identified in the survey responses between *what is desired* and *what exists* with regard to the understandings that canonical governors have about spiritual formation. Some saw the differences as a consequence of the lack of engagement of the broader Catholic community with the call of Vatican II for engagement with the Word of God:

> *I think that the issue of the Word of God, the Scripture, even 40 plus years after Vatican II, [is that] every adult my age is still not sort of steeped in that Scripture, in the Word of God.* (Interviewee H)

Others attributed the differences to the reluctance of some sponsoring institutions to consider or investigate the level of understanding and need for spiritual formation of their governing boards. For example:

> *I think they [leaders of religious institutes] are a bit hesitant because spirituality is often seen as a very personal thing; and the pool of people who are prepared to respond to invitations to be canonical governors (to my way of thinking) tends to be fairly traditionally Catholic.* (Interviewee D)

From this, the interviewee moved to express a view about the need for spiritual formation and the place of the Word of God in that formation:

> *There is spirituality around leadership and stewardship. What we do need to do is to give people some nourishment into that, say from Scripture – so that this dimension of their life is developed.* (Interviewee D)

And added that in considering spiritual formation, it was important to commence with where people were in their lives with the spiritual journey:

When one comes into a group of canonical governors, I think it is important for the sponsoring agency to nourish the spirituality that governors already bring to the responsibility they are taking on. (Interviewee D)

Another interviewee expressed surprise at the result relating to spiritual formation being about living intimately united with the Word of God, in the light of the formation programme used in their organisation:

> *I was kind of surprised that only 46 per cent put it as strongly agree. I guess because we try to [convey] to ourselves and to the people with whom we work, that this is a day by day approach to life. It is the way you grow spiritually.* (Interviewee J)

Spiritual formation for canonical governors entails not only an understanding of the Scriptures as the Word of God, but also an engagement with the meaning of the texts and their implications for their own lives and the spiritual shaping of the ministries in which they are involved. The survey responses and interviewee reflection indicated strong support for engagement with the Word of God as a desirable trait of canonical governors. However, the extent to which this trait was evident in the day to day work of canonical governors was more varied. A number of interviewees attributed this to tentativeness among leaders of religious institutes to provide leadership in formation and engagement with the Word of God for those being encouraged to take up the role of canonical governor. This view is supported by research on senior managers of Catholic ministries undertaken by Cleary (2007) where she argued that the members of the religious institutes previously running the ministries had rarely articulated the mission and belief system because the mission and belief system had never previously been formulated, and nor had the scriptural sources. Other interviewees linked the lack of involvement with the Word of God with the general lack of engagement with the recommendations of Vatican II for Catholics to seek a fuller spiritual life through the Scriptures. The implication for formation from the Thornber study (2012) is that canonical governors require an understanding of the place of the Word of God as a fundamental aspect in their personal development and in their canonical decision making.

Lay Spirituality, Introspection and Openness to Spiritual Formation

One aspect of the spiritual dimension of formation is the changing nature and significance of lay spirituality. The term, lay spirituality, expresses the spirituality of those who live their lives 'primarily as a secular vocation [which means that] they live out their salvation in the context of the saeculum [the secular world], the time created by God within which they are called to build his Kingdom ... this will occur among the many competing commitments of home, work, and family' (Muldoon, 2009, p. 15). This is in contrast to the spirituality of clerics and religious whose way of life was focused on prayer life from which ministry flowed (Wittberg, 2006). Lay spirituality brings other world views and experience (Cleary, 2007, p. 240).

The rise and articulation of lay spirituality has been occurring in the Church since Vatican II. This has been evident on a number of fronts, including the Council's proclamation of the baptismal responsibility of all Christians, as well as the fall in the number of priests and religious. These changes have resulted in positions and roles in the Church which had been taken for granted as belonging to clergy or religious being increasingly filled by lay people. This has raised at least two important issues: the limited understanding of what is entailed for formation for lay leaders for canonical governance; and what are the implications of people who bring a lay spiritual perspective to the nature of such governance? In *Co-Workers in the Vineyard of the Lord*, the US bishops set out a framework for formation for lay ecclesial ministers who work in Church roles in parishes. The expectation was that the formation would be the preparation for the exercise of actual authority in the various roles. Recent literature suggests that this remains very much a work in progress (Fox, 2010b; Hahnenberg, 2009, 2010; Morrisey, 2011; Muldoon, 2009).

The interviewees' reflections on matters of lay spirituality are illustrative of the themes emerging from the recent literature of this topic. For example, in discussing how to address the challenge concerning the current levels (as compared with the desired levels) of understanding that canonical governors have about purpose and various aspects of spiritual formation, interviewees highlighted the impact of the changing backgrounds of the people involved especially the increasing number of lay people invited into canonical governance. The particular issue that they identified was the articulation of a spirituality that reflected the lay life of the people:

> *The development of an appropriate lay spirituality for these groups is still very much in process. So the point of reference is still the founding sponsors, who are, in our case, religious women or religious men.* (Interviewee H)

The notion of lay spirituality is necessarily different to spirituality associated with the priesthood and religious life. It draws from a different set of formative and day to day experiences in their family, community, professional, social and ecclesial life. And it affects the way lay people understand and practice spiritual formation and associated aspects such as 'living intimately with the Word of God', as several interviewees queried:

> *I do not know how they would define spiritual formation. This could be a question of language.* (Interviewee J)
>
> *If we mean being united to the Word of God as [being united to] Jesus – that kind of goes back to 'Do people have a personal spirituality?' Are they living from a relationship with Christ that impels them to service?* (Interviewee H)

The interviewees, particularly those who ran formation programmes, saw that an important element of the spiritual formation process as inviting people into a process of introspection, as one interviewee put it:

> *If I ask somebody about how they understand spiritual formation they would say they are opening themselves up to something within themselves that they were never aware of before, something deeper within them.* (Interviewee J)

In this sense, the task of those who design and deliver formation programmes is to help participants see deeper within themselves, as another interviewee explained:

> *I would expect there to be special 'ah ha!' moments with certain issues, or moments where their insight would be different.* (Interviewee T)

This interviewee gave the example of determining the future of the ministry as a 'ah ha' moment where new and deeper questions emerge, such as:

> *What is the meaning of this work, and is it still God's work? Is this still what God wants? Are we still contributing to the ministry of Jesus Christ by doing what we're doing right now?* (Interviewee T)

Along with providing participants with the opportunity for introspection, the participants themselves need to be open to the idea that spiritual formation underpins the work of canonical governance, as one interviewee concisely put it:

> *You would not put a superb surgeon in as a canonical governor simply because he was a superb surgeon if he did not have that other [spiritual] connection.* (Interviewee C)

This interviewee proffered a reason for the need for a spiritual understanding in the role of canonical governance in these terms:

> *You do need a fairly high degree of faith to be prepared to operate in this industry. My own experience has been on a number of occasions where I think we have been saved by the grace of God.* (Interviewee C)

These comments highlight that appreciating lay spirituality, providing opportunity for introspection, and being open to the possibilities of spiritual formation are necessary underpinnings for formation in canonical governance roles. This is because these foundations assist those in governance roles to bring more informed values and perspectives to their decision making in the light of the mission of their organization, as one interviewee:

In my experience a lot of the canonical type issues you face are issues of reflection. (Interviewee C)

Formation for understanding how to live a life united to the Word of God is an essential element which takes time to develop an approach to spirituality. Religious institutes devote years of preparation to their neophytes in a manner that is not possible for people in other walks of life. Nevertheless, the findings from the Thornber study (2012) emphasise that appropriate time be allocated for introspection in order to deal with the complex issues of the ministry. Moreover the study confirmed the need identified in the literature (Dolan, 2007; Fox, 2005b, 2010b; Fox and Bechtle, 2005; Hahnenberg, 2003; Muldoon, 2009; Wood, 2003) to recognise that changes in approach and greater understanding of lay spirituality are required to underpin approaches formation. Aspects of this recognition would include investigating the meaning and application of key Church concepts and language from the perspective of the lay person; recognising where people are spiritually in their lives; and designing and implementing ways to lead them from there to a deeper understanding of the spiritual significance of their roles. This requires people who are not only skilled in the field of spiritual formation but also have the capability to lead the canonical governors appropriately.

Canonical Governors in the Spiritual Dimension

In this chapter, we have examined the implications for formation from the literature and the findings from the Thornber study (2012) relating to spiritual dimension of canonical governance. Throughout we have adopted the view that spirituality is associated with the belief that there is more to life than is physically observable, i.e. there is a reality beyond human that is regarded as transcendent. Christian spirituality as informed by the Jewish and Christian Scriptures is often termed the Word of God. The other source is the Christian Tradition which is the teaching of the Church that arises from the long, reflected living experience of the Church and its members and tested against the Scriptures (G. Kelly, 1998).

From this basis we discussed the related concepts of baptismal call, vocation, transcendence, lay spirituality and spiritual formation for engagement with the Word of God. We reported the survey responses concerning the spiritual dimension and examined their implications through the reflections of the interviewees relating to the themes identified though the factor analysis (*Sense of Call and Vocation and Call to Spirituality*). From this examination, it is possible to list the ideal features that would inform formation in spiritual dimension. These include:

- Canonical governors recognise their role is based on an informed understanding of baptismal call (Fox, 2003; Hagstrom, 2003; Hahnenberg, 2003; Leckey, 2009; O'Meara, 1999; Wood, 2003).
- Canonical governors experience a sense of vocation to their role (Fox, 2005b; Fox and Bechtle, 2005).
- Canonical governors see their role as a ministry (Lakeland, 2009; Stanek, 2008; Winschel, 2008).
- Canonical governors engage with the Word of God.
- Canonical governors appreciate and are increasingly imbued with a lay spirituality.
- Canonical governors from other faith traditions have opportunity to contribute in distinctive and complementary ways to the mission.
- Canonical governors are open to spiritual formation.

These features are founded on the view that spiritual development is a life journey that may lead people to understand aspects of life differently, as O'Connell Killen and De Beer (1994, p. ix) explain:

> Our capacity to comprehend and live faithfully as Christians exists in direct proportion to our capacity to notice, describe, and discover the revelatory quality of our human experiences. Our capacity to live rich, authentic human lives depends on our capacity to befriend and enter deeply and openly into our Christian heritage. Tapping the inherently dynamic and energy-filled connection between our lives and the Christian heritage is crucial to the survival of our world, our planet and our Church.

In this sense, spiritual formation can be imagined as a journey of developing capacity to appreciate and live the Christian message that is both beyond the limits of experience and grounded in all things. Canonical governors need to be committed to that journey and to what it may call them into the future.

6
Informed and Reflective Canonical Governors: The Intellectual Dimension

What do canonical governors need to know about the Catholic faith? What background should they have in the fundamental disciplines of Theology and Canon Law? How familiar are they with Catholic social teaching and the *Catechism of the Catholic Church*? How capable (and comfortable) are they in explaining how these areas of Catholicism should underpin the operation of their ministry, and how do they apply them in their governance roles? Finally, how are canonical governors encouraged to deepen their understanding of the 'intellectual' dimension of canonical governance and how it relates to the key areas of faith, theology, and Church teaching?

These are questions that focus on the need for canonical governors to not only be informed about matters of faith, Scripture, Tradition, Catholic social teaching, Canon Law and the Catechism, but also how these elements combine to influence their decision making. This combination of elements grounded in a Catholic world view constitutes a particular way of thinking and acting in regard to canonical governance. In the broader sense, the nature and combination of these various elements has been referred to as the Catholic intellectual tradition. For the purposes of this book, we define the term by drawing on the work of Grassl (2009, p. 6-9) as follows:

> Catholic intellectual tradition consists of a style of thought and a worldview where the former defines the way knowledge is appropriated, processed and passed on and the latter refers to the applications of this knowledge to

various regions of reality – to God, humanity, society, and the Church.

Catholic intellectual tradition is centred on the principle of sacramentality described by St. Ignatius as 'the propensity to see God in all things and to understand specific signs as vehicles of grace' (Grassl, 2009, p. 9).

In this chapter, we explore the intellectual dimension of canonical governance with particular emphasis on the elements and understanding of Catholic intellectual tradition. We present findings from the Thornber study (2012) relating to the intellectual dimension, reporting on survey responses and interviewee reflections on the patterns and implications of those responses. The chapter concludes with a call for a greater focus on the intellectual formation of those involved in canonical governance.

The 'Intellectual' Traits of Canonical Governors

In the Thornber study (2012), survey respondents were invited to rate the desirability of various traits and then consider the extent to which those traits currently existed in those in canonical governance roles in Church ministries. Their responses are shown in Table 6.1.

Table 6.1
Desired and Existing Traits of Canonical Governors – Intellectual Dimension (N=92)

Canonical governors	This trait is desirable (%)					The extent to which this trait exists (%)				
understand that the Catholic faith is rooted in God's revelation	51	45	3	-	1	14	38	30	9	9

understand that the Catholic faith is embodied in the living tradition of the Church	49	46	3	-	2	13	41	32	5	9
are aware that formation for ecclesial ministry is a journey beyond catechesis into theological reflection	52	38	7	1	2	16	25	29	19	11
have some background in missiology	29	48	16	1	6	2	26	34	21	17
have some background in ecclesiology	40	47	11	-	2	2	32	39	15	12
have some background in Canon Law	32	48	18	-	2	2	21	42	25	10
can articulate the missiology which underpins the operation of the ministry	46	45	6	-	3	2	33	35	18	12
use Scripture and Tradition to help them understand the needs of the time	38	53	6	1	2	7	28	29	23	13
have a sound knowledge of Catholic Social Teaching	55	37	5	1	2	10	38	36	10	6
have a sound knowledge of the Catechism of the Catholic Church	10	63	21	-	6	3	30	34	17	16

seek to develop their appreciation of the Catholic faith through intellectual formation	30	60	2	2	6	5	34	37	12	12
	Strongly Agree	Agree	Disagree	Strongly Disagree	No Answer	Very High	High	Fair	Low	Unable to Judge/No Answer

The survey responses shown in Table 6.1 underwent a statistical process known as 'factor analysis'. This was done to identify any patterns that may exist in the way that respondents rated the various items. The factor analysis indicated that each item in the intellectual dimension was being responded to in a similar way (see Appendix 2 for the statistical detail). This suggested that there was an underlying theme connecting the items, and therefore enabled the responses to be grouped as one factor. Given the content of the items and their bases in ecclesial literature, the decision was taken to label this single factor Catholic intellectual tradition. The interviewee reflections on the survey responses were then examined in light of this single factor (see Appendix 3 for a listing of interviewee codes and attributes).

The survey responses yielded some intriguing patterns and implications about the desired and existing traits related to Catholic intellectual tradition. When compared with the responses for the other three dimensions of canonical governance (i.e. the human, spiritual and pastoral), those relating to items in the intellectual dimension indicated that the listed traits were both relatively less desirable and less evident than the traits listed under the other dimensions. Several interviewees expressed concern at these findings, for example:

There is a consistent general lack of awareness of how the theological issues are relevant. (Interviewee F)

The perception that canonical governors use theology to help them understand the needs of the time is quite low. That is tricky. They did say that it is important. I do sometimes wonder how much theology is important to the role of [canonical governors]. (Interviewee L)

What did strike me is that the intellectual dimension comes out lower than everything else. I think about this as good people with a spiritual life and a respect for the Church – but with less intellectual understanding or training. That is kind of our profile for these people. It gives me a little heartburn – a lot of heartburn actually! (Interviewee P)

Looking more closely at the survey responses, there was a sizable proportion of respondents who disagreed that certain traits were desirable. For example, 21 per cent of respondents indicated that canonical governors should not have to have a sound knowledge of the Catechism; 18 per cent said some background in Canon Law was not necessary; while 16 per cent and 11 per cent respectively disagreed that some background in missiology and ecclesiology was desirable. Are these findings a cause for concern? Or, is it fair enough that at least some canonical governors do not have background in these areas? It is also worth noting that a substantial share of respondents (i.e. at least one in three) indicated that most traits in the intellectual dimension were only evident to a fair extent or less, with a further significant group being unable to judge. These findings raise issues including: What is a reasonable expectation for canonical governors to know and act upon about the intellectual foundations of their role (i.e. to exhibit traits in the intellectual dimension?) And more fundamentally, given the somewhat esoteric theological and ecclesial language involved – what exactly do these intellectual traits mean? What do they look like? And, how well understood are they? We explore these questions throughout the chapter.

Coming to terms with 'Catechesis' and 'Theological Reflection'

One of the items most heavily laden with ecclesial jargon concerned the desirability and the extent to which canonical governors were aware that formation for Church ministry is *a journey beyond catechesis into theological reflection*. The two key concepts in this item are *catechesis* and *theological reflection*. Catechesis is defined as the systematic introduction of people to the message of the Gospels (McBrien, 1994), while theological reflection is defined by O'Connell Killen and De Beer (1994, p. viii) as the discipline of exploring individual and corporate experience in conversation with the wisdom of a religious heritage.

Around 90 per cent of respondents regarded canonical governors being aware that formation involves an extension of catechesis into theological reflection as a desirable trait. In contrast almost half of the respondents indicated that this trait existed to only a fair extent or less. These findings were a source of concern to many interviewees. Some interviewees saw the practice of theological reflection as being a fundamental part of the governance role. For example:

> *You cannot do it unless you are moderately literate in the theological reflection on the ministry. If you are running a hospital and you do not have a sense of the caring ministry of Jesus, the nature of the holistic person, and how to meet the needs of people's spirituality in the context of health care, then you are not governing a Catholic health care facility.* (Interviewee F)
>
> *As a trustee you are taking account of the long-term, high level milieu in which the organisation operates. I do not think you can involve yourself at that level without significant reflection.* (Interviewee C)

This interviewee went on to explain how the process of theological reflection worked in their governance context:

> *Our trustees have an hour's reflection before every meeting to try and frame the meeting. I think that is what we need to do.* (Interviewee C)

Others spoke of the value of tailoring theological reflection to the issues at hand, for example through the choice of an appropriate Gospel passage at board meetings.

In contrast to the view that there was limited evidence or priority given to theological reflection, some interviewees argued that practice of theological reflection may well be occurring but may not be recognised as such.

Theological reflection is a practice that not too many of us consciously engage in or know that we are engaging in it. (Interviewee D)

In a similar vein, another interviewee who was a member of a PJP reflected on their personal journey to theological reflection:

The survey responses did make me reflect. Maybe I did not understand what I was doing at the time. You reach out in your relationship with God and you are not sure if anything is there, or if there is anyone listening. My sense has always been to keep on rolling along. Then see what happens. For me fortunately in so many different ways, the outcomes have been all right. (Interviewee I)

This interviewee spoke of their journey beyond catechesis into theological reflection in these terms:

There is no doubt I have been brought closer to the Gospel. But I am not a theologian or a scholar; I am a servant and maybe there is a certain level of the catechesis that I have had through the way I have been brought up, and there is more reflection on the Gospel where I am. (Interviewee I)

This comment not only highlights potential links between catechesis and theological reflection, but also points to the integrated nature of formation for canonical governance involving consideration of catechesis and theology along with actual practice in the role, and indeed one's sense of vocation – as this interviewee added:

Being a canonical governor is not only an intellectual thing. There is a lot of other stuff in there. There is something here you have been called to do. (Interviewee I)

Whether from neglect, ignorance or developing awareness of the concept of theological reflection, it was clear to interviewees that canonical governors need more formation in this area, as the following comments demonstrate:

The survey responses are disappointingly low; that given their background sponsors [canonical governors] wouldn't see theological reflection as absolutely core to how they do their work. That says there's a need for some work on that. It's a big disconnect in my mind. (Interviewee T)

I would have expected that desired trait to be higher. For many Catholics their initial formation just opens their eyes to something beyond what they knew about their faith. This needs to be built upon. (Interviewee J)

Along with the need for more formation, it was also recognised that the priority given to theological reflection varies between PJPs. For example:

The thing about theological reflection is that it must vary a lot from group to group. For us, it is built into our mission statement. But when we talk to other PJPs, the issues of theological reflection are not as strong. So I understand the survey responses here. (Interviewee H)

I know some brand new PJPs are focusing specifically on the question of how they 'theologically reflect' on the work they do, and how they take the normal business stuff and manage it in that light. So I think they are taking it very seriously. (Interviewee T)

This range of reflections on the survey responses indicates that theological reflection may be poorly understood, or may not play a prominent role in canonical governance or in associated formation programmes for some PJPs. The question is why might this be the case.

Difficulty with church language was one reason cited by interviewees. They indicated that some respondents simply may not have understood what is meant by *catechesis* and *theological reflection* – as the following quotes testify:

> *When you look at those questions that use the heavy church theological language, I would expect that [the responses] would be low.* (Interviewee N)
>
> *There would be some governors who to my way of thinking would be saying 'well what the devil is catechesis and theological reflection?'* (Interviewee D)

Besides difficult Church language, the other reason cited by interviewees was the problem that canonical governors had finding time to become more aware of how the Gospel might inform their decision making, as one put it:

> *Given the practicality of things, my role as a canonical governor is a part-time role. At times I think maybe I would like to have some more intellectual reflection on theology, [but] there are only so many hours in the day. I am balancing a number of lives.* (Interviewee I)

In summary, theological reflection was identified by survey respondents and interviewees as an important component of canonical governance. Yet how this concept is understood, and the extent to which it is practiced, was found to vary considerably. Issues relating to the difficulty of Church language, the priority given to theological reflection (through the format of board meetings) and the time and other constraints under which canonical governors operate – especially those who are part time – were all found to influence the manner and extent to which theological reflection is understood, practiced and becomes a focus for formation. Despite these issues, there was a high degree of consensus among interviewees of the need to incorporate some theological reflection in the decision making and in the formation of canonical governors. But this call begs the question about what levels of understanding of various theological and ecclesial concepts do canonical governors actually need to perform appropriately in their role.

Understanding Faith, Scripture and Tradition

The Catholic faith is based on the belief in the revelation of God as expressed in the Old and New Testaments, commonly called Scripture. The core documents (Pope John Paul II, 1992; United States Conference of Catholic Bishops, 2005) from the Thornber study (2012) refer to the need for those in Church ministries to understand and interpret Scripture in the light of the times. In fact, the search for insights that Scripture may provide into contemporary issues has been described as an important basis for theological reflection (O'Connell Killen and De Beer, 1994).

As a consequence, the trait that *canonical governors understand that the Catholic faith is rooted in God's revelation* was chosen for investigation in the Thornber study (2012). There was almost unanimous agreement (96 per cent) among survey respondents that this was a desirable trait, yet 39 per cent of respondents indicated that this trait was evident to only a fair degree or less (see Table 6.1).

Several interviewees spoke of the importance of those in governance roles understanding how the Gospel as an element of Scripture should influence their governance decisions, and then being able to reflect on the extent to which it actually does. One interviewee put it this way:

> *I think [canonical governors] should be expected to think very consciously about the Gospel dimensions of the decisions that they make and how these impact on the lives of people. To me it is a vital element of formation for canonical governance. Theological reflection means reflecting upon my actions in light of the Gospel. How do my actions actually line up with the Gospel? It is consciously sitting down and doing that.* (Interviewee D)

The implication for formation from these calls is that canonical governors need opportunities to deepen their understanding of Scripture and how it applies to the governance issues with which they are engaged. The implications and consequences of their decisions need to be considered through well targeted theological reflection that in turn can serve to challenge as well as strengthen their faith. Furthermore, those working in canonical governance need to recognise and incorporate these matters in the design, delivery and evaluation of formation programmes.

Along with Scripture, the Catholic faith is nurtured through the living Tradition of the Church. The term 'Tradition' in this sense refers to the ways in which Scripture has been interpreted and reinterpreted through the ages in light of changing circumstances (McBrien, 1994); and how these ways have become embedded in the philosophical and ideological foundations, the institutional structures and day to day practices of Church ministries. Three ancient theological traditions of the Church are described in Chapter 1 (see also Figure 1.2, pxx). These traditions indicate the breadth of the intellectual engagement evident in Church history and contemporary discourse.

The desire that canonical governors understand that the Catholic faith is embodied in the Tradition of the Church was rated very strongly by survey respondents (see Table 6.1). On the other hand, some 37 per cent of respondents indicated that this trait was evident to only a fair extent or less.

Appreciating the Need and Design Features for Intellectual Formation

The findings from the Thornber study (2012) confirm the passion that many have for involvement in the healing and teaching ministries of the Church. It was also clear that there was a strong desire for this passion to be informed by the intellectual dimension underpinning of the actions of these ministries, i.e. by Catholic intellectual tradition. The findings also suggest that a significant proportion of those currently in canonical governance roles have only a modest understanding of the nature and connections between faith, Scripture and Tradition. This point was highlighted when survey respondents were asked about the desirability and extent to which they believe canonical governors seek to develop their appreciation of the Catholic faith being developed through intellectual formation. The responses to this item, i.e. *canonical governors seek to develop their appreciation of the Catholic faith through intellectual formation*, were again somewhat mixed.

While respondents regarded this trait as highly desirable with 90 per cent expressing agreement, almost half (49 per cent) of respondents indicated that they considered that this trait was evident to only a fair extent or less (see Table 6.1). Interviewees expressed a range of opinions and concerns about this finding, especially in regard to the nature and need for formation:

> *There seems to be an overall appreciation [of the desirability] for the intellectual component, but the low existing scores underscore the need for more understanding of this component in formation programmes.* (Interviewee P)
>
> *If you are going to be a competent governor of a PJP you should have more intellectual formation for the role.* (Interviewee G)
>
> *In stepping back and looking at this category of 'intellectual' again, there is a lot more education that needs to be done around canonical governance.* (Interviewee Z)

Several interviewees added that strengthening the intellectual component might involve a range of strategies – from identifying and sharing appropriate readings to engaging specialist presenters and facilitators.

In general terms, intellectual formation for Church ministry is process that involves coming to a deeper understanding of theology and Canon Law and how these disciplines and areas apply to decision making. The findings from the Thornber study (2012) support the view that those in governance roles require some level of expertise in theology and Canon Law, and that they should be encouraged to continually develop and apply their knowledge of these areas in their role. But what types and levels of knowledge are adequate for the role? And, how and when should canonical governors acquire such knowledge? Opinions varied on these questions. For example, one interviewee expressed the view that significant level of intellectual formation should be a pre-requisite for taking on the role:

> *I would hope that people who are invited to join, or who feel called to join that type of leadership, would have had a really good intellectual formation already. I would think it was solid, and when I say solid, what I mean is some grounding, not necessarily a PhD in theology, but I would hope that they would have more than the 'average Catholic' – let me put it that way.* (Interviewee R)

Is this a realistic view? How feasible is it to expect that prospective canonical governors come prepared and ready for their role and responsibility, appropriately cognisant of the Catholic intellectual tradition?

Other interviewees believe that formation needs to be part of a person's orientation and ongoing involvement in the role. Taking this approach however raises the difficulty of 'pitching the content' at the appropriate level, as one interviewee explained:

> *I often run into problems – at least challenges – from the boards I work with because I really feel we have to introduce the laity who are in these roles to some serious theology. It is not going to be graduate level but the boards and some of the other leaders want a whole lot of reflection. They kind of get stuck at the personal reflection stage of it, but I do not know how we are going to get beyond that.* (Interviewee X)

Similarly, another interviewee grappled with the level of theological knowledge required by comparing it with the professional knowledge needed for other senior or executive roles – for example in finance for senior managers.

Foundations for Formation 145

You have to have some basic understanding of this if you are going to serve. A Chief Executive Officer may not have a degree in finance necessarily — it might be in healthcare administration. But in health administration they probably learned enough about finance to know what questions to ask. But you are going to be in trouble if you are a CEO and you do not have any knowledge of finance nor think it is important. (Interviewee Z)

This analogy warrants serious consideration. After all, a canonical governor is going to be in trouble if they are asked to explain what actually distinguishes their organisation as a 'Catholic ministry' from a neighbouring secular health, education or social service agency. In times where questions of ethics, moral authority and equity are increasingly part of public discourse in the relationship between Church and state, simply stating that 'we are a Catholic hospital' or 'we are a Catholic university' without an accompanying rationale and convincing examples to back it up, is both politically dangerous and morally inadequate.

Interviewees took a similar view. There was a high degree of consensus among them regarding the need for canonical governors to have an appropriate level of intellectual formation to lead the ministries. But the question is: *what is an appropriate level of intellectual formation?* This question can be addressed in several ways. The following is a set of design features that might be considered in planning intellectual formation opportunities.

1. Assess the level of expertise and understanding of board members. This is not as straight forward as it seems. The assessment of relative standards of expertise among board members is not as well developed in the field of governance as it is in other professions. For example:

On our board, we ask people to state their areas of expertise. At one point there were people who said that they thought they had an expertise

> *in ethics. That went everywhere from attending a single workshop to one person who had a master's degree! Nobody said they had a PhD. You know what? No doctor would say that he had an expertise in something unless he had been board certified.* (Interviewee R)

2. Consider what formation has been done in the past – with clergy and religious, as well as lay people. The question of an appropriate level of formation is not new. In fact, several interviewees noted that the theological formation for the religious who had served as canonical governors in the past was not always adequate for the responsibility they were taking on. The following insights highlight this point:

> *Looking from the historical perspective of religious life, they did not look at these things back then, they just assumed and if you were a congregational leader you were elected because you had these abilities. But people didn't.* (Interviewee X)
>
> *I don't know that everybody that has been in leadership roles in congregations has had all of the theology, rather it was very 'ministry oriented'.* (Interviewee P)
>
> *In my experience with religious, a lot of them don't have very strong backgrounds in theology. They have enough in particular or certain things but it's not a very deep.* (Interviewee T)
>
> *There were people serving [as canonical governors] who did not know what they did not know. It borders on somewhat of an ethical issue for me when we say that we are the responsible party for stewardship of this ministry but we are not capable of doing it.* (Interviewee Z)

These comments point to the need to question assumptions about past practice, and to reconsider the formation of religious who are involved as canonical governors – whether in their own institute or in one of the new PJPs. Such involvement must go beyond so-called traditional roles or tokenism, as one interviewee put it:

Sisters are not at the table just to do the opening prayer and make sure the mission piece is being powered. We also have a share of the responsibilities and we have to prepare ourselves and educate ourselves and inform ourselves about those things so we can steward to the best of our ability. (Interviewee Z)

3. Have reasonable and feasible expectations about the level of intellectual formation. Interviewees reflected on how much people in canonical governance roles could be expected to learn. For example:

The question is how much can you realistically expect from people who have not devoted their whole lives to this? (Interviewee X)

Some people run away because it is hard work. Others say, 'You know, I am a lawyer already, a doctor, a psychologist, a social worker and that is my professional arena. Ecclesiology belongs to the Church and I will do my best to understand what I can'. (Interviewee E)

So what is reasonable to expect? Formal qualifications in theology are not an option for everyone. The time for formal study in theology is certainly a disincentive for some.

I am comfortable that I am not expected to be a theologian, and that I don't need to spend my time [doing courses] at a Catholic institute. (Interviewee I)

Less formal, 'in-house' theological formation was a preferred option for others. Such approaches were seen to allow for customisation in content and process, as well as recognise the gifts of the group of canonical governors and how these contribute to learning of others.

I look around at my fellow canonical governors and see that there are complementary skills, complementary gifts. Where I am obviously lacking in some things, there are other persons that are quite high. (Interviewee I)

4. Build the confidence of canonical governors to articulate and debate theological issues. Interviewees reflected on the reluctance of canonical governors expressing their theological ideas in public:

> *We [lay people] are not terribly comfortable quoting Scripture. We are wary of being seen as unqualified preachers. We tend perhaps not to venture into that area, especially outside of our own peer group.* (Interviewee A)

Some explained that this reluctance was due to a lack of connection for lay Catholics between Scripture and their ministerial action borne out of a lack of understanding of theology:

> *I have a sense that for lay Catholics the work is often not as connected with the Scriptures as other people. But I do not think that makes their work any less valuable or profound.* (Interviewee E)

5. Choose appropriate content for intellectual formation. The core documents (Pope John Paul II, 1992; United States Conference of Catholic Bishops, 2005) that provided the basis for the Thornber study (2012) identified three major areas for intellectual formation for clergy and lay ministry: ecclesiology, missiology and Canon Law. While the emphases varied with the 'target group' for each document, it was clear that some background in each of these areas of the Catholic intellectual tradition is needed for those in governance roles; and that therefore, they should form at least some of the content for intellectual formation for Church ministry.

Studying Church, Mission and Canon Law

How do canonical governors understand the Church? How do they see the purpose of their role and value the goals and outcomes of their organization? And, what do they know about issues of ownership and authority, and the rules and regulations governing their decision making?

These are questions that focus on the intellectual dimension of canonical governance, and in particular the disciplines of ecclesiology, missiology, and Canon Law. Let's now look at the literature, and the survey responses and interviewee reflections relating to each of these areas.

Ecclesiology is the study of the Church and its structure and operations (Lakeland, 2007; Lucas, 2007; Lucas et al., 2008; Nichols, 2004; Orsy, 2004; Osiek and Miller, 2005; Putney, 2004; and Sowle Cahill, 2004). This literature consistently puts the case that canonical governors need to understand what they are being asked to be responsible for, especially in relation to Church structure and operation, and that therefore they need some background in ecclesiology. The survey responses generally echoed this view with 87 per cent of respondents agreeing that some background in the workings of the Church was a desirable trait. Some 11 per cent of respondents however held a contrary view, that canonical governors do not need to have some background in ecclesiology! What might this finding imply?

On the practical side, survey responses on the extent to which canonical governors displayed evidence of their background in ecclesiology were more varied. Thirty four per cent (34 per cent) of respondents indicated that canonical governors display some background in ecclesiology to high degree or more, while 54 per cent observed that such background was evident to only a fair degree or less (see Table 6.1).

Interviewees took different perspectives on the issues at the heart of these survey results, though all agreed that some background in ecclesiology was needed. They expressed concern at some findings, referring to the problem of Church language. Sample comments included:

I think most people would not know what ecclesiology is. (Interviewee E)

Ecclesiology is a fairly sophisticated theological concept. To say to a mature lay person who is a governor, 'what is your ecclesiology?' would leave them bemused. (Interviewee D)

While the term, *ecclesiology* may be somewhat puzzling, or even bemusing to the average lay person, the rationale for some background with the concept was summed up neatly by one interviewee as follows:

> *I certainly think you need some background in ecclesiology. You cannot be involved in governance as a canonical governor without some background in what the Church is, how the Church is structured, how the Church is governed, and how the bits of the Church fit together.* (Interviewee F)

Other interviewees expressed concern about whether the survey respondents fully appreciated the importance of an understanding of ecclesiology. For example:

> *I would put a higher priority on ecclesiology because it is how we relate to the Church and understand authority in the Church.* (Interviewee V)
>
> *You absolutely have to have some background in ecclesiology and that is a pathetic figure there of 40 per cent who strongly agree. You have 11 per cent who think you can be a canonical governor without any background in ecclesiology! It is like saying you can be a doctor without any background in medicine! It is very worrying. How can you govern a Church agency without understanding what the Church is? It could be that the people who answered the question did not quite grasp what it meant.* (Interviewee F)

The Thornber study (2012) reported that, of the 92 people who responded to the survey, at least 70 per cent had experienced several years of formation in either a seminary or a religious institute novitiate. As such, it would be expected that they had studied at least some ecclesiology. In this light, the concerns expressed by Interviewee F take on even greater significance. These concerns were echoed by others. For example:

> *I think some of the most important issues healthcare faces today are ecclesiological. Not that there are not important bioethical questions,*

but I think the big picture is about how these ministries will be a part of the church in the future. I think those are the important issues. So the differences here are pretty dramatic. (Interviewee X).

Another interviewee expressed concern at the apparent lack of knowledge of 'models of Church', i.e. different ways of appreciating Church structure and process, if ecclesiology is not well understood:

The ecclesiology actually is a red flag for me. Whether we talk in the most simple way about the Avery Dulles models of the Church, I think people do have to have a sense that there are different ways to view the Church and different ways that the Church expresses itself. (Interviewee H)

However, the interviewee saw a positive possibility from the results in that it provides room and a focus for development, and this was echoed by others:

I see that as a big opportunity for growth. (Interviewee H)

I think if they come to governance without a strong understanding or background in ecclesiology, that to me is not something that hinders, but it is a place where we can do a lot of work. (Interviewee J)

Given the concern about a lack of understanding among canonical governors about ecclesiology as the study of the structure and operations of the Church, there was general agreement that some background in ecclesiology is required for canonical governors to understand the purpose of their ministries in the light of the mission of the Church; and for canonical governors to be able to articulate those understandings. Consequently, there was strong support for formation in ecclesiology.

Missiology was another aspect of Catholic intellectual tradition explored through the Thornber study (2012). Missiology has been generally defined as the study of mission, where the purpose of the mission to reveal the kingdom of God (Abbott, 1966a; Bevans, 2005, 2009; Bevans and Gros, 2009; Bevans and Schroeder, 2011; N. Connolly,

2010; Schroeder, 2008). As one might appreciate from this introduction, missiology is a complex area of theology, and the literature about it is consequently diverse. The term certainly appears to have been somewhat perplexing to survey respondents and interviewees as judged by the range of survey responses and interviewee reflections.

On the one hand missiology has sometimes been associated with a 'study of the missions', i.e. evangelisation of people in foreign lands in order to convert them to the Christian view of the world, as one interviewee put it:

> *Missiology to me refers to people who go to foreign countries do when they embark on planting the Church in a new place.* (Interviewee V)

Other literature makes the point that 'mission' is the activity of the Church, and that it is expressed through daily activity and relationships in all parts of the world – including in local parishes and Church ministries (Bevans, 2009; Schroeder, 2008).

In light of these distinctions, the responses to the item *canonical governors need to have some background in missiology* were intriguing, and even highly disturbing to a number of interviewees. Of note was the comparatively low figure of 77 per cent of survey respondents who agreed that canonical governors should have some background in missiology, together with the 16 per cent of respondents who disagreed that some background was necessary! For some interviewees, the picture appeared even bleaker in moving from the desired to the existing traits, where some 55 per cent of survey respondents indicated that canonical governors in their experience exhibited only a low to fair degree of background in missiology.

When questioned interviewees indicated a level of confusion with regard to the meaning of the term. This had mostly to do with the distinction referred to earlier between missiology as pertaining to 'the work of the missions' and the broader meaning of mission as the activity of the Church, as the quotes listed in Figure 6.1 illustrate.

Figure 6.1 Interviewee comments on the meaning of missiology

> Tell me a little bit more about 'missiology'. Does that relate to the ecclesial community, or what is that? (Interviewee T)
>
> How would you define missiology? I mean I have to be honest. I am a clinician and I don't think in terms of that language. (Interviewee N)
>
> There are people in religious life who don't have a grasp of what missiology is. So I think it is a fairly tall order to expect that governors, fresh on the block, will have handles on missiology. (Interviewee D)
>
> We are not into proselytising with these ministries. Missiology means a lot of different things. I would not want it to proselytise. (Interviewee V)
>
> How many Catholics would you know that can define missiology? I do not think they would have a clue. They would probably think it had something to do with going to the missions. (Interviewee X)
>
> We do not ask the question about missiology because we have an entirely lay organisation. It does not come into our conversations. It has never been mentioned in the church that I go to. But for me I think it is important. (Interviewee E)

Some of the interviewees questioned the relevance of canonical governors having background in missiology on the grounds that they believed that missiology pertained only to 'foreign missions'. It was only after some explanation and discussion with the interviewer that they began to see missiology in the broader sense of the activity of the Church in daily life and relationships. For instance, one interviewee (who had responded to the survey) reconsidered the response they had been made at that time and how they needed to change their view:

> *I was probably thinking too narrowly and not thinking around the mission of the Church. I would probably rethink that one. If by missiology we mean the mission which underpins the operation of ministry that was a big surprise for me because to me, that is critical in recruiting and orienting these folks. This is way more than work. It is way more than a public service in health care, education, or social services. It is about the mission.* (Interviewee H)

Another interviewee similarly changed their view once an explanation of missiology as the study of the mission of the Church was provided:

> *I think as you've explained it, and had it been defined like that, the responses would have been different. This is because our understanding of the mission of our organisation and the charism of our organisation are areas of top priority for those who are preparing people.* (Interviewee N)

Among other things, these reflections indicate that people, given the opportunity to have theological concepts explained, are able to reconsider and perhaps deepen their understanding. Such instances underpin the value of appropriate formation, especially with regard to the complexity and accessibility of ecclesial language.

In summing up, most interviewees agreed that the term *missiology* needed to be more clearly defined and better understood. Their view was that canonical governors of PJPs are committed to their ministry but may have little understanding of the relationship of their ministry to 'the mission' in its broadest and most inclusive sense. They argued that this was a concern because 'mission' is the fundamental reason for the existence of the ministry in the first place, and for the good work that is done by and through it for humanity, as one interviewee put it:

I think it is important when somebody takes on the responsibility of a PJP status that they know what they are on about and what the whole project is on about – that this is a way of continuing the mission of a congregation. (Interviewee D)

From these findings, we suggest that specific formation is needed to assist canonical governors to better understand the meaning and place of mission and the relationships between mission (in the theological sense), the goals and priorities of their organization, and the ministry in which they are engaged.

Canon Law was the third aspect of the Catholic intellectual tradition explored through the Thornber study (2012).

Fr Frank Morrisey is Professor Emeritus of Canon Law, St. Paul University, Ottawa, Canada. He is a significant writer on the interpretation of Canon Law for the establishment and operation of PJPs (Morrisey 1999, 2001a, 2001b, 2002, 2003, 2006a, 2006b, 2006c, 2007a, 2007b, 2007c, 2009). Much of his writing, and that of other canonists (Austin, 2000, 2011; Beal, 2006; Burns, 2006; Cusack, 2006; Di Pietro, 2006, Undated; Dugan, 2006; Euart, 2005; Hite, 2000; Holland, 2001, 2005; King, 2006; McDonough, 2004; P. Smith, 2006a; R. Smith, Brown, and Reynolds, 2006; Sweeney, 2001, 2005) has focused on explaining the relevant canonical concepts regarding PJPs to those without much background in Canon Law who have found themselves having to learn about its implications for the governance of their ministries. These writings have mostly concentrated on options for models of governance. To this point, there has been very little written about formation needs for canonical governors, including the need for them to have appropriate formation in Canon Law. The Thornber study sought to investigate and provide advice in relation to this gap in the literature.

The item, *canonical governors have some background in Canon Law* was consequently incorporated in the survey. Some 80 per cent of respondents agreed that this was a desirable trait, yet 67 per cent indicated that canonical governors only exhibited this trait to a fair extent or less. Added to this, 19 per cent of survey respondents disagreed with the proposition that canonical governors require some understanding of Canon Law (see Table 6.1). A range of issues emerged from these survey responses and subsequent interviewee reflections.

First, how might one explain why 19 per cent of respondents would disagree that canonical governors need some background in Canon Law? Almost one in five respondents believed that this was not a desirable trait. Should this be a concern? Interviewees were divided in their opinion. On the one hand, some interviewees spoke strongly of the responsibility of governors to understand Canon Law. For example:

> *I find that finding amazing because as a trustee, I see one of my primary responsibilities is compliance with Canon Law. You cannot comply with it unless you have a background or understanding of it. These organizations are part of the Church! They are as much a part of the Church as any diocese or parish, and they are [therefore] subject to Canon Law. It is like saying you can govern a civil company while disregarding civil law and your obligations under civil law. You cannot do it. Or if you try, you put yourself at huge risk.* (Interviewee C)

Several interviewees similarly commented with analogies about the need for canonical governors to have appropriate background. For example, they spoke of the responsibility for a medical doctor to be registered before being called a doctor and the need for a Chief Executive Officer to understand finances (even if their background was not finance). Aspects of the Code of Canon Law which are relevant to canonical governors include the law on existence and governance (Book

1 of the Code), the rights of the people of God (Book 2), the mission of the Church (Book 3), and the temporal goods of the Church as they undertake the stewardship of some of those goods (Book 5). The understanding of these elements of the Code was seen as intimately linked with the understanding of Church and mission as set out in the Code and therefore needs to inform the spiritual development of governors.

Other interviewees were more accepting of the discrepancy in the results, explaining that having only a 'fair to low' background in theology was 'fair enough'. For example:

> *I am not surprised. Who reads Canon Law? We have this requirement that people have an appreciation of and a minimum understanding of Canon Law.* (Interviewee E)

Second, many interviewees were concerned that in the setting up of PJPs, much emphasis has been placed on determining the canonical structure while there has been insufficient attention paid the underpinnings of Canon Law for those being asked to lead the ministry. They explained that those involved in the creation of new PJPs often find themselves being required to learn about aspects of Canon Law. This is further complicated by the view that members of religious institutes have themselves limited knowledge of how their ministries are governed (Thornber, 2012; Maltby, 2007). These findings highlight that formation for canonical governance is required for all types of canonical governors (lay, cleric and religious). As those responsible for the stewardship of the Catholicity of the ministry, they need to understand how the relevant elements of Canon Law should guide the canonical governance process.

Others spoke of a background in Canon Law as being part of the basic literacy for the role of canonical governor. For example:

> *How can you be a canonical governor unless you have a sense that this thing that you are governing is part of a broader Church? So you*

> *need a basic literacy in the theology, canon law and pastoral sensitivity.* (Interviewee F)

The sense of one's ministry and its place in Church governance was also reflected on by Interviewee C.

> *You cannot govern canonically I think unless you have a very sound understanding of the theology of the human person. This is in healthcare, and that has to be from the Catholic tradition.* (Interviewee C)

This comment was an example of the inter-relatedness of the various dimensions of canonical governance, in this case between the intellectual and the human. Interviewee C then spoke from experience about lack of formation in Canon Law in leadership groups:

> *The understanding of Canon Law that I find amongst my colleagues as trustees and directors is minimal. They cannot get their heads around the fact that they are subject to legal systems and even senior clergy struggle with the concept of a PJP.* (Interviewee C)

This interviewee elaborated on the difficulty with senior clergy in the role:

> *We found that one of our biggest challenges is actually forming the bishops in this regard. Some of them of course are canonists and have that understanding. But those that are not – those that come from different aspects, different backgrounds – I think they really struggle. I think they do not really have an understanding of what [the PJP] is, where it is placed, and their role in relation to it.* (Interviewee C)

And making comparisons with non-clergy, Interviewee C added:

> *The laity struggle even more.* (Interviewee C).

These views were supported by other interviewees who spoke of their lack of understanding of Canon Law:

> *I would not even know where to start with Canon Law. It is kind of the basic structure of Canon Law even that most people would not have a clue.* (Interviewee E)
>
> *Again I see more of my own inadequacy in a way in some of the more intellectual stuff around the Church. I have been told I should not have to worry about it [but] there are certain things I seek to do by trying to read stuff.* (Interviewee I)

These comments support the argument for including the fundamentals of Canon Law in formation programmes, and providing the opportunity to learn, to question and to apply – as one interviewee put it:

> *I think that some background in Canon Law is a formation need. It is not a question of saying that 'Canon 453-2 says this' – because that is not what it is about.* (Interviewee A)

Some interviewees noted that aspects of Canon Law were beginning to be included in formation programmes, and although modest in scope, were starting to have an impact:

> *We brought in a canon lawyer for a formation. One session does not make a canon lawyer. But he set a nice framework I think.* (Interviewee H)

In summing up, Thornber study (2012) found that there was strong support for more understanding of Canon Law and its relationship to the mission of the Church and the ministry in question.

Addressing Contemporary Needs Through Scripture and Tradition

The use of theological sources of Scripture and Tradition in discerning the signs of the times was a further aspect of Catholic intellectual tradition investigated by the Thornber study (2012). The point is that for a ministry to remain relevant for the mission in changing times, changes may need to be made to the governance structures and processes of the ministry. And this sometimes requires great courage and insight on the part of ministry leaders. This is where the theological sources of Scripture and Tradition are seen to real value (Pope John Paul II, 1992; United States Conference of Catholic Bishops, 2005). The item – *Canonical governors use Scripture and Tradition to help them understand the needs of the time* was consequently included in the survey.

Most survey respondents indicated that this was a desirable trait, with 91 per cent expressing their agreement. A typical comment was:

> *Canonical governors should use theology to help them understand the needs of the time in the light of Scripture and Tradition. I think that is enormously important.* (Interviewee J)

On the other hand, the extent to which this trait was in evidence was more varied, with 52 per cent of respondents indicating that they perceived that canonical governors used Scripture and Tradition to only a fair degree or less (see Table 6.1).

Some interviewees expressed concern at the apparently low profile of Scripture and Tradition, as components of theology. They saw a connection with similarly modest degree of theological reflection that had been identified and highlighted the difficulty of applying theological understandings to contemporary issues. For example:

> *I would connect use of theology with the theological reflection because I think that is what this is – to understand the needs of the time in light of Scripture and Tradition. Arbuckle says that to meet the needs today is to make the leap from the Acts of the Apostles to today. To me that is theological reflection and it is asking a lot of people actually.* (Interviewee H)

Despite the difficulty, there was a strong support for including greater use of Scripture and Tradition in governance practice and formation programmes because they were seen to provide reference points for decision making, as one interviewee explained:

It is where you ground your thinking and what is going to lead you to action. (Interviewee J)

While formal formation programmes have an important role to play in helping individuals develop such as basis, there was concern among interviewees that the basis of the theology being considered is itself in need of examination and refinement in light of the governance arrangements that are being set up:

> *We have to think this out theologically before we act. We may be putting the cart before the horse in a way. We are going to have to go back and do the theology because in many cases, the governance structure has been set up. I think there has been some theological reflection about it not being adequate for what we are dealing with here.* (Interviewee X)

In summary and in common with other aspects of the Catholic intellectual tradition that had been considered, there was much support for the view that Scripture and Tradition should underpin decision making in canonical governance – and that like other aspects there is a need for more considered formation. This pattern of opinion was also evident in the last aspect of Catholic intellectual tradition considered in the Thornber study (2012) – Catholic social teaching.

Appreciation and Application of Catholic Social Teaching

The Catholic intellectual tradition has underpinned the long history of Catholic social teaching (Keehan, 2012) which is a pillar of the Catholic social tradition (Aubert and Boileau, 2003; CHAUSA, 2006b; Naughton, 2006). The social tradition flows from the Hebrew Old Testament writings of dreams for, and failures in creating a world where the vulnerable are supported, particularly in the prophetic writings (Jer 5: 26-31; 1 Sam 2: 1-10; Amos 8: 4-6). Jesus Christ as the Founder of Christianity built on that tradition (Luke 4:18-19); and the account of the life in the early Church demonstrates the Tradition through its focus on service to the widows, orphans (Acts 4:32-35; 6:1-7) and poor communities (Acts 11:27 – 30).

Findings from the Thornber study (2012) support the premise that canonical governors should have a sound knowledge of Catholic social teaching. Some 92 per cent of survey respondents agreed that this was a desirable trait. Again, the extent to which this trait was evidenced in practice was more varied, with 46 per cent of respondents indicating that canonical governors exhibited this trait to a fair degree or less (see Table 6.1).

Catholic healthcare and education ministries were established to assist the poor as an expression of the good news of God's kingdom. The mission statements of the PJPs reflect these commitments – for example, as exemplified by St. Joseph Health System (2007). The principles of Catholic social teaching that relate to the Thornber study (2012) findings indicate that formation for canonical governors should include (among other things) articulating the significance of the values of justice, compassion and respect for persons.

Strengthening the Intellectual Dimension of Formation

There was a common pattern to the findings about the desired and existing traits of canonical governors in relation to the Catholic intellectual tradition. First, all traits were generally considered important – although the meanings of some terms were unclear, at least at first. Second, the traits were 'connected', in that they were seen to be answered in similar ways – hence the single theme identified through the factor analysis. Third, there was general consensus among interviewees that more emphasis needed to be given to the content and process of formation in the intellectual dimension – particularly when compared with other dimensions. For example:

If you look at formation needs, the human, spiritual and pastoral scores are comparable. It is the intellectual one that is the lower both in the desired state and in the perceived reality. (Interviewee N)

Interviewee N contended that there has been overemphasis on spiritual formation at the expense of other dimensions:

There has been probably more sensitivity and awareness to their spiritual development, and less to the theological. Maybe there is a need for more intellectual content.

In reflecting on the likely cause, they saw a pattern in recent formation programmes in relation to the intellectual dimension.

When you look at the newly formed members of sponsored groups, they have only had a small spattering of the intellectual component. That is why I am not surprised that those numbers are lower. (Interviewee N)

Another interviewee similarly reflected on the need to redress the balance between spiritual development and intellectual formation.

It suggests to me that there is a need for more intellectual content in the programme. I have heard arguments that the primary thing needs to be the spiritual formation of those who fulfill the role almost to the, well I won't say exclusion, but definitely the lessening of intellectual content. That is troubling to me. (Interviewee P)

The need for a strengthened intellectual component as a basis for informing the ministry of canonical governance was seen by many interviewees as essential, but the task was not seen as straightforward. In fact because the ministries involve people with personal commitments and aspirations in working for the mission of the Church, canonical governors need to understand how and why theology is relevant in a general as well as a personal sense. In other words, concerns about responsibility to the Church and someone's personal understanding of their vocation to the role are linked, as one interviewee explained:

In terms of understanding personal commitment, that it is not just a board. It is something much more serious – a serious responsibility to the Church and an expression of one's own vocation. (Interviewee X)

This view was supported by others:

I think the programmes need to be clear up front about that and the people being invited to serve. What role do we play in inviting people and making it possible for them to give to the Church and to the world? Until we get over this thing about it being 'our' [religious institute] ministries, then they are not doing us a favour. We are offering them an opportunity to fulfill themselves through this vocational response to the ministries. (Interviewee P)

These observation highlight the difficulty that current 'governance incumbents' have in articulating the theological relevance and substance of their work to those who being invited to the role and who come from different backgrounds of lay spirituality, as well as from outside the ministry altogether.

Special Case: Formation in Governance for Members of Religious Institutes

The Thornber study (2012) was focused on the formation needs for people undertaking canonical governance roles in the PJPs. The expectation was that the main subjects for the study would be lay people. This was based in the assumption that since members of the religious institutes had been conducting governance for some time, and in many cases for centuries, they would already be capable of performing such roles. It was a surprise therefore that the issue of lack of formation for canonical governance for members of religious institutes surfaced.

This issue was noted by an interviewee who had previous experience on a religious institute leadership team, in the following terms.

Do we just assume that they were formed in their early religious life and they have the basis of that and there has never been any need for ongoing formation? (Interviewee Z)

The interviewee reflected that the early religious formation for members of the institute did not include formation for governance, and added that formation in this area needed to be part of ongoing formation:

Coming from the perspective of a religious congregation, those who are elected to congregational leadership are those who end up serving as canonical governors for ministries. I certainly can say from my experience that they have not been well trained to serve in those roles. (Interviewee Z)

There was concern that formation for the contemporary demands and opportunities of canonical governance had not usually been part of formation programmes run through religious institutes or seminaries:

So we cannot assume that the sisters and brothers and priests, by virtue of who they are and their commitment, have what it takes to be canonical governors. There are people coming into the community, coming new into service and healthcare that need the same type of training and formation that I think we are looking at for lay ministry right now. (Interviewee Z)

The interviewee had had experience of leaders of religious institutes seeking help in the area of canonical governance, (or sponsorship as it is called in some circles):

I was struck last year when a number of congregational leaders were coming up to me and saying 'Tell me more about sponsorship. How do you become a sponsor?' (Interviewee Z)

This exchange reinforces the need for a broader and deeper understanding of the nature and practice of intellectual formation for canonical governance as new people come into leadership roles of

PJPs – whether these are religious institutes or separately established ministries, and whether these people are members of the laity or religious institutes.

Towards Greater Theological Literacy in Canonical Governance

Throughout this chapter, there has been a consistent theme, arising from the findings of the Thornber study (2012), that canonical governors require an appropriate level of theological literacy. The findings support the view from the literature that the core issues in contemporary Church governance are essentially theological issues (Arbuckle, 2007a, 2010; Austin, 2011; Beal, 2006; Bevans, 2009; Bouchard, 2008; Casey, 2000; CHAUSA, 2005b; Fox, 2008; Gottemoeller, 2007; Grant, 2001c; M. K. Grant and M. M. Kopish, 2001; McArdle, 2010; Place, 2004; Yanofchick, 2007a).

In this chapter we have examined various elements of the Catholic intellectual tradition including ecclesiology, missiology, Canon Law, Scripture, Tradition, and Catholic social teaching for their significance to the formation needs for canonical governance. The intellectual dimension of formation for canonical governance related to the need for people to engage with the Catholic intellectual tradition and have a basic understanding of the language used (Bouchard, 2009). The survey responses indicated high level of support for canonical governors being basically theologically literate. The Thornber study (2012) findings, however, revealed that this was not necessarily the case. There was particular concern that the intellectual dimension had the lowest desired scores when compared with those relating to the human, spiritual and pastoral dimensions. Several interviewees also made comparisons with people being equipped with specialist knowledge in professional areas such as medicine and business, and were concerned that it was possible to undertake canonical responsibility without related adequate knowledge.

Specialist knowledge in the intellectual dimension requires an understanding of theology. Theology has been described as the study of the relationship of a person and communities with God, and the engagement of the lived experience with the Word of God (McBrien, 1994). An aspect of 'knowing theology' is to understand the meaning of key terms in the ecclesial literature. Theology has a particular set of terms which have their particular meaning. It also has several disciplines. Two particular disciplines treated in this chapter were ecclesiology and missiology. Another relevant intellectual area for canonical governors is an understanding of canon law and its relationship to theology. Further, the Catholic intellectual tradition has helped create Catholic social teaching which in turn, needs to inform social engagement as it is expressed in the ministries.

The implications for formation in the intellectual dimension are profound. Survey responses and interviewee reflections highlighted the need for a clearer understanding of the place that the Catholic intellectual tradition in Church ministries. Capability in the intellectual dimension enables canonical governors to articulate the reasons for the activity – in the name of the Church and in the mission of God. The elements researched in the intellectual dimension were drawn from the elements proposed in the intellectual dimensions of the Church documents for formation needs for priests and ecclesial laity. They were seen as standard basic requirements. The survey results and interviewee reflections support the desirability of these capabilities. The Thornber study (2012) findings indicate that more considered approaches to formation are needed to achieve the desired levels of understanding, articulation and application of the Catholic intellectual tradition – by canonical governors who are well informed and consciously reflective with respect to that tradition.

7

Discerning and Responsible Canonical Governors: The Pastoral Dimension

The pastoral dimension of canonical governance is concerned with the practical aspects of Church ministries – how they operate, why they operate, with whom they operate, and guiding principles upon which the structure and operation of the ministries are based (Arbuckle, 2007a, 2007b; Austin, 2000; Cassidy, Sheehan, and Whelton, 2009; Catholic Health World, 2011a; Fox, 2005a, 2010a; Gottemoeller, 2007; Gray, 2005; W. Johnson, 2010; Keehan, 2009a, 2009b; McCord, 2010; Morrisey, 2003, 2007a, 2010; O'Meara, 1999; Stanek, 2008; Talone, 2004). It requires that canonical governors have an understanding of the 'high level concepts' and exercise leadership based on such understanding. A high level concept is one that is strategic, fiduciary and generative, and is therefore essential for the direction and continuation of the ministry (Chait et al., 2005).

Some examples of high level concepts related to the pastoral dimension of canonical governance include Catholic identity, mission, discernment, spirituality, charism, and canonical responsibility. These concepts were investigated in the Thornber study (2012) through the design and conduct of an online survey and follow-up interviewees and the analysis of the survey responses and interviewee reflections. The content for the survey was mainly drawn from two sources of ecclesial literature: *Pastores Dabo Vobis* (Pope John Paul II, 1992) on priestly formation and *Co-Workers in the Vineyard of the Lord* (United States Conference of Catholic Bishops, 2005) on ecclesial formation of the laity. The survey items were designed to investigate the desirability and the extent to which canonical governors understand selected 'high level concepts' related to the pastoral dimension of governance drawn from these sources.

In this chapter we explore the Pastoral dimension of canonical governance, using the survey responses and interviewee reflections from the Thornber study (2012). The survey responses originally categorised under the Pastoral dimension underwent a statistical process known as factor analysis. This process lead to the identification of two themes: *Catholic Identity and Mission* and *Formation for Canonical Governance*. While both themes refer to the pastoral dimension, the data relating to the first theme *Catholic Identity and Mission* is treated in this chapter. The data relating to the second theme *Formation for Canonical Governance* is discussed in Chapter 8.

Understanding Catholic Identity

Canonical governors need to understand the concept of Catholic identity and appreciate its richness both for the promotion of the ministry, and the defense of their position if and when challenged. How you understand theology influences your understanding and articulation of Catholic identity. Similarly canonical governors need to understand the nature and validity of the particular approach they have to theology and Catholic identity, and be aware of and respect alternative ways of bringing the good news of the Kingdom to the world (Arbuckle, 2007a; D'Orsa and D'Orsa, 2010; Downey, 2003; Gottemoeller, 1999; Hehir, 2008; Hickey, 2006; G. Kelly, 2007; Lucas, 2007; Martinez, 2007; Morrisey, 1999; O'Rourke, 2001). After all, it was St. Paul who spoke of 'different kinds of spiritual gifts, but the same Spirit; there are different forms of service but the same Lord' (I Cor 12:4-5). Our view is that that teaching needs to be given life in formation of canonical governors.

Catholic identity in Church ministries is created and sustained by canonical governors who understand the ministry they lead, discern the signs of the times, inspire a common sense of vision, appreciate their responsibility for the spiritual life of their ministry, are aware of a variety of theological traditions but comfortable in their current one, and understand the responsibilities of bishops with respect to their ministry. Following is an analysis of the survey responses and interviewee reflections in relation to these and associated matters in the pastoral dimension of canonical governance (see Appendices 1-3 for background information relating to the survey questions, factor analysis and interviewees).

The 'Pastoral' Traits of Canonical Governors

The theme of Catholic identity and mission identified through factor analysis grouped several survey items related to the pastoral traits of canonical governors. These traits, along with the survey responses indicating the degree of desirability and the extent to which each trait is evident, are shown in Table 7.1.

There was general agreement that each of the pastoral traits listed in Table 7.1 was desirable. Over 90 per cent of survey respondents agreed that canonical governors need an appropriate level of understanding of their ministry, Catholic identity, their responsibility for the spiritual life of their ministry, and the canonical responsibilities of bishops; together with the capacity to work with others to discern the signs of the times and inspire a communal purpose and vision. The extent to which these traits were evident to survey respondents however was more varied. While traits relating to canonical governors' perceived understanding of their ministry and their responsibility for its ongoing Catholic identity were rated relatively highly, the evidence of the other traits was more modest – with more than one third of respondents indicating their existence to only a fair extent or less.

Table 7.1
Desired and Existing Traits of Canonical Governors – Pastoral Dimension (N=92)

Canonical governors	This trait is desirable (%)					The extent to which this trait exists (%)				
	Strongly Agree	Agree	Disagree	Strongly Disagree	No Answer	Very High	High	Fair	Low	Unable to Judge/No Answer
understand the ministry they lead	76	22	1	-	1	29	46	22	1	2
understand their responsibility for the ongoing Catholic identity of the ministry	74	23	-	1	2	33	44	18	2	3
work together in the ministry of leadership to discern the signs of the times for the mission of the Church	60	35	1	1	3	15	36	36	8	5
inspire communal purpose and vision	60	32	4	1	3	13	37	36	8	6
understand that they have a responsibility for the spiritual life of their ministry	51	41	2	1	5	13	33	38	11	5
understand the responsibilities of the local bishop for the coordination of ministerial services in the diocese	55	37	6	-	2	14	33	35	15	3

These survey responses raise questions about the levels of understanding that canonical governors have regarding their responsibility for the Catholic identity and spiritual life of their ministry and the responsibility of local bishop with regarded to their ministry. They also put the spotlight on the need and capacity of canonical governors to work together in discerning changing contexts and circumstances, and in deciding and developing a common purpose and vision for what needs to be done in light of the mission. From these considerations, we have distilled a series of themes related to the pastoral dimension of canonical governance. These are treated in the following sections of this chapter.

1. Developing and Sustaining Catholic Identity

The first theme to emerge was the role of canonical governors in developing and sustaining Catholic identity. The survey respondents strongly supported the need for canonical governors to understand their responsibility for the Catholic identity of the ministry, with 97 per cent agreement that this trait was desirable (see Table 7.1). Interviewees similarly valued the importance of developing and sustaining Catholic identity, and expressed concern about the level of formation that lay people have to understand these responsibilities. For example:

> *Canonical governors have a serious responsibility. They need to ask does their particular ministry credibly and authentically express the Gospel in this particular place. They have to know what makes the thing authentic, or where it is departing from being authentic or Gospel inspired or Church. Lay people may be a little bit hesitant to embrace this wholeheartedly unless they are given some formation in those areas.*
> (Interviewee D)

The complexity of the concept of Catholic identity was apparent to interviewees. Some (who were canonical governors) noted the difficulty of discerning the most appropriate way of dealing with complex issues in the light of the way they understand and articulate Catholic identity. Others reflected on their experience of canonical governance and outlined the systems in place to ensure that the Catholic identity was a central consideration in the leading and operation of the ministry.

> *In our board committee structure for the health system, we have a committee for clinical quality; a committee for finances; a committee for strategy; and we have a committee for mission and governance. So it is parallel.* (Interviewee V)

They emphasised that the Catholic identity of their ministry was strongly connected to work of the Church.

> *We continually refer to the fact that we are in a particular place within the Church; 'within the Church' is important to us, and it is the 'big C' institutional Church which you have there too.* (Interviewee I)

In fact, one interviewee likened the concept of Catholic identity to the purpose of creating PJPs. They argued that the creation of PJPs was actually designed to develop and sustain Catholic identity, as one interviewee put it

> *See the canonical governance in your new public juridic persons, the idea of PJPs has been to maintain Catholicity, hasn't it?* (Interviewee G)

Others spoke in a related way of the value of pre-existing religious congregations in providing 'a story' or tradition upon which the Catholic identity of the new entity can be built. For example:

> *We are fortunate in that we have a Loreto tradition, or a Christian Brothers', or a Marist Brothers' tradition, and the school is affected by that. Everyone is aware of it. They are continually reminded of it. In a Catholic college that has never had the involvement of a religious teaching institute, or where the link has been lost – it is not nearly as easy to do that.* (Interviewee G)

The implication was that it is more difficult for Catholic laity to lead Catholic secondary schools and maintain Catholic identity in systemic settings where there had been no previous involvement of religious institutes. Is this a valid observation? In contrast, we are aware of many recent instances where, although there had been no connection with religious institutes, these newly established entities drew their Catholic story and identity from the saints after which they were named, as well as from the 'saints of the everyday' – the people they work with and serve, and who serve them in living the mission. This was evident for example in a group of student leaders at a newly established Catholic systemic college with which we are familiar enthusiastically announcing at an assembly to mark the opening of a new wing:

> *At [our college] being in the first group of students is great. It means that when we do something for the first time and it works – it can become a tradition!*

Contrast this with the position of a school or a hospital or another human service agency steeped in tradition where change comes very slowly – if at all. Such organizations may be better described as those who strive to maintain 'the tradition' at all costs though few staff members or clients may really understand the nature and basis of that tradition. These are the types of organizations that are governed by risk-averse bureaucrats, typified by the character of Sir Humphrey Appleby from the BBC series *Yes Prime Minister* (Jay and Lynn, 1987) who once remarked that 'Avoiding precedent does not mean that nothing should ever be done. It simply implies that nothing should ever be done for the first time.'

Our view is that PJPs that evolve from pre-existing religious institutes may or may not be advantaged compared with those that arise through other means (for example from diocesan necessity). Nevertheless in either case, the question arises of how to ensure that those at the operational level (teachers, nurses, managers, principals, vice-chancellors) and those at governance level understand *Catholic identity* and take responsibility for nurturing it. This is a question for canonical governors.

Taking the issue a little further, some interviewees made the case that understanding the term 'Catholic identity' was not sufficient. Rather, they argued that persons in positions of PJP governance should also be members of the Catholic Church and know its tradition, as one interviewee put it:

> *If you are not prepared to sign-up to the Catholic Church, well how can you be a steward of the Catholic Church? You would have to question those juridical bodies that are not insisting that their governors sign up to the Catholic Church. We might have some issues with the authority in the Catholic Church, but in terms of the public identification I think it is really fundamental. I would have trouble contemplating a non-Catholic in the position that I hold – and that is not out of a lack of respect. It is just that you have been invited to make some decisions and to participate in something that is foundational for the Catholic Church.* (Interviewee I)

The debate about the need for canonical governors to be Catholic emerged in the Thornber study (2012) and is also evident in our discussion of other dimensions of canonical governance (see Chapter 4). Our view is that it is possible to resolve the debate by carefully considering the content, process and expectations of formation programmes in light of the background characteristics of those involved.

Against this background, a key component of formation is developing knowledge of the tradition. Interviewees involved in governance of a healthcare ministry reflected on the cause of the concern about the laity ensuring the Catholic identity of the ministries. They were critical of the Church for the lack of integrated education and nurture in people's lives. For example:

> *Do you know one of the things that I have become aware of is the Catholic Church's failure, and I call it failure, at a very early age,*

> *to engage its members with the richness of the Catholic tradition in a way that is meaningful for their lives. Most of the people that we engage as governors are Catholic and they have had no formation since their school years. All they can remember, a lot of them, are the Ten Commandments and hellfire and damnation as an alternative to salvation.* (Interviewee E).

This reflection echoed that of Interviewee G whom we have quoted elsewhere as observing that too many lay Catholics still saw God as an old man with a beard sitting above the clouds. These two interviewees (E from a lay background and G from a clerical background) expressed the concern that in the health and education ministries, there was increasing risk of those invited to leadership roles (such as canonical governance) not understanding their own Catholicity. They contended that this had serious implications for developing and sustaining the Catholic identity of their ministries, arguing that if the leaders' concepts of God were narrow and constrained, then their understanding of Catholic identity would likewise be narrow and constrained.

Developing and sustaining Catholic identity requires that canonical governors understand what is meant by the term (informed by their understanding of the tradition), and how it does and should imbue their ministry. It is therefore a worthy focus for formation.

2. Understanding the Mission

How do those in canonical governance understand the meaning of 'mission'? Throughout this book we take the view that mission refers to responding to the call of Jesus Christ to spread the good news of the Kingdom of God and working to bring it about.

Mission can therefore be understood as involving a series of fundamental premises. Interviewees recognised the difficulty of ensuring that these basics were being addressed in governance practices. For example:

> *The demands of organizational governance now are so huge, unbelievably huge that to 'distract people' – which is what it feels like very often, with the requirements for thoughtfulness about Catholic identity and mission. It is almost like it is too hard for them.* (Interviewee E)

In contrast, several interviewees spoke from experience about how their organisation articulated the relationship between policy planning, implementation and evaluation and the values of mission which underpin these processes. For example:

> *In this organisation we have a framework which every significant decision has to run past – and it is all directed toward missiology.* (Interviewee C)

In this case, as Interviewee C explained, the organization's understanding of mission was closely aligned with the ways in which governance and leadership were exercised, what structures were set up, and how performance was measured. These functions are also regularly reviewed to ensure the organisation remains faithful to its core purpose.

However the meaning of mission is not always as clear as this. The issue of canonical governors seeing 'mission' as the mission of their organisation rather than the ministry being an expression of the mission of the Church was raised by several interviewees. A typical observation was:

> *The thing that I would wonder about is whether they do it for mission for the Church or for their own mission. And I don't know how to answer to that.* (Interviewee R)

This interviewee added that they often heard people saying they worked for the mission of the Church, when in fact they were looking at mission in the light of one particular ministry or organisation:

> *The mission of the Church is obviously important. But many times, what I will hear is people who will seem to discern that, but they*

are looking at it particularly in light of the one particular ministry. (Interviewee R)

Another interviewee (a canonical governor) reflected from their experience on the difficulty of the task in helping others to see the 'bigger mission picture':

I believe that we have formed [canonical governors] for the mission of the health system. Continuing to put that in the context of the mission of the Church is the challenge. I think we have language that does it, but I don't know whether we have formed people enough for the 'big mission'. (Interviewee H)

This concern deserves further consideration. If only the mission of the ministry is being considered, then it could be seen as equating to an attitude of generously 'helping the sisters' in the religious institute as a good thing to do — in and of itself, rather than having some higher or alternate purpose in mind (such as 'working for the mission of the ministry', 'doing it for the Church' or even for one's salvation). But is simply doing something because it seems like the right thing to do necessarily undesirable? Interviewee H reflected on this issue and the related attitudes in their organisation toward understanding the mission of the Church:

I think the folks we are with — at the canonical level, at the governance level, and the system board level — they get the thing about the mission of the health system. They really get that and they are really committed to that. But then if we were to draw back and say 'How does that fit into the mission of the Church?' (Interviewee H)

Others expressed similar concerns about canonical governors' understanding for the concept of mission as the reason for existence of their ministries:

I think the notion of the mission of the broader Church warrants greater consideration — I do not know that we have gotten there yet. (Interviewee R)

We use the language of the healing ministry of Jesus but that is not always connected to the mission of the Church. (Interviewee H)

Does failure to understand the Church mission mean the point may well be being missed in the enthusiasm of people to help in the Church ministries? This concern regarding action without appropriate background knowledge and appreciation of the deeper purpose of agencies was reflected upon by interviewees in the matter of the intellectual gifts needed to discern the signs of the times appropriately.

3. Discerning the Signs of the Times

A third theme to emerge in the pastoral dimension was the ability of canonical governors to discern the signs of the times to see what needs to be done. Discerning the signs of the times is one of those 'high level concepts' described by Chait et al. (2005) that canonical governors need to understand to make good strategic decisions. The call for the Church to scrutinise the prevailing environment, or discern the 'signs of the times' was highlighted in the Vatican document, *Gaudium et Spes* (Abbott, 1966d, n 4). The expectation was that the Church would seek to interpret the 'signs of the times' in the light of the Gospel and consequently act for the good of God's Kingdom.

Discerning the signs of the times requires a combination of the traits. Human maturity borne of significant life experience, theological understanding and reflection, and an informed understanding of the ministry and the mission are all useful characteristics when it comes to making good decisions in complex and challenging circumstances (Grant, 2003; K. Homan, 2004; Moore, 2007; O'Meara, 1999). In times past when canonical governance was the sole province of members of a religious institute, the leaders usually came from the ministry; and if the institute was involved in multiple ministries (e.g., health and education) there would usually be enough people who were knowledgeable from the range of ministries to undertake these leadership roles. These days the picture is very different. We know of cases where people (religious and lay) have been appointed to governance roles with limited substantive background in the ministry. This makes their task of discerning the signs of the times all the more difficult.

We support the premise that some understanding of the ministry is essential for canonical governors to discern the signs of the times and make good decisions. Following a similar line, Cleary (2007, p. 244) expresses the need for leaders to have the ability to transmit the 'meaning system' for which the organisation was established. She explained that while each individual contributes to this meaning system through contributing their particular gifts, some need to be able to take the lead in transmitting the meaning system. Other writers describe this role as that of the 'sense makers' (Chait et al., 2005), whether that be for finance, ethics, law, theology or governance. The sense makers are relied on by others in the group. Cleary argued the faith based organizations need 'faith sense makers' in these critical roles. So put another way, canonical governors who are able to work together in ministry to discern the signs of the times and then make reasoned decisions about what to do might be regarded as 'faith sense makers'. These people are in a most foundational sense, *governing in faith*.

The trait that *canonical governors work together in ministry to discern the signs of the times for the mission of the Church* was regarded as highly desirable by survey respondents with 95 per cent expressing agreement (see Table 7.1). Interviewees strongly supported this finding. On the other hand, some interviewees expressed concern about the 44 per cent of respondents who perceived that canonical governors were only able to discern the signs of the times to a fair extent or less. For example:

> *If you are doing any strategic planning then you have to be looking at the signs of the times. Again I think that it is not just the sign of the*

times for the mission of the Church but it is the signs of the times in the world in which we live. (Interviewee N)

But discerning the signs of the time is not a straightforward exercise. In fact some interviewees argued that proper discernment requires a depth of intellectual understanding, or as the following interviewee proposed – an 'aptitude for discernment':

> *We talk a lot about discernment as a sponsorship [canonical governance] competency but I would argue that discernment cannot be devoid of intellectual understanding. It is not the whole of it certainly, but there has to be some basis there that you are working out of. The aptitude for the intellectual component needs to be considered in the choice of persons we invite to this role. I don't think we have ever talked about that. I think we assume it. I never thought of it as an 'aptitude for discernment', but it might well be*. (Interviewee P)

The implication is that if discernment is not underpinned by appropriate intellectual understanding, then the readings of the issues will be shallow and superficial, and therefore likely to miss significant elements related to the development and sustainability of Catholic identity.

Having the intellectual background for discernment is one factor that contributes to an accurate reading of the 'sign of the times'. Another is actually being open to discernment. Some interviewees expressed concern about this latter factor in commenting about the kind of discernment currently being done by Church leaders, and the consequent difficulties that lay leaders were encountering. For example:

> *Lay spiritual discernment is a great ideal but there are a lot of Church leaders, a la bishops, and even congregational leaders who are not looking at or listening to the signs of the times. They already have a set agenda that they are not prepared to change or vary from, so they say 'Bugger the signs of the times. We know what is orthodox and we are going to hold the line come hell or high water'*. (Interviewee D)

The above comment indicates the leadership tensions that can arise in the difficult task of discerning the signs of the times in the light of the Gospel, and the need for canonical governors to have the background and courage of their convictions to speak out when required, as the interviewee went on to explain:

> *So, it is a brave thing to educate 'mere' lay people to look for the signs of the times and then to suggest to clerical Church leadership, or to religious congregation leadership that we need to go in this direction or we need to shift our focus.* (Interviewee D)

Discerning the signs of the times is a necessary element for serving the mission. The mission comes from Jesus Christ, who instructed his disciples to take the healing and teaching message of the good news of the Kingdom of God to the whole world (Mk 16:15, Mt 28:19). Therefore the ability of canonical governors to work together to discern the signs of the times needs to be carefully nurtured and wisely exercised.

4. Being Responsible for the Spiritual Life of the Ministry

Another theme to emerge from the Thornber study (2012) was the need for canonical governors to understand their responsibility for the spiritual life of their ministry. This trait was considered to be highly desirable by survey respondents, with 92 per cent expressing their agreement. On the other hand, some 49 per cent of survey respondents indicated that canonical governors exhibited this trait to only a fair extent or less.

One of the issues associated with this modest level of evidence of canonical governors being responsible for the spiritual life of the ministry, as noted by the interviewees, was the manner in which spiritual life is expressed. The research of Cleary (2009) is helpful in this regard. She examined the prevalence of symbolic expressions across a range of Catholic human services in education, health and welfare. She noted that the articulation of 'the spiritual', for example through symbols such as statues and writings displayed was more evident in Catholic schools than in Catholic hospitals or welfare sites where there were fewer artifacts indicating the Catholic identity. The reflections of interviewees to the survey responses in the Thornber study (2012) reflected some of the difficulties that Cleary had noted. For example an interviewee (who was a health ministry governor) stated that:

> *When we talk about communicating with the people who work for us and with us, there is almost a need to homogenise the Gospel so that it is not being seen as too Catholic.* (Interviewee A)

Some argued that the downplaying of an overt Catholic identity was a consequence of the variety of religious backgrounds of staff and the challenge of developing an appropriate language for the expression of the Gospel message. For example:

> *In your workforce if you have fifteen per cent practicing Catholics you are doing very, very well. There is that . . . cultural cringe is not the right word. There is a desire to describe the spiritual life of the ministry in more humanitarian language than Gospel language, I think. It does not mean to say that Gospel teachings are not underpinning the humanitarian message. But to relate it to biblical and Gospel teaching is something I do not see an awful lot of.* (Interviewee A)

This preference for humanitarian language raises questions about what type/types of spirituality do and should underpin the work of the canonical governors as they grapple with their responsibility for ensuring the Catholic identity of the ministry. These reflections raise further questions about the nature of canonical governors' involvement and the ways in which they are taking over (or not) the responsibility for spirituality from the religious institutes. One approach for evaluating how governors have carried out their responsibility for the spiritual life of the ministries to this point was explained as follows:

> *I think we are going to have to grow into this one. I think we need to*

> *step back and assess along the way. We need to go back to those who have worked in canonical governance as a lay person, and there are some folks out there who have been doing it for the past 10 years. Talk to them about it now – 10 years later, and ask them what does this say to you? How is this evolving? I think that is important as we look into the future.* (Interviewee Z)

Assessing how and the extent to which canonical governors are effective in exercising their responsibility for the spiritual life of the ministry requires an informed contemporary understanding of Church mission, as related to but distinct from the mission of the religious congregations and the charism which has inspired the operation of the ministry in former times. In fact, part of canonical governors' responsibility for the spiritual life of the ministry is their acknowledging of the potential tension between mission and charism. The spirituality of religious institutes and their engagement with particular charisms can sometimes strain relationships, especially among members of PJPs established from different religious institutes. This can threaten division among those who espouse a shared commitment to the mission, as one interviewee remarked:

> *I do see a lot of reference to the founders [of religious institutes] almost turning organisations into followers of a particular individual or a charism of a particular congregation or group. In some places there is a tendency to use the stories of the founders far more than the stories from the Gospel. That bothers me a little bit because I think it is counterproductive in the broader sense. I think it actually creates divisions between our organisations.* (Interviewee A)

Where such unfortunate divisions occur, the organisations might find that they are not properly discerning the 'signs of the times' and are not understanding that a Scripture-based spirituality that is necessary for the continuation of the ministry. One interviewee (a formator from a religious institute) spoke of the journey that was being undertaken to bring about the needed understanding – both from the point of view of religious moving out of governance and from the perspective of the people being formed to take over the role and understand the responsibility of governance:

> *I mean that is what we have been doing. That is what we have been chipping away at. That has been a journey because canonical governance, not only structurally in the Church, has been tied to the religious congregations.* (Interviewee P)

This reflection provides a powerful insight into the difficulty of moving from a spirituality infused by a charism of a religious institute which was lived by the members of the institute and shaped the operation of the ministry, to a different basis. That new basis is a spirituality which involves people more accustomed to lay spirituality but who are also committed to the ministry in which the religious institute's charism is recognised and valued. This combination of influences shapes the spirituality of those who lead the ministry as they are formed for, and in, their roles as canonical governors.

5. Being Accountable for Spiritual Life and Catholic Identity

Having responsibility for the spiritual life and identity of the Catholic agencies has far reaching implications and requires an appropriate accountability structure, as one interviewee put it:

> *I think that probably one of the biggest challenges that we face for the future is having a suitable accountability and review mechanism. Canonical governors should be reviewing their performance and contribution to the organisation in the light of their role. And there needs to be a process whereby if they are not making an appropriate contribution, they can be held to account.* (Interviewee C)

The issue of accountability in Church ministries is a complex one. It concerns questions about who is responsible to whom for what. For starters, Catholic schools, hospitals and other agencies are accountable to the 'clients', such as the students, the patients and others, that they serve, and to the staff that work there. They can also be accountable to the local community, parish and diocese in which they are located; and of course since these ministries need to operate in compliance with government legislation and regulations, they are also accountable in civil terms. In addition some forms of PJP, known as Pontifical Public Juridic Persons report directly to the Vatican. The appropriateness of accountability requirements for Pontifical PJPs was questioned by one interviewee:

> *My fear with Pontifical PJPs is that the accountability lines are becoming quite stretched. If you are accountable to Rome and someone goes to Rome once a year and spends half an hour or an hour reporting on a significant entity in another country, I do not think that is 'accountability'. I think there needs to be regular communication with an alternate reviewer that has the power to appoint or replace canonical governors.* (Interviewee C)

Given this complexity, exercising proper accountability for the spiritual life and Catholic identity of a local, national or international Catholic ministry demands well focused pastoral formation so that people understand their canonical responsibilities. Along with these responsibilities that flow from the canonical structure of the Public Juridic Person, canonical governors are increasingly taking on responsibilities as civil governors or trustees – and vice versa. This mix of canonical and civil responsibility means that governors essentially need to understand and be evaluated in terms of the criteria that apply to both these spheres of governance. While there is a range of support and guidance available for the corporate or civil sphere of their role (i.e. there is no shortage of lawyers or business consultants), the same cannot be said for the canonical sphere where the individuals or groups able to offer counsel or challenge to the canonical governors is more limited. Several interviewees noted that as these dual canonical and civil roles were becoming more common, there was a corresponding need to distinguish between their associated canonical and civil responsibilities. For example:

> *What we are finding with the new PJPs is that the sponsor board [the canonical governors] and the board of trustees are becoming one and the same. So there is going to have to be a tremendous amount of work in understanding that you cannot get so caught up in the fiduciary responsibility of being 'a governor' and lose what it means to be 'a canonical governor'.* (Interviewee Z)

Our discussion on this aspect of the pastoral dimension of canonical governance highlights the need and the value for formation opportunities for governors that explore what it means to be accountable for the spiritual life and the Catholic identify of a ministry that is called and legislated canonical and civilly to serve the mission and the society respectively and respectfully.

6. Understanding the Role and Responsibilities of the Local Bishop

A sixth theme associated with the pastoral dimension of canonical governance is the ecclesial relationship between the bishop with his pastoral responsibility for the diocese, and the canonical governors with their responsibility for governance of the ministries in his diocese. The relationship between bishops and canonical governors has been a popular topic in the literature (Austin, 2011; Cusack, 2006, 2007, 2008; Euart, 2005; Lucas, 2007; Morrisey, 2007a; Willis, 1986); including that written by bishops themselves (Coleridge, 2009a, 2009b, 2009c; Putney, 2004, 2005, 2007; Sklba, 2007; Skylstad, 2008; Wuerl, 1999).

The role of the bishop in coordinating ministerial services in the diocese was canvassed in the Thornber study (2012) by the survey item: *Canonical governors understand the responsibilities of the local bishop for the coordination of ministerial services in the diocese.* The desirability of this trait was rated very strongly by survey respondents, with 92 per cent expressing agreement. However, their perception that such understanding was in evidence was more varied, with 50 per cent of respondents indicating that they perceived this trait in canonical governors to only a fair degree or less (see Table 7.1).

This latter survey result indicates that the role of the bishop in coordinating of ministries in his diocese is not as well understood as it might be. While interviewees were generally supportive of the bishop's role, they expressed sympathetic concern about the capacity of bishops to grasp the complexities of the operation of the various ministries in their dioceses. Interviewees stressed the need for canonical governors to have good lines of communication with their bishops and develop a more informed understanding – theologically and pastorally, of the issues of most concern to them.

Interviewees reflected on the relationships between the bishops and the canonical governors of the ministries. These reflections were focused on the bishop's responsibility for ministerial coordination and, in some cases, for the ecclesial creation of PJPs; governors' understanding of these coordination responsibilities; and causes of tension between bishops and canonical governors.

Bishops exercise of their authority was found to vary from that as a 'sounding board' characterised by regular discussion, communication flows and feedback to more direct manifestations of the bishops' legitimate power. For example:

> *We were established by [an] ecclesiastical Province of the Bishops. They have certain rights and authorities. We have to report to them. They have the right of suppression of the entity for failure to fulfill the approved mission. They have the right of certain controls over the constitution so the canonical provisions of the constitution cannot be changed without their authority and there is accountability back to the establishing authority.* (Interviewee C)

In contrast, some interviewees were aware of canonical governors who did not realise that the bishop had a role in coordinating their ministry. Sample quotes included:

> You hear some people say well why do we need to go and talk to the bishop? They do not understand that we are in his diocese and we serve in his diocese and the bishop oversees of the ministries of his diocese. (Interviewee Z)
>
> Canonical governors usually do not understand the bishop's responsibilities – that is for sure. But they learn quickly. It is important we have it there as a desired trait. (Interviewee J)

Several interviewees also reflected on the difficulties that bishops are facing with the emergence of the new governance models associated with the newer PJPs. One spoke of the importance of the bishop and the different roles that he might have with regard to a particular Public Juridic Person:

> Our bishops have up to four different roles in our organisation and we have identified each role. They can be a member. They can be part of the establishing authority. They can be a combination of those, or they can simply be the chief pastor in the area in which we operate. There are canonical responsibilities in each of those roles, and they have to be very aware of which hat they are wearing when they undertake any action.

They added that:

> Bishops have certain authorities in terms of the coordination of the services, the appointment of chaplains, the oversight of the pastoral services and for those things that we have accountability to them as chief pastor. (Interviewee C)

One of the issues cited by interviewees was the capacity of bishops to grasp the complexity of the range of ministries in their dioceses, for example as one interviewee explained:

> There is the aged care industry, the health industry, employment

industry, the child protection industry. But it is beyond the bishops. Sorry, it is beyond them. How can they possibly be aware? I cannot be aware, even as chair, of all of the industry coordination requirements and my experience is there is a huge lot of trust and I value that trust enormously. (Interviewee E)

This interviewee spoke of their experience with a bishop regarding the closure of a part of the ministry for which they had delegated responsibility:

I had not said to him that we were going to close it. I had said that we were likely to close it. But his comment was that I should have consulted him. And I said 'I am sorry, I can consult you about the fact that it is going to be necessary and whether there is anything else we can possibly do to save it but not if it means the rest of the organisation going bankrupt or going belly up.' (Interviewee E)

In the light of this experience, Interviewee E reflected further on the coordination responsibilities of the bishop, the operational demands of the PJP, and the need for the bishop to be consulted and came to the conclusion that this had been an appropriate issue about which to consult the bishop – 'for better or for worse'.

This example also highlights issues regarding the nature and timing of consultations. For example, questions such as why, how and when should consultation take place – and who should be involved need to be considered. Given the complexity and the dynamics of the ministries involved it is not always possible (or preferable) to consult the bishop about every strategic decision. This emphasizes the need for bishops who hold the canonical authority for the ministry and canonical governors who have delegated responsibility to develop and agree upon some decision making principles about why, when and how consultation should take place.

The codes of practice for maintaining effective relationships, communication flows, and accountabilities between canonical governors and bishops vary with the context and the people involved, as one interviewee put it:

> *Our experience has been that it varies with the bishops. It varies with their capacity, and it varies with what they have on their plate. It varies with the complexity of what we are doing. It varies with what one hears about the sort of person they are, and how much they may want to get involved in operational matters. This is a real messy one for me.* (Interviewee E)

Context, personality and in some cases gender were cited by interviewees as potential sources of tension between bishops and canonical governors. In fact, some noted that such tensions between Church hierarchy (as represented by the bishops) and older PJPs (namely the religious institutes) has a long history:

> *The women religious in particular have often done work in spite of a bishop, and they have done great work – sometimes supported by the local bishop, but not always. So there are deep roots for some tension that to some extent continues today and in some ways is getting worse but in different ways.* (Interviewee T)

In recognising both the potential and existing tensions, interviewees called for bishops and canonical governors to work together in ways that mutually recognise and support each other's roles.

> *I do not think the bishops can afford to be disinterested in the growth of these organisations. Equally I do not believe that the PJPs can afford almost consciously to develop structures that negate the role of the bishops.* (Interviewee A)

> *Okay there are some of the bishops who have issues with PJPs, so keeping the relationship with the big Church is kind of important.* (Interviewee I)

In this context, interviewee I went on to explain what needed to be understood by canonical governors and those who were appointing them.

> *There are certain fundamentals; we are part of the Church and we may not agree necessarily with all the decisions. But there are some fundamental things, and if you are not signed up to that then your organisation must drift somewhere.* (Interviewee I)

The notion of 'mission drift' (i.e. circumstances where the core purpose of a ministry is neglected, or poorly understood and enacted – or at worst forgotten altogether) can arise when PJPs do not place sufficient importance on their relationship with bishops. This inevitably leads to tensions which then need to be solved by better governance. For example:

> *When there is a tension between the sponsored ministries and the larger church, this is usually expressed in the relationship of their local bishop.* (Interviewee T)
>
> *Co-ordination of ministerial services is distinctly and qualitatively different. You know the guy in charge has got to know what is going on. That is not a problem. Communication is not a problem. Governance is a problem.* (Interviewee P)

While the tensions around relationships between canonical governors bishops were recognised, there was a widespread and genuine respect for the role of the bishop among interviewees. Our view is that this respect can continue to serve as a basis for bishops and canonical governors for developing the understanding and respect of each other's roles and the relationships necessary for good canonical governance. Bishops and canonical governors may come with different gifts, but they are parts of the one body of the Church.

Implications for Pastoral Formation for Canonical Governance

This chapter has reported on the pastoral dimension through reference to the survey responses and the reflections of interviewees. The findings that we have reported from the Thornber study (2012) support the view that canonical governors need to understand what their being discerning and responsible means for their ministry. Because their ministry exists in a changing environment, canonical governors need to keep the ministry in touch with the mission, and discern where the ministry might need to be directed in the light of such discernment. What's more in light of the broader context of Church ministry and governance, they need to be cognizant of the responsibility of the bishop for the coordination of ministries, and the relationship which needs to exist between the bishop and themselves as canonical governors.

There are several implications for pastoral formation for canonical governance. First, formation needs to ensure that canonical governors grasp the significance of the mission of the Church and are able to articulate it as 'good news' to those served through their ministry. Second, canonical governors need to understand the relationship between the mission of the Church and the mission of their organisation and ministry.

Finally in light of the evident tensions as well as the genuine respect surrounding the role of bishop in coordinating the ministries of the diocese, we believe that a more informed and inclusive pastoral dimension of governance is possible. Hence we contend that the topic of *roles and relationships with bishops* should constitute a significant aspect of formation for canonical governors, including for the bishops themselves.

8
Developing a Framework for Formation

A framework is a set of related elements that provides a way of understanding a complex phenomenon, and taking action in regard to it. From this perspective, a framework for formation of canonical governors can be understood to incorporate the following elements:

1. Definition of formation and its foundations in the ecclesial literature on canonical governance
2. Means of identifying formation needs based on the idea of determining differences between what is desired and what is currently evidenced in terms of the traits of those engaged in, or invited to roles as canonical governors
3. Principles that should underpin the process of formation and the design of formation programmes.

In this chapter we treat each of these elements in turn, drawing upon the ecclesial literature on formation and canonical governance, the approach taken to investigating formation needs used in the Thornber study (2012), and the survey responses and interviewee reflections that highlighted important issues and possibilities for formation processes and programme design.

What do we mean by 'formation'?

One of the early realizations from the Thornber study (2012) was the lack of detail in the ecclesial literature about what 'formation' actually meant. The literature usually referred to formation in terms of needs or expected outcomes of formation rather than providing a definition. For example, The Code of Canon Law, *Pastores Dabo Vobis* (Pope John Paul

II, 1992) on priestly formation and *Co-Workers in the Vineyard of the Lord* (United States Conference of Catholic Bishops, 2005) on ecclesial formation of the laity, each appear to assume that readers have or share a common understanding of the meaning of 'formation'. In the secular world, formation is commonly described as the process of creating something, or by which something develops or takes a particular shape [Encarta Dictionary: English (UK)]. While one might assume that clergy and religious would be familiar with the meaning of the term through their own experience and induction into ecclesial roles, we believe that this gap in the literature is certainly not helpful to those (such as lay canonical governors) who may be relatively unfamiliar with Church language and concepts. So for the Thornber study (2012), it was necessary to create a definition of formation. It read as follows:

> Formation is a reflected development on one's gifts and how the gifts contribute to the need in hand providing an holistic preparation of a person for a role – human, spiritual, intellectual, pastoral – including reflection on the experiences of their own life which might highlight some lacks in development or knowledge that are essential for that need (Thornber, 2012).

This definition was developed from existing literature and researcher experience. It emphasises that formation is a process of development of the whole person. It underlines the value of recognising and reflecting upon one's gifts, and highlights the importance of identifying gaps in knowledge or understanding as an essential step in seeking to better understand and meet the needs of those served by one's ministry.

Interviewees were invited to comment on the 'reasonableness' of this definition of formation. (See Appendix 3 for a listing of interviewee codes and attributes). They were generally supportive of what was proposed and offered some further insights. For example:

> *I think you are picking up the essential concepts that are important*

in formation. You must have human formation, spiritual formation, intellectual formation and pastoral formation, particularly for the role that we are talking about here in this context. (Interviewee D)

Another reflected on the definition in the light of the approach taken to formation programmes in their ministry.

It is similar to the definition that we have developed for use in our formation programme and I think the particular points of similarity are the discussion of one's gifts. (Interviewee X)

Others commented on the appropriate scope of the definition:

I can see it as developing people for a role, a specific role and it includes all those aspects, human, spiritual, intellectual and pastoral. So I think that is valid. (Interviewee C)

Another said:

It covers all the things that I would expect. (Interviewee E)

One interviewee while agreeing with the need for certain traits, was concerned about the degree to which those currently in canonical governance roles had acquired them:

While everyone agrees that you need certain traits. I think the understanding is that we are a long way from people having yet acquired them. (Interviewee F)

Several interviewees commented on elements in the definition relating to 'reflective development on one's gifts'. For example:

I think certainly you start with a reflective development on one's gifts and then how those gifts relate to the particular activity that is proposed. In this case, the question is what it is that you are governing. (Interviewee F)

Another interviewee reflected on the idea that the gifts were being developed for a particular purpose and context, and how these are relevant to different roles in the ministry:

> *That brings in your point that it is a reflected development. How you contribute to the need. The need in this case is canonical governance. In another case it might be how to be a board member or a director of mission.* (Interviewee N)

Another expressed support for highlighting the place of reflection and gifts in the definition, as well as the importance of developing the whole person:

> *Reflection and personal gifts – how those contribute to the role of canonical governance, and using that as a basis for holistic preparation – I thought that was really important.* (Interviewee P)

Several interviewees commented on the importance of the lived experience of people as the starting point for formation, and supported the recognition of that concept in the definition:

> *We definitely try to connect formation experience with their own personal experience, so I think there are many similarities here and I think this is a very adequate definition.* (Interviewee X)

Another interviewee spoke similarly:

> *Well you have a reflected development on one's gifts, it is also about beginning with the gifts that you have and developing them.* (Interviewee F)

However, this interviewee was also concerned that the wording might leave a person believing that reflection on the gifts was all that was required:

> *There is a little too much on the reflection. You have to begin with an assessment of one's gifts and then an assessment of what one needs to do to build on those gifts in order to meet the outcome which is fitness for canonical governance.* (Interviewee F)

While the general opinion was that the definition developed for the Thornber study was appropriate, there were some areas of concern. For instance, some interviewees noted that the "need for technical competence" seemed to be neglected in the proposed definition. They argued that canonical governors should know about the technical issues surrounding the need in hand in order to be able to make reasoned decisions. For example:

> *A governance role requires certain technical skills that would relate to management of people and certain technical skills relating to the particular enterprise that is being governed. If you are governing schools you need to have some technical knowledge of schools, if you are governing hospitals I think you would need some technical knowledge of hospitals.* (Interviewee F)

Another interviewee commented that:

> *Depending on the institution they are governing, they will need specific knowledge. I was not sure that I saw it there. For instance you will not want a good person with human gifts, with spiritual gifts, intellectual gifts and pastoral gifts who does not know tiddly-winks about higher education or about healthcare to be in canonical governance. There is a body of professional information that they have to have to be credible.* (Interviewee V)

By referring to technical competence, these interviewees were not seeking to make it a substitute or addition to certain elements of the definition formation. Rather they saw it as a necessary area of competence for governance roles. We accept this and see it as an important aspect of the intellectual dimension of formation.

Finally, there were several comments about the value of the definition in indicating that formation was for a purpose. For example:

> *There has to be a personal orientation towards service in ministry, and an understanding of how the work we do in governance or in any*

element of healthcare or education is an extension of God's work and our part in that. (Interviewee T)

This interviewee made the point that formation should also take the needs of the ministry into account:

Formation [is] not just for the individual, but also for the sake of the organisation that the person serves. (Interviewee T)

Given the responses and insights provided by the interviewees, our view is that the definition of formation used in the Thornber study is generally sound and can provide a useful basis for investigating the desired traits and needs for formation of canonical governors. While the definition is related to formation for canonical governance in PJPs, it could also fit formation for a range of other senior positions including senior executives of Catholic health, education and welfare agencies, school principals and university roles. For instance, it could be used as a basis for considering the question: how is one formed to become a professor of education or theology, or a vice-chancellor/president, or a member of the governing body in a Catholic university to ensure that the mission of the Church is being fulfilled? Before tackling such questions, we need to consider how to identify formation needs.

How do we identify formation needs?

The Church documents that provided the foundation for the Thornber study (2012) investigating the formation needs of canonical governors were *Pastores Dabo Vobis* (Pope John Paul II, 1992) on priestly formation and *Co-Workers in the Vineyard of the Lord* (United States Conference of Catholic Bishops, 2005) on lay ecclesial formation. These documents used the same dimensions (i.e. human, spiritual, intellectual and pastoral) when referring to formation. The content of both documents with regard to these dimensions was similar, though customised to the different audiences (for example, the priestly formation is required to take six years of full time engagement whereas this is not an expectation for ecclesial workers).

Both documents emphasise the need for development of a personal spirituality informed by the Scriptures and a theology informed by the Church tradition. While the pastoral emphasis varied with the ministry being addressed, a common feature of both was that the dimensions are said to be interlinked. We believe that is crucial for development of the whole person. For example, a developing intellectual knowledge of Scripture and theology would be expected to influence one's personal spirituality and faith relationship with God. This would then be expected to assist the person in shaping their response to the mission for which the organisation exists and to which the person has been called to leadership. The implication for those engaging in formation for canonical governance is that they need to recognise and appreciate the value of the links between the human, spiritual, intellectual and pastoral dimensions.

Using *Pastores Dabo Vobis* (Pope John Paul II, 1992) and *Co-Workers in the Vineyard of the Lord* (United States Conference of Catholic Bishops, 2005) provided an authoritative basis upon which to develop a means of deciding on desired traits and identifying formation needs of canonical governors. The research instrument used to investigate these traits and formation needs was a survey consisting of items drawn from both documents and classified under one of the four dimensions: human, spiritual, intellectual, and pastoral. Survey respondents were invited to indicate their level of agreement about the desirability of various traits and the extent to which they saw those traits in action. Statistical analyses of the results indicated a high level of agreement about the desirability of the nominated traits, but a degree of concern from interviewees about the extent to which survey respondents perceived that the traits were evidenced in practice. The disparity between the desirable and existing traits of those in canonical governance roles was evident across each of the four dimensions, and provided an indication of the types and levels of need for formation in various areas.

The development and application of the four dimensions of formation, drawn from Pope John Paul II (1992) and USCCB (2005) proved to be worthwhile for considering the identification of formation needs. These dimensions were seen as valuable and comprehensive by the interviewees. However the survey results and interviewee responses indicated a range of understandings about concepts and language associated with formation and canonical governance. One explanation cited by several interviewees was the failure of Church leaders, themselves struggling with the implications of what was being asked by the bishops of Vatican II, to educate their congregations in what had been decreed without much preparation (Arbuckle, 1993; Confoy, 2008; Gallagher, 2003; Schweickert, 2002). The Vatican Council documents came out over a period of two years proclaiming a different way of seeing the Church while most formation programmes and Church practices were operating in the model of Church that was being downplayed by the Council. The changes that have since occurred in the Church and the world indicate that the further education is necessary to understand the differences in the approach that lay people, clerics and religious have. For example, Cleary (2007) speaks of the 'multiple world views' which lay people are bringing to their work in the Church compared with the specialised view of clerics and religious of the past. Coming to an understanding of these various world views is necessary to allow those in canonical governance roles to undertake their responsibilities for discerning the signs of the times and proclaiming the good news through their ministry. It needs to be a key component of formation processes and programmes for such roles.

The survey responses underwent factor analysis to validate and identify emergent themes relating to each dimension. These themes are shown in Figure 8.1.

Figure 8.1 Themes Identified from Factor Analysis of Canonical Governance Traits

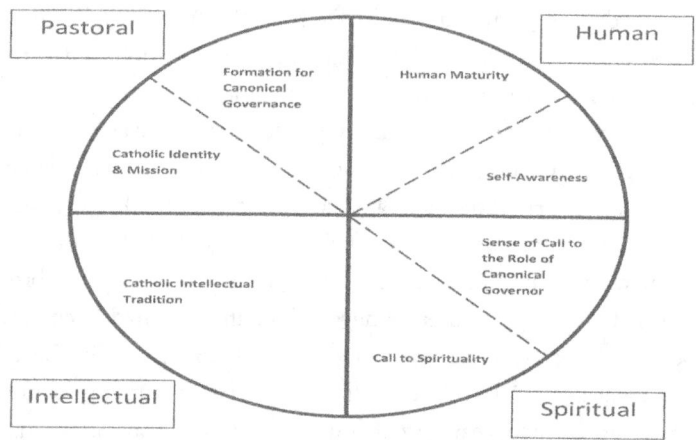

The themes identified from the factor analysis indicated that canonical governors should have particular groups of characteristics and areas of competency, namely that those in canonical governance roles should:

i. be mature and aware of their gifts (from the human dimension);

ii. have a sense of call or vocation to the role and an involvement with the transcendent, spiritual aspects of life (from the spiritual dimension);

iii. engage with the Catholic intellectual tradition (from the intellectual dimension) – meaning that canonical governors understand that the Church has developed a coherent intellectual tradition that is based on its values and underpins its actions, and that the canonical governors should be aware of and literate in that tradition;

iv. understand their responsibility for the Catholic identity of the ministry (from the pastoral dimension); and

v. have appropriate formation in these matters (i-iv) to prepare them for the role (from the pastoral dimension).

The Thornber study (2012) showed that formation needs can be identified through a combination of survey development, distribution and analysis. It found that the conduct of interviews was an important component of the process of determining formation needs. The interviews enabled the interviewer and interviewee to raise questions and help clarify the meanings of terms and concepts as well as consider the extent to which various traits are desirable and evident in canonical governance. Whether there is a need for formation will depend on one's assessment against these traits. The Thornber study (2012) highlighted that such assessments have *objective* as well as *subjective* aspects. The objective nature of the needs assessment includes reference to authoritative ecclesial literature as a means of mapping the range of traits required – in general terms at least. The Thornber survey is an example of a research instrument in the objective sphere. It is not designed to identity needs; rather, its role is to provide information for discussion. The subjective element, on the other hand, involves a degree of reflection about the gifts that individuals 'bring to the table' as canonical governors in the work of the Church. From the perspective of those invited to the role, the following questions come to mind: *Why am I interested in this role? What can I bring to it?* From the viewpoint of those involved in the selection and formation of such individuals, matters for consideration include: *What gifts does this person have that are valuable to the ministry? What are their needs for formation? How do I know?* And, *how might these needs be best addressed?* In summary, the identification of formation needs has to be negotiated between those invited to, or undertaking the role and those responsible for selecting and supporting them.

What principles should underpin formation processes and programme design?

The third element of the formation framework for canonical governors is the principles that underpin the process of formation and the design of formation programmes. We have distilled the following principles from the ecclesial literature and research findings of the Thornber study (2012), and recommend them as useful touchstones for those involved in developing and running formation programmes.

Principle 1: Understand what is meant by 'formation' for canonical governance.

Having an agreed understanding of 'formation' and its bases in the ecclesial literature are fundamental. We need to be clear about the meaning of formation and why it is important before going about the task of identifying needs, and designing and delivering formation programmes. To help with this, we believe that the definition of formation that was validated through the Thornber study (2012) and ecclesial literature associated with it are useful foundations.

Principle 2: Have an appropriate means of identifying formation needs.

Allied with an understanding of formation is the importance of having an appropriate means of identifying formation needs. Our view is that the approach developed through the Thornber study (2012) presents a worthwhile template for such investigation. This is because the identification of formation needs involves comparing what is desired with what is being evidenced in the beliefs and actions of those in canonical governance roles. In this sense the Thornber study (2012) provides a starting point for identifying formation needs by determining desirable traits, and noting the nature of any discrepancy between those desired traits and what is evidenced in practice. One point of caution for those engaged in this type of investigation is that what is desired and considered as a discrepancy will vary from person to person and from context to context. So beware of identifying needs that may not exist – or failing to identify those do! Identifying formation needs is a complex and collaborative undertaking. Don't rely on your judgment alone.

In addition to having an agreed definition of formation and an appropriate means of identifying formation needs, what other principles should underpin formation processes and programme design?

In the following sections, we draw from the survey responses and reflections of interviewees relating to specific items from the pastoral dimension of the Thornber study (2012) survey. These items were grouped under the factor 'formation for canonical governance' identified through the factor analysis. The survey responses are presented in Table 8.1.

Over 84 per cent of survey respondents agreed that having an appropriate way of calling those leading the operation of the ministry to account, understanding organisational systems and dynamics, and using mission-based criteria in selecting and forming their successors were desirable pastoral traits for canonical governors. However between 35 per cent and 43 per cent felt that these traits were only evident to a fair extent or less. These findings suggest that there is a need for further investigation around the issue of whether exhibiting a trait to a *fair* extent is 'fair enough' – i.e. is it sufficient or is it indicative of a need for formation?

Table 8.1
Desired and Existing Traits of Canonical Governors – Formation for Canonical Governance (N=92)

Canonical governors	This trait is desirable (%)					The extent to which this trait exists (%)				
	Strongly Agree	Agree	Disagree	Strongly Disagree	No Answer	Very High	High	Fair	Low	Unable to Judge/No Answer
have an appropriate way of calling those leading the operation of the ministry to account	62	31	2	1	4	10	40	32	10	8
understand organisational systems and dynamics	38	51	7	1	3	10	40	35	8	7
use mission-based criteria in selecting future governors	50	35	7	1	7	14	38	25	10	13
use mission-based criteria in forming future governors	50	40	3	1	6	12	34	30	12	12

Principle 3: Use mission-based criteria for canonical governor selection and formation

Survey respondents were invited to consider the use of mission-based criteria in the selection and formation of canonical governors. The term, mission-based criteria refers to principles of decision making drawn from Catholic social teaching and the special spiritual and religious character and gifts (or charism) that underpin the particular ministry and are applied and demonstrated in the work of that ministry.

The respondents clearly valued the use of mission-based criteria in canonical governor selection and formation; with 50 per cent strongly agreeing and 35 per cent agreeing with regard to the former, and 50 per cent strongly agreeing and 40 per cent agreeing with regard to the latter (see Table 8.1). However their perceptions about the degree to which mission-based criteria were actually being applied in selection and formation programmes were more varied. For example with respect to the selection of canonical governors, 14 per cent of respondents considered the trait currently existed to a very high extent, 38 per cent to a high extent, 25 per cent to a fair extent and 12 per cent to a low extent. Similar variation was evident with respect to the use of mission-based criteria in the formation of canonical governors. Twelve per cent of respondents answered that the trait currently existed to a very high extent, 34 per cent to a high extent, 30 per cent to a fair extent, and 12 per cent to a low extent.

These variations caused concern among several interviewees. A number of interviewees cited the difficulty of having and finding canonical governors who have sufficient understanding of Catholic social teaching and background in the ministry (and its charism) to be able to apply mission-based criteria to the selection and formation of colleagues and successors. As one interviewee explained:

I mean it is just a big hill to climb and the first part of formation for canonical governance is finding the people, recruiting them. (Interviewee V)

Moreover, these findings emphasise the need for selection and formation processes for canonical governors to be explicitly and comprehensively underpinned by mission-based criteria; criteria that are understood by those doing the selecting and providing the formation opportunities as well as by those who are being selected and participating in those opportunities. In fact given appropriate priority and properly handled, we believe that the use of mission-based criteria in formation processes can assist canonical governors in two related areas of potential need, shown in Table 8.1. By integrating specific Catholic social teaching and charism elements with relevant aspects of management and organisation theory in the content of formation, canonical governors can develop their understanding of organisational systems and dynamics, along with their capability in calling those responsible for the operation of the ministry to account.

Principle 4: Formation involves more than going to courses

There are two broad approaches to formation. One approach involves formal programmes where those with existing roles and responsibilities or those who are potential candidates for canonical governance participate in a structured programme, as one interviewee put it:

> *There are programmes such as the XX and YY and so on. These are programmes that have a beginning, middle and an end. Like an overall orientation, four weekends over sixteen months.* (Interviewee V)

As we have previously explained, formation programmes should be designed on the basis of the needs that have been collaboratively identified, i.e. where there is agreement among those involved about the desired ends, any discrepancy between the existing and the desired traits, and the means of meeting the needs that have been identified. Each programme can then be evaluated in terms of how well it has addressed the discrepancy between the existing and the desired traits of canonical governors.

The second approach to formation is *ongoing formation*. This involves a combination of strategies and learning activities of varying 'formality', format and duration. It can include aspects of 'just-in-time' learning as issues and opportunities arise, as well as structured experiences (such as inviting potential governors to meetings). The former means may involve some coaching or mentoring by experienced colleague, while the latter might be used to assess the suitability of people being considered for governance roles as well as allow opportunity for them to learn about what is involved and reflect on their sense of vocation to the role, as one interviewee described:

> *We are bringing on interns to let them see what the role of the PJP is and whether or not they think this is a call for them and if they can contribute to it in a meaningful way.* (Interviewee J)

Our view is that formation is most effective when it extends beyond formal courses to include ongoing formation. This perspective was supported by several interviewees:

> *If you have only [the formation course], [then] people will have something to tick off. You know, 'I have had that formation, now I am done. I have gone through that'. This is something that is supposed to be ongoing.* (Interviewee V)

Another spoke about the limitations of formation as 'going to courses' in these terms:

> *What bothers me about formation as I have seen it is that it has been more like a journey of going to courses. I do not denigrate the importance of courses. But it is almost as if, 'Well, I have been to the course. Now I am going back to work'.* (Interviewee A)

This insight highlights the issue of individuals seeing little or no connection between the formation they attend and the way they operate in the ministry. One way to address this is to alter the format of meetings so that concepts and understandings that have been highlighted in formation courses can be recapped and reinforced, as one interviewee explained:

> *At every one of our board meetings we take 30 to 40 minutes for formation and that never ends.*

Some interviewees expressed concern if prior to the creation of a PJP, candidates for canonical governor roles were required to undertake compulsory formal formation. For example:

> *One of the things that troubles me and it came from my last retreat actually was the notion that before you form a PJP the members should have undergone one, two, three years, or whatever of formation.* (Interviewee E)

The interviewee spoke of how ongoing formation for canonical governors in their organisation incorporates regularly scheduled formation programmes which are run internally:

We have biannual formal retreat formations as well as our stewardship formation which is bimonthly. We have two Sisters who head up the stewardship and are responsible, with the director of mission, for growing the formation for all board members. (Interviewee E)

The organisation referred to above was criticised for its method of formation, as explained:

The accusation that has been offered to me is that we should not have done that without having organised a solid period of formation prior to establishing the PJP. (Interviewee E)

In response, the interviewee was convinced of the appropriateness of their method of formation:

What I can absolutely say without a shadow of doubt is that, unless the formation that we have done had been done in the way we have done it, we would not have as strongly formed a board as we have. If we had had to choose only from people who had undertaken a programme of formation previously, we would not have the richness that we have. (Interviewee E)

The point being emphasised here is that ongoing formation, run by people within the organisation, can serve as a means of inducting canonical governors as well as supporting the further growth and understanding of the role of those more experienced on the role. At the same time, it is important to be open to the possibility of integrating externally developed formation programmes with what is being offered internally, particularly as a means of discerning the signs of the times and formation needs into the future, as Interviewee E explains:

We will move to some new formation needs and have to provide new opportunities. [From this perspective] it would be really good to have some formation opportunities that people could buy into.

This sentiment was reflected by other interviewees as they spoke of the need to provide timely, initial and ongoing high quality formation opportunities for current and prospective canonical governors. Such formation, they said, needs to take account of changing circumstances and be led and delivered by different groups and individuals from what has happened in the past. As one interviewee put it:

> *Many were formed, as I was, by sisters or brothers with the idea that we would be the next tier of succession of governance.* (Interviewee C)

With lessening involvement of religious and increasing involvement of laity in canonical governance, new approaches to formation are called for. These approaches need to go beyond the development and delivery formal courses and take on an ongoing character in order to ensure the mission of the ministries is sustained.

Principle 5: Take an adult learning approach to formation

Research on formation for canonical governance has shown that it needs to be based on the principles of adult learning (Connolly, 2002). These principles include an acknowledgement by those designing and delivering formation programmes of the background knowledge and experiences of the participants. This point was emphasised by several interviewees. For example:

> *Many people who are moving into a canonical governance role have a skill set in one area and there is a learning process in the other. There are some areas that when you look at a whole organisation, they may have more work to do in one area versus another.* (Interviewee N)

One area of adult learning where the background knowledge and experience of participants was recognised in the Thornber study (2012) was the integration of the spiritual and theological aspects implicit in the role of canonical governors with the skills and understandings that participants bring from their work life. Several interviewees noted that formation experiences were pivotal in helping individuals integrate the theological and spiritual with the practical aspects of their role. For example:

> *To me it is about trying to understand the theological and the spiritual and all of the other implications of everything that you do every day. [Finding ways of] bringing all of those other aspects more genuinely into all of the practical things are important.* (Interviewee A)

Allied with this endeavour is the need to recognise the perspectives which lay people (some of whom may have decades of professional background in secular institutions) bring to the formation process; and how these compare with the viewpoints, experiences and expectations of the priests and religious as a consequence of their ecclesial lifestyle. One interviewee highlighted this point with an example:

> *I think the first challenge is with the people who are doing the formation. Sister XX wrote an article and in it she said one of the men said 'are you trying to make us mini novices?'* (Interviewee L)

Applying the principles of adult learning in this instance means realising that lay people may develop a spirituality that is different from that traditionally associated with priestly and religious life and, what is more, they may not have the ecclesial language to articulate it, as the interviewee went on to explain:

> *I think that it has to be different in terms of lay people. There has to be some points of focus that take account of the fact that grace works in their lives within the relationships that are central to their own lives rather than in the community that they become part of in the ministerial work of governance.* (Interviewee L)

This comment is helpful in distinguishing the bases of formation for life compared with formation for ministry. Members of religious institutes who ran the ministries were formed to live in community and to work together in ministry. Often, the focus was on the ministry as the source of satisfaction for living, and the community was a base to come from and go to. For lay people on the other hand, the starting point is the relationships in their lives. It is the gift they bring to the ministry. Taking an adult learning approach means recognising the spiritual journey that people bring to the formation process. Furthermore, differences in background should be expected to lead to differences in outcomes. The interviewee clarified the point:

> *You cannot conflate the points of emphasis of religious life with the points of emphasis of lay life. Some lay people have a sense of we cannot do this the way the sisters did it. The answer is no, you are not supposed to. [My advice is] find your way of doing this.* (Interviewee L)

Another interviewee in supporting the need to employ an adult learning approach went to suggest a particular area of sacramental theology as needing attention in formation for canonical governors:

> *Yes, I think, part of [the] formation [that] people need to be taken through, in an adult education way, [is] the notion of baptismal commitment to mission. I do think they need some formation in sacramental theology particularly around the sacrament of baptism.* (Interviewee D)

The interviewee described something of what such an approach might entail:

> *What is it exactly? Without driving them silly, I think it should be done through practical example and illustration. That is part of the formation bag I think.* (Interviewee D)

Some understandings that might flow from engagement with people on their own spiritual journey as they prepare for and perform canonical governance roles are explained in the following terms:

> *It is still an area that needs exploration and some of the main points of people coming to a certain trust of their own spirituality that 'God has indeed called you as you are, and to grow further as you are. But as*

> *you are – as a married person, as a family member, as a single person, as a member of the community in which you live, the town'. That is the stuff of the life of a person.* (Interviewee L)

This interviewee taught university students and had experience of the personal development that is possible when an adult learning approach is taken to formation:

> *We had a formation programme for the lay students involved in pastoral ministry, and what I would say was significant was the gradual growth in their sense of themselves as spiritual beings in their own right, not trying to be like the sisters, or not trying to be like the priests. And that is hard.* (Interviewee L)

The interviewee provided some insights into the educational experiences which contributed to this development:

> *Theological reflection is useful [as well as] spiritual experiences of mini retreats, retreats that draw out the themes of everyday life. I think that one of the graces of this moment is some breaking down of the sacred-secular categories and a greater possibility of seeing God's action in all that is.* (Interviewee L)

The interviewee reflected on the changes being effected for lay students preparing for activity in pastoral roles:

> *I think that the new [thinking] invites us to think about the very world we live in. And the teachings of the Vatican Council about God's presence in all things, invites us to think that way. The fact of lay people, not people living in convents and rectories but people living in the world, the fact of that contributes to this and can lead to a greater discovery of God's presence in all things.* (Interviewee L)

While these reflections stem from involvement with young lay students, we believe that they can be applied to the formation for canonical governors. In fact, those responsible for formation might expect to have deeper spiritual engagement from people bringing a more mature life experience to the formation process. The interviewee's insights for development were tempered with a concern about not engaging with the opportunity which the present times seemed to offer:

> *On the other hand we could domesticate all of this and effectively put everybody in convents, intellectually, relationally. I think that is not what this moment calls for.* (Interviewee L)

We agree. Our view is that engagement with adult learning approaches is an essential principle in formation for canonical governors.

Principle 6: Consider the time commitment for the role of canonical governor

Experience, as well as findings from the Thornber study (2012) tells us that there is considerable time involved in being a canonical governor. Interviewees generally thought that the time required was a major influence on who might be willing to make themselves available to be selected for roles in canonical governance. Their view was that effective governance processes take time, and the types of individuals who are invited to governance roles are typically busy people. Added to this is the likely different background of people (i.e. lay compared with clerics or religious) who might be available for governance roles in the future compared with those who currently occupy such positions. As a consequence, several interviewees noted that more time was likely to be required to meet the formation needs of canonical governors into the future. Further, such time would be in addition to that involved with the actual practice of canonical governance. In referring to this issue, one interviewee said starkly:

> *What you want are canonical governors who do not have fulltime jobs elsewhere.* (Interviewee C)

This interviewee went on to outline the time expectations for the role in the ministry with which they were associated.

We demand of our governors probably two retreats a year and a strategic planning session a year which are residential things. Plus we meet over two days. We expect them to visit between two and four site locations [each year] which are a day visit. We do not believe we should turn up at a site, walk straight into a trustee meeting and leave. We go and visit our site. We have presentations. We socialise with the facility management and then we hold our meetings. So, it is not a token visit. (Interviewee C)

This description of the requirements of trustees, who are also the canonical governors, highlights a substantial time commitment. The interviewee reflected on what this commitment might be:

I suspect that if you added up the time that our trustees spend, it is probably 30 or 40 days a year in the role. (Interviewee C)

In the light of this evidence, the interviewee returned to the claim that a full-time employee could not be selected for the role:

A full-time employee cannot do that. (Interviewee C)

These comments reflect a general concern about the nature and extent of time required for effective performance in the role, especially by people who were holding down full-time jobs. In the light the significance of this issue, the Thornber study (2012) sought data from other ministries regarding time expectations of canonical governors. One said 15 days a year. Another said 18 days for most governors and 70 days for the Chair. A third said 60 days minimum a year (including meetings taking two days, preparation, annual pastoral visits to all facilities, meetings with bishops, conferences and private meetings.

The issue of time commitment for formation and acting in the role of canonical governor is a pragmatic pastoral matter. It is handled in different ways in light of the different demands and contexts of various ministries. The range of time expectations given by respondents in existing PJPs suggests that the time requirements and expectations need to be very carefully thought through by those seeking to set up PJPs and inviting others to participate in such bodies.

Principle 7: Address the implications of generational change in background of canonical governors

Many currently involved in canonical governance are, or have been members of religious institutes and have some background in the ministry, governance and the charism. Many of the lay people currently in canonical governance roles have been mentored by those with a substantial formation background. The next generation of canonical governors selected and invited to these roles will not have had some level of mentoring support from religious institutes and will be dependent on the 'second generation' governors. Abeles (2008, p. 32) explains this concern:

> In some ways, however, we have placed our ministry at risk because we have not been as careful with their formation as were women religious with second generation leaders. In sum, because we may not have been as intentional with their formation, these leaders may not fully understand the theology that underlies this ministry of the Catholic Church, and how to enact it in the full context of all they do.

Related to this concern, several interviewees reflected on the predicted loss of the religious institute members at board and operational level while expressing the hope of retaining their contribution at the canonical governance level for an extended time. For example:

> *We will be going into the next few years where there are likely to be no religious on our board. I think there will probably be religious as long as we have them amongst our governors if we can get them.* (Interviewee E)

This interviewee was involved with a PJP which had works in several ministries – health, welfare and education. The view was shared by Interviewee C who was engaged in governance in the health ministry:

> *I think that is one of the biggest challenges that we will face. In the next five or ten years I suspect we will see the total removal of religious from these organisations, not only within the organisation but at governance level.*

The interviewee then reflected on various religious institutes' projections of people available and capable of being canonical governors:

> *The various congregations that have traditionally run Catholic health will not be able to continue to effectively sponsor or oversee their historical ministries in [say] ten years' time. I mean genuinely whether they will have people capable of doing it or willing to do it.* (Interviewee C)

The interviewee went on to express concern about the future and the importance of appropriate governance (canonical and civil) of the ministry of health for the mission of the Church:

> *It is a very, very significant enterprise worldwide [in the Church]. It needs to be governed at the highest standards of governance and I think the religious will not be in a position to do that en masse the way they have done it in the past. There will be individuals who will be capable, but not en masse.* (Interviewee C)

Our book is premised on this understanding and the need to address these changing circumstances in the Church. Similarly, Interviewee C noted the importance of formation in preparing people who would be available for taking on governance roles:

> *Therefore, if it is going to be governed effectively and in a way that it deserves to be, you have to create a whole range of canonical governors out of the laity. And I think they need significant formation.* (Interviewee C)

The interviewee was hopeful that there were a sufficient number of people able and willing to undertake canonical governance roles, particularly in the health ministry:

> *I think one of the challenges is that there are a whole lot of people working within the sector that I think will, for a whole range of reasons, make perfectly wonderful future [canonical] governors.* (Interviewee C)

Others were not so optimistic:

> *Where do we even find these people who would be willing to undergo this formation, who have the natural gift for it, the background?* (Interviewee V)

Several difficulties were identified in attracting and selecting individuals for governance roles. The first is the expectation that it is an honorary role. The second is that the role required people with energy:

> *We need to develop processes whereby we can give outstanding leaders within the organisation cross fertilization. But you can't take someone say, who is the chief executive of [a ministry], and say at age 50, 'how about stepping down to be a canonical governor? Oh, but we do not actually pay you'. But the difficulty is you should not wait until they retire because at that stage they are older, tired and probably not at their prime.* (Interviewee C)

The interviewee added that the task of seeking and selecting canonical governors from the executive ranks requires reconsideration of the concept of career path and associated remuneration:

> *You need to have a career path by which these people can reach the top of management and move beyond but still have the capacity to earn, because these people will need that.* (Interviewee C)

Along with the need to address with issues of remuneration and career path, the interviewee advocated having people with appropriate background knowledge of the sector:

There is clear advantage in having people with high level experience. It is quite risky getting a group of canonical governors that do not understand the sector. It is big business and unless you understand that, unless you understand it is a very difficult sector, it is very easy to make mistakes in it. And history is littered with people who thought they knew how to run hospitals and did not. And [they] created disasters.
(Interviewee C)

In summing up, our view is that the seven principles shown in Figure 8.2 should underpin the process of formation and the design of formation programmes. Our hope is that these principles provide a useful reference point for those responsible for formation.

Principle 1: Understand what is meant by 'formation' for canonical governance.

Principle 2: Have an appropriate means of identifying formation needs.

Principle 3: Use mission-based criteria for canonical governor selection and formation.

Principle 4: Formation involves more than going to courses.

Principle 5: Take an adult learning approach to formation.

Principle 6: Consider the time commitment for the role of canonical governor.

Principle 7: Address the implications of generational change in background of canonical governors.

Figure 8.2 Principles to underpin the process of formation and the design of formation programmes for canonical governance

In this chapter we have presented a framework for formation of canonical governors that incorporates the definition of formation and its foundations in the ecclesial literature, a means of identifying formation needs, and the principles that should underpin formation. In *Gaudium et Spes* (1964, n. 4), the Council had called on the Church to move to 'discern the signs of the times' (Abbott, 1966d). Such discernment requires us to be open to changes in the needs of the Church and its ministries. Our task is to understand the dramatic changes and be able to interpret how to deal with them in the light of the mission of the Church. The framework that has been developed from the findings of the Thornber study (2012) is designed to assist in that task.

9

Forming Foundations for the Future

Formation for the role of canonical governor is based on the principle that people who undertake these roles require certain traits and associated types of support and preparation experiences. As we have discussed throughout this book, canonical governance is a multifaceted responsibility and process. It involves attention to the human, spiritual, intellectual and pastoral dimensions of governance and how these influence decisions about the purpose, priorities, policies, programmes and performance of the Church ministries. Consequently, we have argued that canonical governors require a range of knowledge, skills, beliefs and other attributes associated with these dimensions to perform effectively and authentically in their roles.

The Thornber study (2012) set out to identify the traits that canonical governors need for their ministry and to examine and explain the extent to which canonical governors are currently exhibiting those traits. It drew upon recognised sources in the ecclesial literature, including *Pastores Dabo Vobis* (Pope John Paul II, 1992) on priestly formation and *Co-Workers in the Vineyard of the Lord* (United States Conference of Catholic Bishops, 2005) on ecclesial formation of the laity, to develop a listing of potential traits across the four dimensions of human, spiritual, intellectual and pastoral formation. This listing of traits was then converted into a survey where respondents were asked to indicate their level of agreement about desirability of the various traits and the extent to which they perceived those traits to be evident. The survey respondents consistently expressed high levels of agreement about the desirability of the listed items, but also considered that these traits were generally less evident than what might be expected given their perceived importance (see Chapters 4-7).

This discrepancy between *what is desirable* and *what is evident* provided the basis for identifying potential formation needs as well as suggesting specific content and design features for formation programmes. The survey responses were then examined through interviews with people with experience and expertise in the fields of canonical governance, spirituality, Canon Law and theology. While the interviewees similarly expressed their agreement with regard to the desirability of the listed traits, they were concerned at the consistent discrepancies between what was desired and what was evident. They saw this phenomenon as providing the impetus for more informed and concerted efforts in the formation of canonical governors.

In general terms the types of knowledge, skills and other attributes identified through the Thornber study (2012) were that canonical governors require:

a) the maturity to deal justly and compassionately with the demands of their ministry;

b) the ability to engage with, and be responsible for the spiritual life of their ministry;

c) an appreciation of Catholic intellectual tradition;

d) an awareness of the concept of Catholic identity; and

e) an understanding of the role and responsibilities of bishops.

In this chapter we will present a set of key messages and themes for the future that we have distilled from our analysis of survey responses and interviewee reflections gathered through the Thornber study (2012). Our hope is that these will offer a basis for reflection and planning for those involved in the design and delivery of formation programmes for canonical governors, as well as providing useful background information for those contemplating, and those undertaking roles in the canonical governance of Church ministries.

Key Messages for 'Governing in Faith'

1. Canonical governance is an area for leadership development in the Church. The nature of canonical governance is undergoing profound change. As religious institutes are either unavailable or have diminishing capacity to lead Church ministries and as more lay people understand and take canonical responsibility for those ministries, traditional approaches to governance are no longer viable or appropriate. The demise of the stable and certain world of canonical governance since Vatican II brings challenges as well as opportunities. Despite the changes, the role of canonical governors remains an essential element for the continuing mission of the Church as expressed through its various ministries in education, health, aged care and social welfare. In the increasingly diverse and evolving world of canonical governance, those charged with the responsibility for continuing the mission need to understand the importance of their leadership role. It follows therefore that developing the leadership capabilities of canonical governors through needs-based, informed, engaging and sustainable formation opportunities needs to be a major priority of our contemporary Church.

2. Canonical governors require certain traits. The role of a canonical governor requires particular areas of knowledge and skill related to the human, spiritual, intellectual and pastoral dimensions of their work. The choice and priority given to certain traits or combinations of traits may vary from ministry to ministry and from context to context depending on the circumstances and the people involved. The listing of traits developed through the Thornber study (2012) provides a reference point for thinking about what traits should be considered and which traits should be given priority in particular situations. To use the findings of this study fruitfully, ministry leaders need to develop a shared understanding of their goals and mission, and therefore what is required of canonical governors to serve those aspirations. Formation programmes can then be designed and delivered in light of this. These should be programmes that take account of the needs, knowledge, skills, interests and motivations of 'would-be' and existing canonical governors – and the traits to be developed.

3. Formation requires commitment and appropriate resourcing. Preparing to become a canonical governor and performing appropriately in the role entails a willingness and commitment to engage in formation opportunities. Invitees and experienced practitioners alike need to be open to what formation may hold for them, and enter into it willingly. There is also considerable time involved – time that may take them away from their 'mainstream' professional endeavours as well as their families. Such commitments need to be recognised and moderated so that the roles remain feasible and the programmes sustainable. Consequently, we argue that appropriate resourcing (in terms of funding and time allowances, and administrative support) is necessary to provide the opportunities for both new and experienced canonical governors to develop their human, spiritual, intellectual and pastoral gifts to enable them to better achieve the goals of their ministry.

4. Canonical governance has language and traditions. The Thornber study (2012) identified two problems with Church language. First, the survey responses and the interviewee reflections indicated that people involved in Church governance are using key terms differently. For example, concepts such as justice, compassion, respect for persons and Catholic identity were frequently noted as having different meanings for different people in different contexts. Second, the study found that a relatively low level of theological literacy among the current crop of canonical governors. This was evident, especially in the responses to survey items and interview questions relating to the purpose of the Church (missiology) and how it operates (ecclesiology). Our view is that without some grounding in these areas it is extremely difficult for canonical governors to discern, for example how the mission of their ministry aligns with how mission is understood in the Church. In other words, for them to be able to appreciate how what they do as canonical governors might be reasonably termed as 'Catholic'. And this is not as straightforward as it might seem. There is, always has been, and is always likely to be, a range of theological views in the Church. Canonical governors need to have sufficient theological understanding to appreciate this, and therefore be able to discern what might be most appropriate in context of their ministry.

Because of this, we suggest that an important element of formation of canonical governors has to be developing an understanding of Church concepts and language. One means of addressing this need is to consider authoritative writing in the areas of models of Church (Dulles, 1987), types of theology (Bevans and Schroeder, 2004; Ormerod, 1997) and conceptual frameworks for theology (Bevans, 2002). The writers in these areas drawn upon and explain the nature of ancient traditions in the Church, their legitimacy and their application to current circumstances. Importantly canonical governors would need to understand that the Catholic identity which flows from each tradition emphasizes different aspects of the mystery of God in the world, and a follower of one tradition who had no understanding of the others – and was closed off from learning about or dialoguing with those others (Bevans and Schroeder, 2011) – would likely to question or even ignore the validity of the Catholic identity of the other. Anthropologist Arbuckle (1993, 2000, 2001, 2007a, 2010) has written extensively on the cultural implications of this issue, particularly from his viewpoint and critique of postmodernism. His writings are supported by theologians (Muldoon, 2009; Ormerod, 2008; Putney, 2008), educators and missiologists (Bevans and Schroeder, 2011; D'Orsa and D'Orsa, 2010; Gallin, 2000) and canonists (Beal, 2006; Morrisey, 1999, 2001a, 2003, 2011).

Findings from the Thornber study (2012) indicate that canonical governors generally lack awareness of the different, and legitimate intellectual traditions of the Catholic Church. We believe that this can have serious implications for their pastoral work and decision making, and therefore regard their engagement with these aspects of the Catholic intellectual tradition as a vital part of their formation. In this sense we concur with Cleary (2007, p. 263) about the need for canonical governors to have the intellectual capacity to integrate the range of theological perspectives of the Church with the history and tradition of their ministry and sponsoring group, while holding in balance the needs of a civil corporation that provides human services in an increasingly complex environment. In short this is not a role for the faint-hearted or the empty-headed!

5. Canonical governance involves choices and ethical dilemmas.
Another of the challenges for canonical governors confirmed through the Thornber (2012) was the difficulty of leading when the types and levels of need far outstrip the resources available to the ministry. Interviewees who had experience as canonical governors described how their decisions had sometimes been criticised as unjust or lacking in compassion by those who were either not directly involved in the decision making process or were not privy to all the facts. They found this difficult as they reasoned that they had genuinely sought to apply the values of justice and compassion, but this was not always recognised. In fact, they explained that they experienced ethical dilemmas in their role that often challenged them not to choose between 'right' and 'wrong', but between 'two rights' in order to serve the greater, or common good. The sort of analysis, soul searching and justification involved in these types of decisions should not be underestimated. In these circumstances, mere recourse to statements such as 'we have based our decision on Gospel values' is simply not good enough. Such replies too easily disguise the fact that values such as justice and compassion are often in tension and cannot be easily accommodated in difficult decisions, as John Henry Thornber puts it:

When justice is meted out to us, we might beg for mercy;
When someone is given a lenient decision, the cry is 'where's the justice in that?'

Canonical governors' understanding and capacity to deal with these types of choices, tensions and dilemmas would be assisted by formation in Catholic social teaching.

6. Canonical governors need to be mature human beings. Canonical governors need to be people with a well-developed sense of themselves and the relevant professional and personal experiences to be able to deal with the complexity of issues involved in Church ministries. Put simply, they need to be mature human beings, who are able to deal with unexpected turns of events, a range of client and stakeholder demands and opportunities, and the capacity to accept praise and criticism about the ways in which they carry out their governance responsibilities with magnanimity.

7. Canonical governors need to have their vocation nurtured. People are invited and called to be canonical governors but this can lose its appeal in the busyness of everyday life with its completing demands and shrinking timeframes. Therefore it is important to set aside opportunities for canonical governors to nurture their sense of vocation. This requires a framework of lay spirituality with a 'different richness' to that those formed for and by clerical and religious life. Recognising the background that lay people brings to the role requires trust and understanding on the part of Church leaders to believe that 'different' is not 'wrong' (Kirkwood, 2012a). A growing sense of the vocation is an integral element on the spiritual journey of canonical governors from their baptismal call (which was the message of renewal from the bishops of Vatican II), and needs to be a fresh and relevant focus for their formation.

8. Canonical governors need some background in Canon Law.

The legal basis for canonical governance – Canon Law – is not as well understood as it should be. Canonical governors need to be better informed about the aspects of Canon Law most closely related to their governance roles. These include the law on governance, the rights of people, the mission of the Church and the temporal goods of the Church. Indeed, we contend that one's background in Canon Law should at least be given comparable priority to one's background in civil law, particularly for those governors whose role which requires them to undertake both canonical and civil responsibilities.

9. Canonical governors need to be open to the Word of God. The Thornber study (2012) highlighted the concern about people who are not Catholic being appointed to the role of canonical governor, a position that has responsibility for aligning the ministry with the mission of the Church. In response, we maintain that leading a Catholic ministry requires a clear, informed and practical understanding of mission and ministry. Consequently formation needs to be directed toward deepening one's understanding of Catholic identity and developing one's capacity to articulate that identity for those working in the ministry. In particular ministries, the mission and charism of a founding religious institute can also be an inspiring influence. Canonical governors need to understand the relationship between the mission of the Church and the mission of the ministry in order to maintain the Catholic identity and integrity of the institution and its ministry. This requirement applies to both the baptised and the non-baptised. What matters most is that canonical governors are open to the Word of God and its possibilities for them – and through them for others.

10. Formation for canonical governance involves religious and clergy as well as lay people. One 'surprise finding' from the Thornber study (2012) was that 'it is not all about what the lay people need'. While some bishops and others may express the concern that lay people may not be capable of undertaking the role, we argue that there has been a misplaced perception that the leaders of religious institutes understood their responsibilities for governance. Evidence from a number of interviewees identified examples that showed that while leaders of religious institutes may have come to the role with significant theological background, they had limited understanding of governance – canonical or civil. As a consequence we propose that formation into the future is designed and delivered with religious and clergy as well as lay people in mind.

Formation Themes for the Future

1. Knowing the meaning and purpose of formation. Another surprising outcome of the Thornber study (2012) was the need to create a definition of 'formation'. The review of the literature indicated that writers in the area assumed that their readers understood the meaning of the term, and tended to describe and analyse the purpose and outcomes of formation rather than what was involved in the process itself. This might be attributed to the traditional use of term in clerical and religious formation where patterns of formation have been established and entrenched for centuries.

As lay candidates and practitioners in canonical governance have not and do not undergo these patterns of formation, the term needed to be more appropriately defined. The following definition was subsequently developed by Thornber (2012) and validated by the interviewees:

> Formation is a reflected development on one's gifts and how the gifts contribute to the need in hand providing an holistic preparation of a person for a role – human, spiritual, intellectual, pastoral – including reflection on the experiences of their own life which might highlight some lacks in development or knowledge that are essential for meeting that need.

This definition is similar to that given by Bouchard (2009, p. 40) who while couching his terminology in religious language, also sees formation as a developmental or 'transformative process', as follows:

> Formation is a transformative process rooted in theology and spirituality that connects us more deeply with God, creation and others.

Self-reflection, as a key element of formation opens us to God's action so that we derive deeper meaning from the work we do, grow in awareness of our gifts, increasingly see our work as vocation, and build a greater communal commitment to the ministry. As a consequence, we recommend that a definition of formation drawn from the above definitions and related literature, be articulated as a core component of formation programmes. This would provide some welcome clarity for participants and facilitators alike on the meaning and purpose of the teaching and learning activity involved.

2. Understanding the canonical concept of the Public Juridic Person (PJP). One of the difficulties encountered in the Thornber research (2012) was the understanding of the term PJP. It was not well known, even by religious. One reason may be that the term only came into Church language in the 1983 Code of Canon Law and was not widely spoken about or examined until the need for alternative governance models emerged in the late 1980s (Austin, 2011). Religious Institutes, dioceses and parishes were regarded as 'moral persons' under the previous 1917 code (Austin, 2011, p. 69). As a result of the changes in ministry leadership since then, more has been written about the meaning of the PJP. However, this emphasis on new canonical structures, as the Thornber study (2012) revealed, has not been matched by the level of theological understanding deemed desirable for appropriate canonical governance (Bouchard, 2008).

In light of this, we suggest that formation for canonical governance include a focus on the meaning and forms of PJPs and their purpose and connection with Canon Law.

3. Appreciating that different people have different needs in different contexts. Formation needs can vary from person to person and from context to context. Two significant sources of variation were identified in the Thornber study (2012).

The first arose during interviews in relation to questions about 'who' needs to be formed for canonical governance across different types of PJPs. For example in one type of PJP, individual members (i.e. 'natural persons') are appointed as canonical governors. Sometimes these people are referred to as trustees and are readily identified as participants for formation. Other types of PJP have (other) PJPs as the members. These PJP members may be dioceses, parishes, religious institutes or a combination of these entities. In this case, each member is represented by a natural person and these natural persons usually elect or appoint people to conduct the ministry at a civil governance level. For the operation of the ministry in the name of the Church, the natural persons representing the PJPs as well as those appointed to conduct the ministry may be regarded as candidates for formation. Importantly though because their canonical governance responsibilities vary, the scope and mode of their formation may also need to be different. For example, the representatives of PJPs, having appointed the civil governing group, may have minimal involvement in governance (barring any unexpected catastrophes, of course) until the next Annual General Meeting, and their formation would need to reflect this. Hence, canonical governance responsibilities in PJPs can be different for different groups. For example, representatives of member PJPs may have responsibility for choosing the leadership group as well as formation of that group to ensure that they understand the canonical as well as civil accountabilities of their ministry. Trustees on the other hand may or not have either of these responsibilities.

A second source of variation concerns the appointment of people who are 'not in communion with the Catholic Church' to the role of canonical governor and the implications that this has for formation. In the light of the concerns that were raised in the Thornber study (2012) and the fact that we are entering 'new territory' with regard to the question of who can be canonical governors, we believe that the Congregation for Institutes of Consecrated Life and Societies of Apostolic Life (CICLSAL), as the Church authority responsible for such matters has a key role to play in developing the rationale for appointment (or non-appointment) of persons in this situation. This issue, like those linked to the particular types of PJP being considered clearly highlight that more work needs to be done to clarify and articulate the eligibility and responsibilities of member representatives and appointed trustees. This would provide a firmer base upon which formation for different people in different contexts can be most appropriately designed and implemented.

4. Engaging with the teachings of Vatican II. The Thornber study (2012) found that there was a disturbing lack of understanding about how the teachings of Vatican II should apply to the process of canonical governance. Some interviewees argued that this was the result of a lack of attention on the part of some Church authorities, and that the consequent lack of understanding is having undesirable implications for current thinking and practice of mission and ministry (Confoy, 2008). To address this issue, these interviewees maintained that a stronger intellectual and spiritual foundation is needed.

In light of these findings, we encourage Church leaders to engage current and potential canonical governors in the teachings of Vatican II. This would involve formation in aspects such as understanding and responding to baptismal call, engaging with the Word of God and appreciating the role of canonical governors in the mission of the Church. Associated with these efforts is the need to define key ecclesial and theological concepts as a basis for engaging with the teachings of

Vatican II, exploring what they mean and how they apply to particular ministries. Greater efforts along these lines would provide more fertile ground for responding to the call to the ministry of governance.

5. Naming canonical governance as a ministry. Ministry has been broadly defined as a public service to the Church (O'Meara, 1999). From this perspective, naming canonical governance as a ministry seems appropriate. While there is limited literature on recognising canonical governance as an ecclesial ministry, the Thornber study (2012) indicates that canonical governors are fulfilling an important public service for the Church but there is some confusion among bishops, religious leaders and lay appointees as to the actual status of canonical governance as a ministry.

Certain conditions for appointment to ecclesial ministry in a diocesan or parish setting were set out in *Co-Workers in the Vineyard of the Lord* (United States Conference of Catholic Bishops, 2005). These included appropriate authorisation to serve, leadership in a ministry, and close mutual collaboration with the pastoral ministry of the relevant clergy. These appear to be similar and relevant conditions for what is asked of canonical governors. A further condition related to the provision of appropriate preparation and formation for the level of responsibility being assigned. Again, this is a condition that applies to canonical governors. On these bases, we believe that canonical governance should be recognised as a Church ministry, and that appropriate formation that takes into account the level of responsibility being assigned become accepted practice and be resourced accordingly. A useful resource to inform these efforts would be Hahnenberg's (2003) work on the nature of diocesan ministry and the role of the bishop.

6. Seeing the role of canonical governor as a vocation. We contend that a person's involvement as a canonical governor is a vocation or call, and that this impacts on their spiritual development or 'holiness'.

Canonical governors take on responsibility for an aspect of the mission of the Church and need to understand that such responsibility requires their commitment to that mission. Accepting that responsibility impacts on their beliefs and formation is needed to help them explore those beliefs.

In taking this approach in formation, it is expected that some 'candidates' will come to a realisation that, for a range of reasons, canonical governance is not for them and will decide to withdraw. The term 'candidate' has been used because the preparation is seen as a process of becoming formed to enter a role with an appropriate understanding and that appointment will not be automatic. Consequently candidates require the human maturity to appreciate that what they are undertaking is a path in their life's journey, in lay spirituality. This journey is asking them to trust what God might be calling them to in their life as a consequence of their baptism. Some may see that they do not wish to continue on the journey. Others may be advised that their talents lie elsewhere. Such invitations and journeys involve risk and challenge. In light of these possibilities, we would advise that formation for canonical governance include opportunities to engage candidates in the exploration of their calling to the ministry of governance.

7. **Valuing the place of holiness.** The history of ministries involving the religious institutes was that people joined the institute in search of personal salvation and the ministries were the 'good works' that the members became involved with as part of the process of self-sanctification or the finding of God in one's life and co-operating in the mission of Jesus. Wittberg (2006) described the role of religious as that of *religious virtuosi*. The reality is that the ministries are now beyond what the religious are capable of (Gottemoeller, 2005; Grant and Vandenberg, 1998; Schweickert, 2002; Wittberg, 1991, 1993, 1994, 1998, 2000, 2006). Consequently, questions arise as to whether, and in what respects the ministries may be regarded as 'Catholic ministries'

and 'places of holiness'; and whether and how people seek a personal engagement with God in these ministries (Lennan, 2005).

The contemporary challenge for the religious institutes is how to involve lay people in canonical governance and formation that recognizes their spirituality rather than imposes a regime of religious life (Abeles, 2008; Casey, 2010; Fox, 2005a). The Thornber study (2012) argued that further research is needed into understandings of holiness in lay spirituality and the role of the ministries in leading people into a deeper relationship with God through their role as canonical governors. The research might usefully build on the work of Casey (1991, 2005), Fox (2003, 2005a, 2010b), Hahnenberg (2003, 2004, 2009, 2010), and Wood (2009, 2003). The research might also investigate whether the canonical governors become the *religious virtuosi* as described by Wittberg (2006) and if not, where this role may lie in the new governance arrangements for Church ministries.

8. Consulting bishops about formation for canonical governance.
The Thornber study (2012) found that the responsibility of the bishop for the pastoral guidance of the diocese and the coordination of ministries is relatively well understood. The study also noted that a bishop can have multiple roles in a PJP. In some cases, the diocese is a member of a PJP. Some bishops have opted to be the member's representative. Others have appointed another person. In other cases, a group that wishes to set up a PJP may need the approval of the bishop. In still other cases, the group wanting to set up a Pontifical PJP might need the opinion (and hopefully support) of the bishop. It is not surprising therefore given this range of possibilities that bishops are concerned about the continuing Catholic identity of the ministries in their diocese, as these new canonical governance structures emerge.

The question of Catholic identity is a theological issue but the emphasis to date in setting up PJPs has been on the canonical structures rather than theological development (Austin, 2011; Beal, 2004; Di Pietro, 2006; Euart, 2005; Hagstrom, 1996; Hite, 2000; Morrisey, 2007a; Sweeney, 2001, 2005). The Thornber study (2012) found little literature on formation needs for canonical governors and the survey responses reflected that the fruits of formation were not being perceived to the levels desired.

Given their responsibilities for ministry coordination and Catholic identity, our view is that bishops would be more confident that PJPs were being set up in an appropriate fashion if they were consulted about the formation programme being used. Consequently we suggest that the design and delivery of formation programmes for canonical governors are discussed with bishops as a matter of course as part of the setting up and continuing validation of a PJP.

9. Exploring the concept of Catholic identity. The Thornber study (2012) explored the use of the term 'Catholic identity'. Awareness has grown among Catholics that what was once taken for granted as 'Catholic', with its signs, symbols, practices and language can no longer be assumed to be imbued in the culture. Cleary (2007) explored this cultural development and the impact on 'meaning systems' of Catholic identity when dealing with managers of Catholic human services. Meaning systems refer to the way people create meaning through their life and values, not just as individuals, but as a group and culture. The issue of Catholic identity applies to the governance level as well. If the language of 'Catholic identity' is not to be reduced to a catch-cry or to one theological way of seeing the world, canonical governors need to understand what is involved in the concept and how their ministry attends to the question of 'Catholic identity'. They will be assisted in this through engagement with the long history of the Catholic intellectual tradition, particularly its current expression in Catholic social teaching. Those who design and deliver formation programmes for canonical governance candidates would benefit from an understanding of this change in meaning systems that has been happening with accelerating pace in the Church and in the world since Vatican II.

10. Evolving and evaluating formation programmes for canonical governance. The ministry of canonical governance is an area of development in the Church. As with any change, one can expect difficult times and painful lessons as well as findings of opportunity and promise to celebrate. While formation programmes for canonical governance (termed *sponsorship* in North America) have been in place for some time, the Thornber study (2012) found that while there were high levels of agreement about the proposed desirable traits of canonical governors, the extent to which those traits were evident was much more varied. In fact for many of the items up to one third of respondents indicated that the nominated traits were only evident to a fair extent or less. This raises the question as to why outcomes from programmes in place are not being perceived to be bearing more fruit.

Beside this somewhat puzzling or even gloomy picture, there are signs of hope and guidance. The Thornber study (2012) on which this book is based has done much to point the way. It has proposed a definition of formation, a series of traits drawn from the ecclesial literature and validated by survey respondents and interviewees with experience and expertise in the field, described a means of identifying the formation needs, and provided a set of principles, messages and themes upon which to tackle the complex issues of formation for canonical governance. Our view is that it is timely to take a more informed look at formation programmes that builds on this work.

First, we need to realise that formation programmes have to evolve to meet the changing talents, needs and aspirations of those called to the governance ministry – and the complex demands and opportunities facing Church ministries as a whole. Our hope is that this book can provide some support for this evolution. Second, any changes we make to formation programmes need to be based on evidence about what works. This calls for a more informed approach to evaluating formation programmes. Part of this involves the selection and use of criteria to investigate the value of such programmes. To this end, we propose that those design, delivering and responsible for formation consider the criteria and questions listed in Figure 9.1. While these criteria are taken from the public policy literature (Dunn, 1981), we believe that they have application in the area of formation for canonical governance.

Criterion	Question
Effectiveness	Has a valued outcome been achieved?
Efficiency	How much effort was required to achieve a valued outcome?
Adequacy	To what extent does the achievement of a valued outcome resolve the problem?
Equity	Are the costs and benefits distributed equitably among different groups?
Responsiveness	Do program outcomes satisfy the needs, preferences or values of particular groups?
Appropriateness	Are the outcomes actually worthwhile or valuable?

Source: Dunn, W. N. (1981) Public Policy Analysis: An Introduction. Englewood Cliffs, NJ: Prentice-Hall, p 343.

Figure 9.1 Criteria for Evaluation

There are many ways to assess the value of a formation programme. For example, this can be done on the basis of *effectiveness* in terms of what was achieved, of *efficiency* in terms of the cost, or of *adequacy* in terms of a reasonable outcome for the effort expended. Then there questions about who benefits (*equity*) and whose needs are being responded to (*responsiveness*). Finally when 'all is said and done' and taking into account the extent to which these preceding criteria are met, a programme can be judged on the degree to which it is considered *appropriate* for the context and people involved. If your formation programmes take into account the messages and themes highlighted in this chapter and are evaluated in terms of the degree to which they meet these criteria, then you can be more confident that you are 'governing in faith'.

Closing Reflection

In this book, we have presented the background and contemporary context of governance in Church ministries, and the individuals charged with the responsibility for ensuring those ministries they serve remain authentic to the mission for which those ministries were established. We have examined the findings from the Thornber study (2012) on the formation needs of canonical governors, proposed a framework for addressing those needs, and identified some key messages and important themes for the future with regard to the formation of canonical governors.

We have reviewed the literature drawing on various traditions for formation in the Catholic Church. Canonical governance is an evolving filed. Continuing change in the Church and in the world means that the Church's past forms of governance are no longer sustainable for many ministries. This is complicated by the fact that lay people (as clergy and religious) are undertaking governance roles with limited understanding of their canonical responsibilities.

In this book, our aim has been to provide a resource to assist those involved in canonical governance to meet the future with a more informed sense of hope. We have identified relevant traits to provide a focus for formation efforts, as well as a framework within which formation programmes can be created, using dimensions already promoted and in use in formation in the Church. If formation for canonical governance can be undertaken with courage and trust, as called for in *Ad Gentes* (n.

25), the call of the Council will become a reality in a field the Council did not, at the time, imagine:

> 'A sower went out to sow his seed; And as he sowed, some fell on the path and was trampled, and the birds of the sky ate it up. Some seed fell on rocky ground, and when it grew, it withered for lack of moisture. Some seed fell among thorns, and the thorns grew with it and choked it. And some fell on good soil, and when it grew, it produced fruit a hundredfold.' After saying this, he called out, 'Whoever has ears to hear ought to hear.' (Luke 8:5-8)

Good soil isn't everywhere and it needs preparation and, at times, further cultivation to be able to maintain the responsibility for what is dreamed and expected from it. May the fruits of this book aid that cultivation!

References

Abbott, W. (Ed.). (1966a). *Ad Gentes: Decree on the Church's missionary activity.* London: Geoffrey Chapman.

Abbott, W. (Ed.). (1966b). *Apostolicum Actuositatem: Decree on the Apostolate of the laity.* London: Geoffrey Chapman.

Abbott, W. (Ed.). (1966c). *Dei Verbum: Dogmatic Constitution on Divine Revelation* London: Geoffrey Chapman.

Abbott, W. (Ed.). (1966d). *Gaudium et Spes: Constitution on the Church in the modern world.* London: Geoffrey Chapman.

Abbott, W. (Ed.). (1966e). *Lumen Gentium: Dogmatic constitution on the Church.* London: Geoffrey Chapman.

Abbott, W. (Ed.). (1966f). *Optatam Totius: Decree on priestly formation.* London: Geoffrey Chapman.

Abbott, W. (Ed.). (1966g). *Perfectae Caritatis: Decree on the appropriate renewal of religious life.* London: Geoffrey Chapman.

Abeles, J. (2008). Leadership formation: A Call to action: How can the next generation of leaders carry Jesus' healing ministry in Catholic health care? *Health Progress, 89*(2), 32-37.

Alberigo, G. and Komonchak, J. (Eds.). (1995). *History of Vatican II, Vol 1, Announcing and preparing Vatican Council II toward a new era in Catholicism* (Vol. 1). Maryknoll, NY: Orbis Books.

Andrews, D., Nonnecke, B., and Preece, J. (2003). Electronic Survey Methodology: A Case Study in Reaching Hard-to-Involve Internet Users. *International Journal of Human- Computer Interaction, 16*(2), 185-210. Retrieved from http://www.informaworld.com/10.1207/S15327590IJHC1602_04

Arbuckle, G. (1987). *Strategies for growth in religious life.* Homebush, NSW: St Paul Publications.

Arbuckle, G. (1993). *Refounding the Church: Dissent for leadership.* (Australian ed.). Homebush, NSW: St Paul Publications.

Arbuckle, G. (1995). Leadership for refounding: understanding contemporary tensions in the Church. *The Australasian Catholic Record, 72*(2), 143-150.

Arbuckle, G. (2000). *Healthcare ministry: Refounding the Mission in tumultuous times.* Collegeville, MN: Liturgical Press.

Arbuckle, G. (2001). Ministry and postmodernism: The New Age has both positive and negative implications for Catholic health care. *Health Progress, 82*(2), 14-19.

Arbuckle, G. (2005). Maintaining prophetic cultures. *Health Progress, 86*(5), 19-24.

Arbuckle, G. (2006). Sponsorship's Biblical roots and tensions *Health Progress, 87*(5), 13-16. Arbuckle, G. (2007a). *Crafting Catholic identity in postmodern Australia*. Canberra: Catholic Health Australia.

Arbuckle, G. (2007b). Retelling "The Good Samaritan". *Health Progress, 88*(4), 20-24. Arbuckle, G. (2010). *Culture, inculturation and theologians – a postmodern critique*. Collegeville, MN: Liturgical Press.

Arbuckle, G. (2013) *Catholic Identity or Identities? Refounding Ministries in Chaotic Times*. Collegeville, MN: Liturgical Press.

Ascension Health. (2011). Retrieved from http://www.ascensionhealth.org/

Aubert, R., and Boileau, D. A. (2003). *Catholic Social Teaching: An Historical Perspective*. Retrieved from http://site.ebrary.com.ezproxy1.acu.edu.au/lib/australiancathu/docDetail.action?docID=100 49147

Austin, R. (2000). *Swallow hard and jump – the alternative may be oblivion: Church Law and CHA Regional Structures*. Paper presented at the Catholic Health Australia National Conference, June 26, 2000.

Austin, R. (2011). *Things both old and new: Shaping a future for Apostolic works of Religious Institutes*. 45th Annual Conference of Canon Law Society of Australia and New Zealand, Melbourne, Vic, 12-15 September, 2011.

Barnett, J. (2005). *Between towns: Religious life and leadership during a time of critical change* Unpublished doctoral dissertation Australian Catholic University, Strathfield, Sydney. Retrieved from http://dlibrary.acu.edu.au/digitaltheses/public/adt-acuvp92.29052006

Beal, J. (1995). The Exercise of the Power of Governance by Lay People: State of the Question. *The Jurist, 55*, 1-92.

Beal, J. (2004). It shall not be so among you! Crisis in the Church, crisis in Church law. In F. Oakley and B. Russett (Eds.), *Governance, accountability, and the future of the Catholic Church* (pp. 88-102). New York, NY: The Continuum International Publishing Group Inc.

Beal, J. (2006). From the heart of the Church to the heart of the world: Ownership, control and Catholic identity of institutional apostolates in the United States. In R. Smith, W. Brown and N. Reynolds (Eds.), *Sponsorship in the United States: Context, theory and praxis* (pp. 31-48). Alexandria, VA: Canon Law Society of America.

Beale, J. and McMullen, B. (1998). Ongoing CHA Project Addresses Lay Sponsorship. *Health Progress,* 79(1), 13-15.

Bechtle, R. (2005). Giving the Spirit a home: Reflections on the spirituality of institutions. In Z. Fox and R. Bechtle (Eds.), *Called and chosen – Toward a spirituality for lay leaders.* (pp. 99-112). Lanham, MD: Bowman and Littlefield Publishers.

Berg, B. (2004). *Qualitative research methods* (5th ed.). Upper Saddle River, NJ: Pearson. Berger, P. (1969). *A rumour of angels.* Harmondsworth, UK: Penguin Books Ltd.

Bevans, S. (2002). *Models of contextual theology* (Rev. ed.). Maryknoll, NY: Orbis Books.

Bevans, S. (2005). Wisdom from the margins: Systematic theology and the missiological imagination. *Australian E-Journal of Theology, August* (Issue 5). Retrieved from http://dlibrary.acu.edu.au/research/theology/ejournal/aejt_5/bevans.htm

Bevans, S. (2009). The Mission has a Church, the mission has ministers: Thinking missiologically about ministry and the shortage of priests. *Compass,* 3, 3-14.

Bevans, S. and Gros, J. (2009). *Evangelization and religious freedom – Ad gentes, Dignitatis humanae.* Mahwah, NJ: Paulist Press.

Bevans, S. and Schroeder, R. (2004). *Constants in context: A Theology of mission for today.* Maryknoll, NY: Orbis Books.

Bevans, S. and Schroeder, R. (2011). *Prophetic dialogue: Reflections on Christian mission today.* Maryknoll, NY: Orbis Books.

Bogdan, R. and Biklen, S. (2007). *Qualitative research for education: An introduction to theory and methods* (5th ed.). Boston: Pearson.

Bonnell, M. (1992). *Franciscan sponsors and lay trustees: Partners in sustaining the Franciscan mission in higher education* Unpublished doctoral dissertation Saint Louis University, St Louis, MO. Retrieved from http://proquest.umi.com/pqdweb?did=746277941andFmt=7andclientId=18921andRQT=309andVName=PQD

Bouchard, C. (2008). Health care as "Ministry": Common usage, confused theology. *Health Progress, 89*(3), 26-30.

Bouchard, C. (2009). The promise and challenge of board formation *Health Progress, 90*(5), 40-44.

Brennan, F. (2011). Indonesian and Australian justice. Retrieved from http://www.eurekastreet.com.au/article.aspx?aeid=26631

Brueggemann, W. (1978). *The prophetic imagination*. Minneapolis, MN: Fortress Press. Brueggemann, W. (1993). *Texts under negotiation: The Bible and postmodern imagination*. Minneapolis, MN: Fortress Press.

Brueggemann, W. (1997). *Theology of the Old Testament*. Minneapolis, MN: Fortress Press. Brueggemann, W. (2000). Together in the Spirit – Beyond seductive quarrels. In P. Miller (Ed.), *Deep memory exuberant hope: Contested truth in a post-Christian world* (pp. 29-40). Minneapolis. MN: Fortress Press.

Brueggemann, W. (2007). *Mandate to difference – An invitation to the contemporary church*. Louisville, KY: Westminster John Knox Press.

Burns, H. (2006). Reflections on Sponsorship: One Congregation's perspective. In R. Smith, W. Brown and N. Reynolds (Eds.), *Sponsorship in the United States: Context, theory and praxis*. (pp. 1-16). Alexandria, VA: Canon Law Society of America.

Bush, T. (2007). Authenticity in research – reliability, validity and triangulation. In A. Briggs and M. Coleman (Eds.), *Research methods in educational leadership and management* (2nd ed.) (pp. 91-105). London: Sage.

Campbell, R., and Aherns, C. (1998). Innovative community service for rape victims: an application of multiple case study methodology. *American Journal of Community Psychology, 26* (537-71).

Canales, D. A. (2008). Forming leaders in the business of health care: Trinity Health uses a disciplined process rooted in Christian spirituality and theology. *Health Progress, 89*(2), 27-31.

Candy, P. (1989). Alternative paradigms in educational research. *Australian Educational Researcher, 16*(3), 1-11.

Casey, J. (1991). *Food for the journey: Theological foundations of the Catholic healthcare ministry*. St Louis, MO: CHAUSA.

Casey, J. (2000). Holy memory, faithful action: The Catholic identity of Catholic Health East, based in memory, has important implications for the future. *Health Progress, 81*(2), 28-31

Casey, J. (2005). Sponsorship as a unique ministry [Audio CD]. St Louis, MO: CHAUSA. Casey, J. (2010). Formation for Lay Ministry: Learnings from religious life. In Z. Fox (Ed.), *Lay Ecclesial Ministries – Pathways towards the future* (pp. 143-155). Lanham, MD:Rowman and Littlefield Publishers.

Cassidy, T., Sheehan, M. and Whelton, P. (2009). Beyond reform: Catholic health care matters even when all can pay. *Health Progress, 90*(1), 52-55

Catholic Health Australia. (2011). *Guide for understanding the governance of Catholic health and aged care services*. Draft June 8, 2011. Retrieved from http://www.cha.org.au/site.php?search_text=Governanceandsearch_submit=Goandid=63andsea rch_type=allandoutput=site

Catholic Health East. (2011). Retrieved from http://www.che.org/

Catholic Health Initiatives. (2011). Retrieved from http://www.catholichealthinit.org/

Catholic Health World. (2011a). Ministry leaders explore how best to equip people for sponsor roles. *Catholic Health World,27*(18). Retrieved from http://www.chausa.org/Pages/Publications/Catholic_Health_World/Catholic_Health_World_Archive/2011/October_15/Ministry_leaders_explore_how_best_to_equip_people_for_s ponsor_roles/

Catholic Health World. (2011b). St. Joseph caregivers dig deep to show authentic respect.

Catholic Health World, June 1, 2011. Retrieved from http://www.chausa.org/Contenttwocolumn.aspx?pageid=4294968095

Catholic Healthcare Limited. (2011). *Annual Review 2010/11*. Sydney, NSW: Catholic Healthcare Limited.

Chait, R., Ryan, W., and Taylor, B. (2005). *Governance as leadership: Reframing the work of nonprofit boards*. Hoboken, NJ: John Wiley and Sons.

CHAUSA. (2005a). *Sponsorship: Resources for Sponsors – Research study of successful practices*. St Louis, MO: CHAUSA.

CHAUSA. (2005b). *Sponsorship: Resources for Sponsors – Toward a Theology of Catholic health care Sponsorship*. St Louis, MO: CHAUSA.

CHAUSA. (2006a). *Core elements for Sponsorship: A Reflection guide*. St Louis, MO: CHAUSA.

CHAUSA. (2006b). Leadership formation module: Catholic Social Tradition [DVD]. St Louis, MO: CHAUSA.

CHAUSA. (2007a). *Core elements For leaders of Catholic ministry: A Reflection guide*. St Louis, MO: CHAUSA.

CHAUSA. (2007b). *One vine, different branches: Sponsorship and governance in Catholic ministries; A Collection of resources for health care, education and social services*. St Louis, MO: CHAUSA.

CHAUSA. (2007c). *Personal development plan for leaders in Catholic ministries: Sponsor – Trustee – Executive*. St Louis, MO: CHAUSA.

CHAUSA. (2009). *Competencies for Mission Leaders* (Vol. 2009). St Louis, MO: CHAUSA. Cleary, M. (2007). *Management dilemmas in Catholic human service – Health care, welfare and education*. Lewiston, NY: Edwin Mellen Press.

Cleary, M. (Ed.). (2009). *Public Juridic Persons in the Church*. Marsfield, NSW: Governance and Management.

Clifton, R. and McEnroe, J. (1994). A synergy of values: Catholic healthcare leaders must implement their organization's mission and model its values. *Health Progress, 75*(5), 37-39

Coleridge, M. (2009a, May). Best for ACT if Catholic provider remains. *The Catholic Voice*, No 265, pp. 1-28 Retrieved from http://www.cg.catholic.org.au/news/newsletterarticle_display.cfm?loadref=70andid=593

Coleridge, M. (2009b). Statement on proposed takeover of Calvary Hospital by ACT Government. (26 October). Retrieved from http://www.cg.catholic.org.au/about/default.cfm?loadref=86

Coleridge, M. (2009c). Time to encourage homes of 'the burning heart'. *The Catholic Voice*, No 249. Retrieved from http://www.cg.catholic.org.au/news/newsletterarticle_display.cfm?loadref=70andid=688

Compendium of the Catechism of the Catholic Church. (2008). (A.C.B.C.S.P. Publications, Trans. World Youth Day ed.). Strathfield, NSW: St Pauls Publications.

Confoy, M. (2008). *Religious Life and Priesthood*. Mahwah, NJ: Paulist Press.

Confraternity of Christian Doctrine. (1988). *The new American Bible with revised New Testament*. Mission Hills, CA: Benziger Publishing Company.

Congregation for Institutes of Consecrated Life and Societies of Apostolic Life. (2002).

Starting afresh from Christ: A renewed commitment to consecrated Life in the third millenium. Retrieved from http://www.vatican.va/roman_curia/congregations/ccscrlife/documents/rc_con_ccscrlife_doc_20020614_ripartire-da-cristo_en.html

Congregation of Christian Brothers. (1996). *Constitutions*. Rome: Congregation of Christian Brothers.

Connolly, J. (2002). *Sponsorship of Catholic health care: An adult education model for preparing the Laity*. (Unpublished doctoral dissertation Northern Illinois University, DeKalb, IL. Retrieved from http://proquest.umi.com/pqd web?did=727397921andFmt=7andclientId=18921andRQT=309andV Name=PQD

Connolly, N. (2010). God has a liberating plan for the cosmos. [Editorial]. *The Far East, 92*(1), 1-24.

Conway, E. (2003). The Communitarian Tradition: The Church's social teaching guides Our ministry toward collaboration, not individualism. *Health Progress, 84*(1). Retrieved from http://www.chausa.org/Pub/MainNav/News/HP/Archive/2003/01JanFeb/articles/hp0301i.htm

Coriden, J. (2000). *Canon Law as ministry – Freedom and good order for the Church*. Mahwah, NJ: Paulist Press.

Coriden, J. (2004). *An Introduction to Canon Law* (Rev. ed.). Mahwah, NJ: Paulist Press. Cornish, S. (1993). Catholicism, an incarnational faith and social transformation. *The Australasian Catholic Record, 70*(4), 443-448.

Covenant Health Systems. (2011). Retrieved from http://www.covenanths.org/

Creswell, J. (2008). *Educational research: Planning, conducting and evaluating quantitative and qualitative research* (3rd ed.). Upper Saddle River, NJ: Pearson Education International.

Crotty, M. (1998). *Foundations of social research*. Sydney: Allen and Unwin.

Cunningham, A. (1986). Power and Authority in the Church. In J. Mallett (Ed.), *The Ministry of Governance* (pp. 80-97). Washington, DC: Canon Law Society of America.

Curran, C. (1997). The Catholic identity of Catholic institutions. *Theological Studies, 58*(1), 90-108.

Cusack, B. (2006). The Role of the Diocesan Bishop in relation to Catholic health care: Eighth in a series on Canon Law. *Health Progress, 87*(4). Retrieved from http://www.chausa.org/Pub/MainNav/News/HP/Archive/2006/07JulAug/Articles/Features/ hp0607m.htm

Cusack, B. (2007). How does the "Communion of the Church" apply to Catholic health care?: Fourteenth In a series on Canon Law. *Health Progress, 88*(5), 14-15

Cusack, B. (2008). Bishops and Religious Institutes: Building collaboration. *Health Progress, 89*(3), 1-132.

D'Orsa, J. and D'Orsa, T. (2010). *Explorers, guides and meaning-makers: Mission and theology for Catholic educators* (Vol. 1). Mulgrave, Vic: John Garrett Publishing.

Darlaston-Jones, D. (2007). Making connections: The relationship between epistemology and research methods. *The Australian Community Psychologist, 19*(1), 19-27.

de Vaus, D. (2002). *Surveys in social research* (5th ed.). Sydney, NSW: Allen and Unwin.

Di Pietro, M. (2006). A juridic meaning of Sponsorship in the formal relationship between a Public Juridic Person and a healthcare corporation in the United States. In R. Smith, W. Brown and N. Reynolds (Eds.), *Sponsorship in the United States: Context, theory and praxis* (pp. 101-122). Alexandria, VA: Canon Law Society of America.

Di Pietro, M. (n.d.). Sponsorship: A word of caution. *The Legal Bulletin*, No 78, 21-30.

Dixon, R. (2005). *The Catholic community in Australia* (Rev. ed.). Adelaide, SA: Christian Research Association.

Dolan, M. (2007). *Partnership in lay spirituality*. Dublin: The Columba Press.

Downey, M. (2003). Ministerial identity. In S. K. Wood (Ed.), *Ordering the Baptismal Priesthood* (pp. 3-25). Collegeville, MA: Liturgical Press.

Downey, M. (2005). "Without a vision the people perish": Foundations for a spirituality of lay leadership. In Z. Fox and R. Bechtle (Eds.), *Called and chosen – Toward a spirituality for lay leaders* (pp. 17-30). Lanham, MD: Bowman and Littlefield Publishers.

Dugan, P. (2006). The Sponsorship relationship: Incorporation and dissolution civil and canon law perspectives. In R. Smith, W. Brown and N. Reynolds (Eds.), *Sponsorship in the United States: Context, theory and praxis* (pp. 73-84). Alexandria, VA: Canon Law Society of America.

Dulles, A. (1987). *Models of the Church* (2nd ed.). Dublin: Gill and MacMillan Ltd.

Dunn, B.K. (1995). *Sponsorship of Catholic institutions, particularly healthcare institutions, by the Sisters of Providence in the western United States* (Unpublished doctoral dissertation University of Ottawa, Ottawa, Canada. Retrieved from http://proquest.umi.com/pqdweb?did=739322171andFmt =7andclientId=18921andRQT=309andV Name=PQD

Eck, P. and Morris, T. (2005a). Continuing Bon Secours' mission. *Health Progress, 86*(1), 48-50

Eck, P. and Morris, T. (2005b). Sponsorship: Developing Sponsorship competencies. *Health Progress, 86*(3), 60-63.

Eisenhardt, K. M. (1989). Building theories from case study research. *Academy of Management Journal, 14*(4), 532-550.

Euart, S. (2005). The Role of the Bishop. *Health Progress, 86*(5). Retrieved from http://www.chausa.org/Pub/MainNav/News/HP/ Archive/2005/09SepOct/articles/Features/ hp0509n.htm

Ferrera, S. (2000). *How lay presidents in Xaverian Brothers Sponsored schools implement the charism of the Xaverian Brothers* Unpublished doctoral dissertation Fordham University, New York. Retrieved from http://proquest.umi.com/ pqdweb?did=732096641andFmt=7andclientId=18921andRQT=309andV Name=PQD

Field, A. (2000). *Discovering statistics using SPSS for Windows*. London: Sage Publications Ltd.

Fox, Z. (2003). Laity, ministry and secular character. In S. K. Wood (Ed.), *Ordering the Baptismal Priesthood* (pp. 121-151). Collegeville, MA: Liturgical Press.

Fox, Z. (2005a). *New Ecclesial Ministry – Lay Professionals Serving the Church* (Rev. ed.). Chicago, IL: Sheed and Ward.

Fox, Z. (2005b). Why did you choose your work? Reflections on Vocation. In Z. Fox and R. Bechtle (Eds.), *Called and chosen – Toward a spirituality for lay leaders* (pp. 3-16). Lanham, MD: Rowman and Littlefield Publishers.

Fox, Z. (2008). Continuing the mission: How do health care leaders keep Catholic identity alive in today's world? *Health Progress, 89*(2), 23-26.

Fox, Z. (2010a). Strengthening ministrial leadership: Perspectives from systems theory. In Z. Fox (Ed.), *Lay Ecclesial Ministries – Pathways towards the future* (pp. 197-212). Lanham, MD: Rowman and Littlefield Publishers.

Fox, Z. (Ed.). (2010b). *Lay Ecclesial Ministries – Pathways towards the future*. Lanham, MD: Rowman and Littlefield Publishers.

Fox, Z., and Bechtle, R. (Eds.). (2005). *Called and chosen – Toward a spirituality for lay leaders*. Lanham, MD: Bowman and Littlefield Publishers.

Gaillardetz, R. (2010). The theological reception of *Co-Workers in the Vineyard of the Lord*. In Z. Fox (Ed.), *Lay Ecclesial Ministries – Pathways towards the future* (pp. 17-30). Lanham, MD: Rowman and Littlefield Publishers.

Gallagher, M.P. (2003). *Clashing symbols: an introduction to faith and culture* (Rev. ed.). London: Darton, Longman and Todd.

Gallin, A. (2000). *Negotiating identity: Catholic higher education since 1960*. Notre Dame, IN: University of Notre Dame Press.

Gascoigne, R. (1995). Evangelization and Catholic identity. Paper given at the July 1994 meeting of the Australian Catholic Theological Association, Melbourne. *The Australasian Catholic Record, 72*(3), 269-279.

Giganti, E. (2004). What is "Leadership Formation" now? A new statement describes formation for health ministry leadership and the changes it can help bring about. *Health Progress, 85*(5), 18-221.

Golden, P. (2006). Sponsorship in higher education. In R. Smith, W. Brown and N. Reynolds (Eds.), *Sponsorship in the United States: Context, theory and praxis* (pp. 85-100). Alexandria, VA: Canon Law Society of America.

Gottemoeller, D. (1991). Institutions without Sisters. *Review for Religious, 50*(4), 564-571. Gottemoeller, D. (1999). Preserving our Catholic identity: If the health ministry is to remain faithful to its basic elements, it must first spell them out. *Health Progress, 80*(3), 18-21

Gottemoeller, D. (2005). Catholic institutional ministries: Their history and legacy. In Z. Fox and R. Bechtle (Eds.), *Called and chosen – Toward a spirituality for lay leaders* (pp. 53-65). Lanham, MD: Bowman and Littlefield Publishers.

Gottemoeller, D. (2007). The privilege of continuing His work: Some thoughts on quality, safety, and the mission of Catholic health care. *Health Progress, 88*(6), 64-67.

Grant, M.K. (2001a). Creating a Mission-based culture. *Health Progress, 82*(3), 53-54.

Grant, M.K. (2001b). Reframing Sponsorship: The time has come to make sponsorship itself a ministry Introduction. *Health Progress, 82*(4), 38-40.

Grant, M.K. (2001c). Toward a theology of the community. *Health Progress, 82*(4), 10. Grant, M. K. (2003). Exercising Sponsorship: Five essential tasks. *Current Issues in Catholic Higher Education, 23*, 61-66.

Grant, M.K. and Kopish, M. (2001). Sponsor leadership formation. *Health Progress, 82*(4). Retrieved from http://www.chausa.org/Pub/MainNav/News/HP/Archive/2001/07JulAug/Articles/SpecialSection/HP0107t.htm

Grant, M.K. and Kopish, M.M. (2001). Sponsorship: Current challenges and future directions Introduction. *Health Progress, 82*(4), 24-26.

Grant, M.K., and Vandenberg, P. (1998). *After we're gone: Creating sustainable Sponsorship.* Mishawaka, IN: Ministry Development Resources.

Grassl, W. (2009). *Is there really a Catholic intellectual tradition?* Paper presented at the American Academy of Religion, Montreal, Nov 7-10, 2009. Retrieved from http://snc.academia.edu/WolfgangGrassl/Papers/219666/Is_There_Really_a_Catholic_Intellectual_Tradition

Gray, K. (2005). New Sponsorship model responds to needs. *Health Progress, 86*(1), 51-52.

Greeley, A. (2004). *Catholic revolution: New wine, old wineskins, and the Second Vatican Council.* Berkeley, CA: University of California Press.

Hagstrom, A. (1996). Can lay people govern the church? *America, 174*(5), 20-21.

Hagstrom, A. (2003). The secular character of the vocation and mission of the laity: Toward a theology of Ecclesial lay mission. In S. K. Wood (Ed.), *Ordering the Baptismal Priesthood* (pp. 121-151). Collegeville MA: Liturgical Press.

Hahnenberg, E. (2003). *Ministries: A relational approach.* New York: Herder and Herder. Hahnenberg, E. (2004). Think globally, act locally: Responding to lay ecclesial ministry. *New Theology Review* (November), 13, 52-65.

Hahnenberg, E. (2009). Lay? ministry? Christian mission in a pluralist world. In T. Muldoon (Ed.), *Catholic Identity and the Laity: College Theology Society Annual Volume, 2008* (Vol. 54, pp. 207-219). Maryknoll, NY: Orbis Books.

Hahnenberg, E. (2010). Theology of lay ecclesial ministry: Future trajectories. In Z. Fox (Ed.), *Lay Ecclesial Ministries – Pathways towards the future* (pp. 67-83). Lanham, MD: Rowman and Littlefield Publishers.

Hehir, B. (2008). Identity and institutions. *Health Progress, 89*(3), 18-23.

Hellwig, M. (2005). "The reign of God Is among you": Biblical and theological themes for lay leadership. In Z. Fox and R. Bechtle (Eds.), *Called and chosen – Toward a spirituality for lay leaders.* (pp. 45-51). Lanham, MD: Bowman and Littlefield Publishers.

Hester, D. (2000). Practicing governance in the light of faith. In T. P. Holland and D. C. Hester (Eds.), *Building effective boards for religious organisations: A handbook for trustees, presidents and church leaders* (pp. 58-79). San Francisco: Jossey-Bass.

Hickey, D.E. (2006). *Identifying and maintaining religious heritage amidst conflict and diminishing religious presence in a Catholic high school* (Ed.D.), University of Pennsylvania, Philadelphia. Retrieved from http://proquest.umi.com/pq dweb?did=1144190601andFmt=7andclientId=18921andRQT=309and VName=PQD

Hite, J. (2000). *A Primer on Public and Private Juridic Persons: Applications to the healthcare ministry.* St. Louis, MO: The Catholic Health Association.

Holland, S. (2001). Sponsorship and The Vatican. *Health Progress, 82*(4), 32-37.

Holland, S. (2005). Vatican official provides "checklist" of PJP criteria. *Catholic HealthWorld, 21* (August 31).

Homan, K. (2004). Formation and governance: Catholic organizations should institute theological and spiritual formation programs for their Trustees. *Health Progress, 85*(5), 23-29.

Homan, S.M., Domahidy, M.R., Gilsinan, J.F., Brennan, D.G., Flick, M.J., Schonhoff, R.M. and Behrman, G. (2003). Formation for love and justice in graduate school and professional education. *Current Issues in Catholic Higher Education, 23(1)*, 55-71.

Huels, J. (1986). The Role of Canon Law in the light of Lumen Gentium. In J. Mallett (Ed.), *The Ministry of Governance* (pp. 98-120). Washington, DC: Canon Law Society of America.

Huels, J. (2000). *The Power of Governance and its Exercise by Lay Persons: A Juridical Approach.* Paper presented at the Canon Law Society of Australia and New Zealand Proceedings of the Thirty-Fourth Annual Conference, 23-26 October 2000, Narrabundah, ACT.

Hume, S. (1999). Catholic theology informs thinking on healthcare reform. *Health Progress, 80*(3), 43.

Hursthouse, R. (2007). Human dignity and charity. In J. Malpass and N. Lickess (Eds.), *Perspectives on human dignity* (pp. 59-72). Dordrecht: Springer.

Johnson, E. (2003). *Truly our sister: A Theology of Mary in the communion of saints.* New York: The Continuum International Publishing Group.

Johnson, W. (2010). The call of *Co-Workers in the Vineyard of the Lord* for cultural diversity in lay ecclesial ministry. In Z. Fox (Ed.), *Lay Ecclesial Ministries – Pathways towards the future* (pp. 159-179). Lanham, MD: Rowman and Littlefield Publishers.

Kaiser, L., Tersigni, A., Serle, J. and Dover, J. (2007). A successful reconfiguration: In Washington State, an acute care facility begins a new life as a "Critical Access Hospital". *Health Progress,88*(4), Retrieved from http://www.chausa.org/Pub/MainNav/News/HP/Archive/2007/07July-Aug/Articles/Features/hp0707g.htm

Karam, J. (2008). Living the mission in a business model of health care. *Health Progress, 89*(3), 38-39.

Keehan, C. (2009a). Health Reform: Remember Why We Got Into This. *Health Progress, 90*(6), 4.

Keehan, C. (2009b). Yes! The Time is Now: Health Care Reform Can Help the Country's Economic Recovery Process. *Health Progress, 90*(1), 18-19.

Keehan, C. (2012). Our greatest treasures. *Health Progress, 93*(1), 4-5.

Kelly, G. (1998). Grounded in faith. In R. Lennan (Ed.), *An introduction to Catholic theology* (pp. 56-79). New York: Paulist Press.

Kelly, G. (2007). The Relationship between mission and identity: A case study from theological education. *The Australasian Catholic Record, 84*(1), 35-44.

Kelly, M. (2007). A collaborative formation programme for Sponsors. *Health Progress, 88* (1 January-February), 16-21.

Kelly, M. and Mollison, M. (2005). Journey into Sponsorship's future. *Health Progress, 86,* (July 3), 50-53.

Keogh, D. (2008). *Edmund Rice and the first Christian Brothers*. Dublin: Four Courts Press. King, W. (2006). Sponsorship By Juridic Persons. In R. Smith, W. Brown and N. Reynolds (Eds.), *Sponsorship in the United States: Context, theory and praxis* (pp. 49-72). Alexandria, VA: Canon Law Society of America.

Kirk, J. A. (2000). *What is mission? Theological explorations*. Minneapolis, MN: Fortress Press.

Kirkwood, P. (2012a). Flattening the Church – Work of Robert Fitzgerald. *Eureka St*. Retrieved from http://www.eurekastreet.com.au/article.aspx?aeid=30443

Kirkwood, P. (2012b). Lifting the laity – Work of Zeni Fox. *Eureka St*. Retrieved from http://www.eurekastreet.com.au/article.aspx?aeid=30606

Klimoski, V. J., O'Neil, K. and Schuth, K. (2005). *Educating leaders for ministry: issues and responses*. Collegeville, MN: Liturgical Press.

Kothari, C. (2004). *Research methodology: Methods and techniques*. Retrieved from http://site.ebrary.com.ezproxy1.acu.edu.au/lib/australiancathu/docDetail.action

Lakeland, P. (2004). Governance, accountability, and the future of the Catholic Church. *Theological Studies, 65*(4), 885-886.

Lakeland, P. (2007). *Catholicism at the crossroads: How the laity can save the church.* New York, NY: Continuum.

Lakeland, P. (2009). Maturity and the lay vocation: From ecclesiology to ecclesiality. In T. Muldoon (Ed.), *Catholic Identity and the Laity: College Theology Society Annual Volume, 2008* (Vol. 54, pp. 241-260). Maryknoll, NY: Orbis Books.

Larrere, J. and McClelland, D. (1994). Leadership for the Catholic healing ministry: A CHA study identifies key competencies of outstanding leaders in Catholic healthcare. *Health Progress, 75*(5), 28-33.

Leckey, D. (2006). *The laity and Christian education: apostolicam actuositatem, gravissimum educationis.* Mahwah, NJ: Paulist Press.

Leckey, D. (2009). From Baptismal font to ministry: The surprising story of laity stirring the Church. In T. Muldoon (Ed.), *Catholic Identity and the Laity College Theology Society Annual Volume, 2008* (Vol. 54, pp. 19-33). Maryknoll, NY: Orbis Books.

Lennan, R. (2005). Holiness, "Otherness", and the Catholic school. *The Australasian Catholic Record, 82*(4), 399-408.

Lennan, R. (Ed.). (1998). *An introduction to Catholic theology.* New York: Paulist Press.

Lichtman, M. (2006). *Qualitative research in education: a user's guide.* Sage, CA: Thousand Oakes.

LimeSurvey. (2010). *LimeSurvey – The open source survey application.* Retrieved from http://www.limesurvey.org

Lucas, B. (2007). Mission and identity of faith-based organisations – the role of the Bishops. *The Australasian Catholic Record, 84*(1), 45-55.

Lucas, B., Slack, P., and d'Apice, W. (2008). *Church administration handbook.* Sydney: St Pauls Publications.

Lynch, P. (1998). Tested By practice. In R. Lennan (Ed.), *An introduction to Catholic theology* (pp. 164-183). New York: Paulist Press.

MacLennan, B. and Marr, R. (2008). Giving flesh to dry bones: God's Spirit in strategic planning. *Health Progress, 89*(3), 52-56.

Mallett, J. (Ed.). (1986). *The Ministry of Governance.* Washington, DC: Canon Law Society of America.

Maltby, T. (2007). Pilot programme is for potential Sponsors: The "Sponsorship Pilot" helps people decide whether they should join the ministry. *Health Progress, 88*(1), 24-25

Martinez, S. (2007). *Strengthening Catholic identity: The role of an academic dean in strategic planning* (Unpublished doctoral dissertation University of Southern California, Los Angeles. Retrieved from http://proquest.umi.com/pqdweb?did=1407499321andFmt=7andclientId=18921andRQT=309and VName=PQD

McArdle, P. (2010). Ministry? Mission? Catholic Health Care? In 10 years will we have an adequate theology of health care? In 10 years who will be theologians of health care?. Paper presented at the Catholic Health Australia August 23-25, 2010, Adelaide, SA.

McBrien, R.P. (1994). *Catholicism* (Rev. ed.). North Blackburn, Vic: Collins Dove.

McClellan, R., and Dominguez, R. (2006). The uneven march toward social justice. *Journal of Educational Administration, 44*(3), 225-238.

McCord, R. (2010). Co-Workers in the Vineyard of the Lord: A pastoral perspective on its reception. In Z. Fox (Ed.), *Lay Ecclesial Ministries – Pathways towards the future* (pp. 3-15). Lanham, MD: Rowman and Littlefield Publishers.

McDonough, E. (2004). Religious Institutes as Juridic Persons in reconfiguration. *Review for Religious, 63*(3), 323-328.

McLaughlin, D. (2009). Research paradigms, methodologies and methods – EDFD707 – 2009 Research Term B, Online. Retrieved from http://blackboard.acu.edu.au/webct/cobaltMainFrame.dowebct

McTernan, B. (2005). The notion of grace. *Health Progress, 86*(5), 28-30.

Merriam, S. (1985). The case study in educational research: A review of selected literature. *Journal of Educational Thought, 19*(3), 204-217.

Modern Healthcare. (2011). Modern Healthcare – Healthcare Systems Ranked By 2010 Net Patient Revenue. Retrieved from http://www.modernhealthcare.com/section/lists?djoPage=product_detailsanddjoPid=23117and djoTry=1323211226

Moore, B. (2007). Sponsorship transformation at Ascension Health: A large system with multiple sponsors takes steps to ensure that its mission is perpetuated. *Health Progress, 88*(1), 26-28.

Morrisey, F. (1999). Catholic identity in a challenging environment: What criteria determine the Catholicity of Catholic healthcare organizations? *Health Progress, 80*(6), 38-42.

Morrisey, F. (2001a). *Catholic identity in a world of "Weird Arrangements"*. Unpublished paper, Grandin [OMI] Province Sponsorship Conference, Grey Nuns' Regional Centre, Edmonton, AB, March 31, 2001.

Morrisey, F. (2001b). Toward Juridic Personality. *Health Progress, 82*(4), 27-31.

Morrisey, F. (2002). Trustees and Canon Law: An increasingly lay leadership in Catholic health care must remember its responsibilities to the Church. *Health Progress, 83*(6) 11-18.

Morrisey, F. (2003). Improving the identity of Catholic health care institutions' structures. *Dolentium hominum, 52*(18), 128-134.

Morrisey, F. (2006a). Canon law and mortgages: Sixth in a series on Canon Law. *Health Progress, 87*(2), 46-47.

Morrisey, F. (2006b). *Select Canon Law Issues for Higher Education or Other Ministries*. Unpublished paper presented at the Conference for Mercy Higher Education, Sacred Heart Seminary, Plymouth, MI, 9 February 2006.

Morrisey, F. (2006c). Various types of Sponsorship. In R. Smith, W. Brown and N. Reynolds (Eds.), *Sponsorship in the United States: Context, theory and praxis* (pp. 17-30). Alexandria, VA: Canon Law Society of America.

Morrisey, F. (2007a). Does Canon Law speak of Sponsorship of Catholic works? *Health Progress, 88*(1), 29-30.

Morrisey, F. (2007b). *Ecclesiastical Structures in North America*. Paper presented at the How the Catholic healthcare ministry is adapting to meet new challenges, Pontifical Council for Health Pastoral Care, May 3-5, 2007, Vatican City.

Morrisey, F. (2007c). What does Canon Law say about the quality of Sponsored works?: Eleventh in a Series on Canon Law. *Health Progress, 88*(2), 10-11.

Morrisey, F. (2009). Public Juridic Persons in the Church. In M. Cleary (Ed.), *Public Juridic Persons in the Church* (pp. 11-38). Sydney, NSW: Governance and Management. Morrisey, F. (2010). A guide for Church stewards. *Health Progress, 91*(March-April), 62-63.

Morrisey, F. (2011). *The right of the baptised to be involved in the Church's mission*. Paper presented at the On Sacred Ground Conference, Brighton-le-Sands, Sydney, NSW, 21-23 September 2011.

Mudd, J. (2005). From CEO to mission leader. *Health Progress, 86*(5), 25-27.

Muldoon, T. (Ed.). (2009). *Catholic Identity and the Laity* (Vol. 54). Maryknoll, NY: Orbis Books.

Naughton, M. (2006). Catholic Social Tradition: Teaching, thought, practice. *Health Progress, 87*(1), 44-45.

Nichols, T. (2004). Participatory hierarchy. In S. Pope (Ed.), *Common calling: The laity and governance of the Catholic Church* (pp. 111-126). Washington, DC: Georgetown University Press.

Nicholson, P. (2011). *Panacea or Pandora's Box*. Paper presented at the On Sacred Ground Conference, Brighton-le-Sands, Sydney, NSW, Sept 21-23, 2011.

NVivo 8 Fundamentals. (2008). QSR International.

O'Connell Killen, P. and De Beer, J. (1994). *The art of theological reflection*. New York, NY: Crossroad Publishing Co.

O'Meara, T. (1999). *Theology of ministry* (Rev. ed.). Mahwah, NJ: Paulist Press.

O'Rourke, K. (2001). Catholic hospitals and Catholic identity. *Christian Bioethics, 7*(1), 15-28.

Oakley, F. and Russett, B. (Eds.). (2004). *Governance, accountability, and the future of the Catholic Church*. New York, NY: The Continuum International Publishing Group Inc.

Ormerod, N. (1997). *Introducing contemporary theologies: The what and the who of theology today*. (Rev. ed.). Sydney: E J Dwyer (Australia).

Ormerod, N. (Ed.). (2008). *Identity and Mission in Catholic Agencies*. Sydney, NSW: St Pauls Publications.

Orsy, L. (2004). The Church of the third millenium. In S. Pope (Ed.), *Common calling: The laity and governance of the Catholic Church* (pp. 229-251). Washington, DC: Georgetown University Press.

Osiek, C. and Miller, R. (2005). *Lay ministry in the Catholic Church: visioning church ministry through the wisdom of the past: a symposium with Carolyn Osiek ... [et al.]*. Liguori, MS: Liguori.

Peters, S. (2005). Embodying the spirit of those who came before. In Z. Fox and R. Bechtle (Eds.), *Called and chosen – Toward a spirituality for lay leaders* (pp. 113-126). Lanham, MD: Bowman and Littlefield Publishers.

Peters, S., Conroy, B., Lunz, M., Mollison, M. and Munley, A. (2003). Beyond the present: The shape of Sponsorship in the 21st century. *Current Issues in Catholic Higher Education, 23*, 67-69.

Pirola, T. (1995). Church professionalism – When does it become "Lay Elitism"? In R. Lennan (Ed.), *Redefining the Church: Vision and Practice* (pp. 71-87). Sydney: E J Dwyer (Australia).

Place, M. (2004). Toward a Theology of Sponsorship: Reflections. *Health Progress, 85*(1), 6-9.

Pope John Paul II. (1988). *Christifideles laici*. Retrieved from http://www.vatican.va/holy_father/john_paul_ii/apost_exhortations/documents/hf_jp-ii_exh_30121988_christifideles-laici_en.html

Pope John Paul II. (1992). *Pastores dabo vobis*. Vatican: Roman Catholic Church.

Pope John Paul II. (1996). *Vita consecrata*. Retrieved from http://www.vatican.va/holy_father/john_paul_ii/apost_exhortations/documents/hf_jp-ii_exh_25031996_vita-consecrata_en.html

Pope John XXIII. (1962). *Opening speech to Vatican II Council*. Retrieved from http://www.saint-mike.org/library/papal_library/johnxxiii/opening_speech_vaticanii.html

Putney, M. (2004). Health care and the Church's mission: An Australian Bishop reflects upon the health care ministry's role in the larger work of the Catholic Church. *Health Progress, 85*(1), 19-25.

Putney, M. (2005). The Catholic School of the future. *The Australasian Catholic Record, 82*(4), 387-398.

Putney, M. (2007). Evangelisation in Australia. *The Australasian Catholic Record, 84*(1), 80-87.

Putney, M. (2008). Catholic Identity and Mission. In N. Ormerod (Ed.), *Identity and Mission in Catholic Agencies* (pp. 14-37). Sydney, NSW: St Pauls Publications.

Ranson, D. (2006). Forming a new generation of leaders for Catholic schools. *The Australasian Catholic Record, 83*(4), 415-421.

Ranson, D. (2010). Priesthood, ordained and lay: One in the heart of the Other. Possibilities and challenges for the Australian pastoral context. *The Australasian Catholic Record, 88* (April), 146-161.

Reid, S., Dixon, R. and Connolly, N. (2010). See, I am doing a new thing!: A report on the 2009 survey of Catholic Religious Institutes in Australia (pp. 1-52). Sydney, NSW: Catholic Religious Australia.

Rinere, E. (2003). Canon law and the emerging understandings of ministry. In

S. K. Wood (Ed.), *Ordering the Baptismal Priesthood.* (pp. 68-86). Collegeville, MA: Liturgical Press.

Rivera, J. M. (2011). Generation, interiority and the phenomenology of Christianity in Michel Henry. *Continental Philosophy Review, 44* DOI: 10.1007/ s11007-011-9176-7(2), 205-235. Retrieved from http://www.springerlink.com.ezproxy1.acu.edu.au/content/q8p065303km3n510/fulltext.ht ml

Robinson, B. (1997). *Capital punishment.* Retrieved from http://www.religioustolerance.org/execut3.htm

Roman Catholic Church. (2013). *The Council of Trent.* Retrieved from http://www.thecounciloftrent.com/ch5.htm. 14 April 2013.

Roman Catholic Church. (1983). *The Code of canon law.* Sydney: Collins Liturgical Australia.

Rush, O. (2007). The spirit of lay ministry. *The Australasian Catholic Record, 84*(4), 437-443.

Sachs, W. (2000). The religious mission of the board. In Thomas Holland and D. Hester (Eds.), *Building effective boards for religious organisations: A handbook for trustees, presidents and church leaders* (pp. 44-57). San Francisco, CA: Jossey-Bass.

Schneiders, S. (1986). *New wineskins: Reimaging religious life today.* Mahwah, NJ: Paulist Press.

Schneiders, S. (2001). *Selling all: Commitment, consecrated celibacy, and community in Catholic religious life.* Mahwah, NJ: Paulist Press.

Schroeder, R. (2008). *What is the mission of the Church? A guide for Catholics.* Maryknoll, NY: Orbis Books.

Schuth, K. (1999). *Seminaries, theologates, and the future of Church ministry – An analysis of trends and transitions.* Collegeville, MN: Liturgical Press.

Schweickert, J. (2002). *Standing at the crossroads: Religious orders and reconfiguration.* Chicago, IL: Convergence Inc.

Seasoltz, K. (2003). Institutes of consecrated life: Identity, integrity, and ministry. In S. K. Wood (Ed.), *Ordering the Baptismal Priesthood* (pp. 228-255). Collegeville, MA: Liturgical Press.

Senge, P. (1990). *The fifth discipline – The art and practice of the learning organisation.* New York, NY: Doubleday.

Shaykh, M. i. A. a.-K. (2005). *The Legal Penalty for Stealing.* Retrieved from http://qa.sunnipath.com/issue_view.asp?HD=1andID=1895andCATE=12

Sklba, R. (2007). God at work at work: Even the filing of a patient's chart involves creation, redemption, and sanctification. *Health Progress, 88*(5), Retrieved from http://www.chausa.org/Pub/MainNav/News/HP/Archive/2007/09Sept-Oct/Articles/SpecialSection/hp0709c.htm

Skylstad, W. (2008). Serving God's people. *Health Progress, 89*(3), 24-25.

Smart, N. (1984). *The religious experience of mankind* (3rd ed.). New York: Scribner.

Smith, P. (2006a). Sponsors and sponsored ministries. In R. Smith, W. Brown and N. Reynolds (Eds.), *Sponsorship in the United States: Context, theory and praxis* (pp. 123-136). Alexandria, VA: Canon Law Society of America.

Smith, P. (2006b). What are "Indults" and "Dispensations"? Ninth in a Series on Canon Law. *Health Progress, 87*(5), Retrieved from http://www.chausa.org/Pub/MainNav/News/HP/Archive/2006/09SeptOct/Articles/Features/HP0609h.htm

Smith, R., Brown, W. and Reynolds, N. (Eds). (2006). *Sponsorship in the United States: Context, theory and praxis*. Alexandria, VA: Canon Law Society of America.

Sowle Cahill, L. (2004). Feminist theology and a participatory church. In S. Pope (Ed.), *Common calling: The laity and governance of the Catholic Church* (pp.127-150). Washington, D.C.: Georgetown University Press.

St Joseph Health System. (2007). *Fact Sheet*. Retrieved from http://www.stjhs.org/view/AboutUs/mvvfolder/default

Stanek, R. (2008). Bridging the mission-business gap in health care: How can Catholic health ministries close the gap between business and mission? *Health Progress, 89*(3), 35-37.

Stanley, T. (2007). Can ministry members collaborate for Formation of the next generation of Sponsors? *Health Progress, 88*(1), 12-15.

Statuto, R. (2004). Words, actions, beliefs: The mission at work. *Health Progress, 6*, 10-11. Sullivan Clark, C. (2005). Sponsorship: The JRK Study. *Health Progress, 86*(1), Retrieved from http://www.chausa.org/Pub/MainNav/News/HP/Archive/2005/01JanFeb/Articles/Features/ HP0501O.htm

Sweeney, B. (2001). *Incorporation and governance of Catholic schools – A canon law perspective for inclusion in the constitution of a Catholic school*. Unpublished paper prepared for the QCEC Governance Working Party, July 28, 2001, Brisbane, Qld.

Sweeney, B. (2005). *Governance! – What does it mean?* Paper presented at the Thirty

Ninth Annual Conference, Canon Law Society of Australia and New Zealand, Mercure Hotel, Geelong, September 12-15, 2005, pp. 6-21.

Sweeney, B. (2011). *Canonical responsibilities of Trustees*. Unpublished paper presented at the CHA Governance Conference 2011, Coogee, NSW, April 14-15, 2011, Retrieved from Catholic Health Australia, http://www.cha.org.au/site.php?id=1143

Talone, P. (2004). Budgeting as theological reflection: True stewardship of resources requires realism, generosity of spirit, and commitment to the common good. *Health Progress, 85*(1), 14-16.

Talone, P. (2005). The Theology of Community Benefit; our tradition obliges us to reach out beyond our hospital walls. *Health Progress, 86*(4), 20-21. Retrieved from http://www.chausa.org/Pub/MainNav/News/HP/Archive/2005/07JulAug/articles/SpecialSection/hp0507h.htm

Talone, P. (2009). Introduction – Forming leaders: Handing on the Tradition. *Health Progress, 90*(5), 19-20.

Taylor, C. (1999). A Catholic modernity? In J. Heft (Ed.), *Catholic Modernity?: Charles Taylor's Marianist Award Lecture, with Responses by William M. Shea, Rosemary Luling Haughton, George Marsden and Jean Bethke Elshtain*, pp. 13-37 New York, NY: Oxford University Press.

The Congregation for Institutes of Consecrated Life and Societies of Apostolic Life. Retrieved from http://www.vatican.va/roman_curia/congregations/ccscrlife/documents/rc_con_ccscrlife_p rofile_en.html

Thornber, J. (2012). *Cultivating fertile ground – Formation for Canonical Governance*. PhD Thesis. Canberra: Australian Catholic University.

Thornber, J. (2009). *Ensuring fertile ground – Preparing people for canonical governance*. Paper presented at the HAND IN HAND – 2009 National Conference Catholic Healthcare Australia, Hobart, Aug 17-19, 2009. Retrieved from http://www.cha.org.au/site.php?id=176

Thornhill, J. (2007). Influential 'New Ecclesial Movements' face the challenge of inculturation. *The Australasian Catholic Record, 84*(1), 67-79.

Tracy, D. (1983). The Foundations of Practical Theology. In D. Browning (Ed.), *Practical theology: The emerging field in theology, church, and world* (pp. 61-82). San Francisco, CA: Harper and Row.

Trinity Health. (2011). Retrieved from http://www.trinity-health.org/

Turner, N. (1986). *Which Seeds shall grow? Men and women in religious life.* North Blackburn, Vic: Collins Dove.

United States Conference of Catholic Bishops. (2005). Co-Workers in the vineyard of the Lord – *Development of lay ecclesial ministry.* Retrieved from http://www.usccb.org/search.cfm?q=Co-workers

United States Conference of Catholic Bishops. (2006). *Laity, marriage, family life and youth.* Retrieved from http://www.usccb.org/laity/laymin/index.shtml

Weisenbeck, M. (2007). Holding fast to the mission and works proper to the institute. *Health Progress, 88*(4), 13-14.

White, K. (1996). *Catholic healthcare: Isomorphism or differentiation?* Unpublished doctoral dissertation Virginia Commonwealth University, Virginia. Retrieved from http://proquest.umi.com/pqdweb?did=743262371andFmt=7andclientId=18921andRQT=309andV Name=PQD

White, K., Chou, T.-H. and Dandi, R. (2010). Catholic hospital services for vulnerable populations: Are system values sufficient determinants. *Health Care Management Review, 35*(2), 175-186. Retrieved from http:/ovidsp.tx.ovid.com.ezproxy2.acu.edu.au/sp-3.4.1b/ovidweb.cgi?

Willis, R. (1986). Ministry, Governance and Relational Growth. In J. Mallett (Ed.), *The Ministry of Governance* (pp. 160-192). Washington, DC: Canon Law Society of America.

Winschel, D. (2008). Formation path in the workplace: How does it work? *Health Progress,* 89(2), 20-22.

Wittberg, P. (1991). *Creating a future for religious life: A sociological perspective.* Mahwah, NJ: Paulist Press.

Wittberg, P. (1993). Residence stability and decline in Roman Catholic religious orders of women: A preliminary investigation. *Journal for the Scientific Study of Religion,* 32(1), 76-81.

Wittberg, P. (1994). Women in the vanishing cloister: Organizational decline in Catholic religious orders in the United States (Book Review). *Contemporary Sociology,* 23(1), 137-138. Retrieved from http://search.ebscohost.com/login.aspx?direct=trueanddb=a9handAN=9406060810andsite=ehos t-live

Wittberg, P. (1998). Ties that no longer bind. *America,* 179(8), 10-14.

Wittberg, P. (2000). Declining institutional Sponsorship and religious orders: A study of reverse impacts. *Sociology of Religion,* 61(3), 315-324.

Wittberg, P. (2006). *From piety to professionalism – and back? – Transformations of organised religious virtuosity*. Oxford, UK: Lexington Books.

Wood, S. (2009). Health care sponsorship: From charism to ecclesial ministry. *Health Progress*, 90(5), 45-48.

Wood, S. (Ed.). (2003). *Ordering the baptismal priesthood*. Collegeville, MA: Liturgical Press.

Wuerl, D. (1999). Catholic health ministry in transition: Church's unique vision remains stable in shifting healthcare landscape *Health Progress*, 80(3), 14-16.

Yanofchick, B. (2007a). Mission and outreach: Whose work are we about?: Mission and leadership. *Health Progress*, 88(4), 8-10. Retrieved from http://www.chausa.org/Pub/MainNav/News/HP/Archive/2007/07July- Aug/Articles/Columns/hp0707r.htm

Yanofchick, B. (2007b). Servant leadership: Bring it home: Mission and leadership. *Health Progress*, 88(5), 6-7. Retrieved from http://www.chausa.org/Pub/MainNav/News/HP/Archive/2007/09Sept-Oct/Articles/Columns/hp0709r.htm

Yin, R. (1994). *Case study research: design and methods* (Vol. 5) (2nd ed.). Thousand Oaks, CA: Sage.

Appendix 1: Online Survey
Section 1　Demographics

For each of the following questions, please indicate the option that best describes your background with regard to the formation for canonical governance.

What is your role in ministry? (indicate as many as apply to you)	
Member of a Religious Institute	
Board member of a ministry	
Involved in formation for Public Juridic Person/Sponsorship	
Leadership position in a Religious Institute	
Member of Trustees	
Member of Public Juridic Person	
Senior manager in a ministry	
Representative of Public Juridic Person	
Theologian	
Canonist	
What is your role in the Church?	
Religious Sister	
Lay person not a member of a Religious Institute	
Religious Brother	
Religious Priest	
Priest	
Bishop	
What is your range of involvement with Public Juridic Persons?	
Involvement with more than one Public Juridic Person	
Involvement with one Public Juridic Person	
Neither	
What is your length of involvement with Public Juridic Persons?	
> 25 years	
16 – 25 years	
11 – 15 years	
6 – 10 years	
1 – 5 years	
< 1 year	
In which country are you currently living?	
Australia	
United States of America	
Canada	
Other (specify)	

Section 2 Desirable and Existing Traits

For each of the following items, please indicate
- your level of agreement about the desirability of the particular trait, and
- the extent to which you regard that trait to be currently evident in those with roles as canonical governors

Canonical governors	This trait is desirable					The extent to which this trait exists				
	Strongly Agree	Agree	Disagree	Strongly Disagree	No Answer	Very High	High	Fair	Low	Unable to Judge/ No Answer
are people of integrity										
exhibit balance in judgment										
possess a deep sense of justice										
are genuinely compassionate										
show a genuine concern for others										
possess well-developed personal maturity										
demonstrate self-knowledge										
respect every person										
are aware of their gifts										

demonstrate an ability to learn from praise									
exhibit balance in behaviour									
understand their baptismal call to mission									
have a sense of vocation to their role									
are aware that spiritual formation requires individuals to be open to the transcendent									
view their role as a ministry of governance									
understand that spiritual formation is about living intimately united to the Word of God									
demonstrate an ability to learn from criticism									

Canonical governors	This trait is desirable (%)					The extent to which this trait exists (%)				
	Strongly Agree	Agree	Disagree	Strongly Disagree	No Answer	Very High	High	Fair	Low	Unable to Judge/ No Answer
are committed to the mission of the Church										
are aware that spiritual formation aims for a daily growing in love of God and neighbour										
understand that they are a bridge for people to Christ										
enjoy a public identification with the Catholic ecclesial community expressed in a variety of ways										
pray and practice other forms of spirituality										
understand that the Catholic Faith is rooted in God's revelation										
understand that the Catholic Faith is embodied in the living tradition of the Church										
are aware that formation for ecclesial ministry is a journey beyond catechesis into theological reflection										

have some background in missiology									
have some background in ecclesiology									
have some background in Canon Law									
can articulate the missiology which underpins the operation of the ministry									
use theology to help understand the needs of the time in the light of Scripture and Tradition									
have a sound knowledge of Catholic social teaching									
seek to develop their appreciation of the Catholic faith through intellectual formation									
understand the ministry they lead									
understand their responsibility for the ongoing Catholic identity of the ministry									
have a sound knowledge of the *Catechism of the Catholic Church*									

Canonical governors	This trait is desirable (%)					The extent to which this trait exists (%)				
	Strongly Agree	Agree	Disagree	Strongly Disagree	No Answer	Very High	High	Fair	Low	Unable to Judge/ No Answer
work together in the ministry of leadership to discern the signs of the times for the mission of the Church										
have an appropriate way of calling those leading the operation of the ministry to account										
understand the responsibilities of the local bishop for the coordination of ministerial services in the diocese										
use mission-based criteria in forming future governors										
understand organisational systems and dynamics										
understand that they have a responsibility for the spiritual life of their ministry										
inspire communal purpose and vision										
use mission-based criteria in selecting future governors										

Section 3 Follow-up

Would you be willing to participate in a follow-up interview? If so, please email us at [the researcher's email]

Thank you for your participation in this survey!

Appendix 2

Statistical Results from the Factor Analysis of Survey Responses

Table A2.1   Factor Analysis Human Dimension Traits

Human Item	Factors for Indicated Component*			
	Desirable		Existing	
	1[a]	2[b]	1[c]	2[d]
People of Integrity	.450	.276	.707	.141
Balance in Judgement	.808	.208	.613	.168
Deep Sense of Justice	.853	.036	.712	.445
Genuinely Compassionate	.687	.464	.750	.234
Concern for Others	.750	.422	.718	-.039
Personal Maturity	.776	.339	.657	.388
Demonstrate Self-knowledge	.594	.461	.522	.492
Respect Every Person	.756	.355	.771	.206
Balance in Behaviour	.438	.656	.597	.147
Learn from Criticism	.278	.725	.116	.850
Aware of their Gifts	.172	.676	.130	.713
Learn from Praise	**.183**	**.832**	**.197**	**.727**

*Component 1 = Human Maturity. Component 2 = Self Awareness
[a]Cronbach's Alpha = .914 on 9 items, [b]Cronbach's Alpha = .715 on 3 items
[c]Cronbach's Alpha = .879 on 9 items, [d]Cronbach's Alpha = .713 on 3 items

Table A2.2 Factor Analysis Spiritual Dimension Traits

Spiritual Item	Factors for Indicated Component*			
	Desirable		Existing	
	1[a]	2[b]	1[c]	2[d]
Understand Baptismal Call	.243	.854	.330	.737
Sense of Vocation	.337	.746	.491	.634
See Ministry of Governance	.145	.803	.277	.764
Committed to Mission of Church	.603	.320	.145	.820
Identification with Ecclesial Community	.647	.019	.137	.692
Practices of Prayer and Spirituality	.745	.364	.665	.431
Open to Transcendent	.719	.321	.743	.307
United to Word of God	.799	.231	.822	.250
Growth in Love	.799	.287	.878	.076
Bridge for People to Christ	.474	.389	.669	.242

*Component 1 = Sense of Call. Component 2 = Call to Spirituality
[a]Cronbach's Alpha = .713 on 5 items, [b]Cronbach's Alpha = .850 on 5 items
[c]Cronbach's Alpha = .834 on 5 items, [d]Cronbach's Alpha = .857 on 5 items

Table A2.3 Factor Analysis Intellectual Dimension Traits

Intellectual Item	Factors for Indicated Component*	
	Desirable	Existing
	1[a]	1[b]
Faith Rooted in God's Revelation	.542	.666
Faith Embodied in Living Tradition	.480	.738
Journey to Theological Reflection	.689	.757
Some Background in Missiology	.669	.677
Some Background in Ecclesiology	.768	.775
Some Background in Canon Law	.777	.695
Articulate Missiology for Ministry	.648	.715
Understand needs in Light of Scripture and Tradition	.755	.751
Knowledge of Catholic Social Teaching	.589	.746
Catechism of Catholic Church	.376	.691
Appreciation of Faith through Intellectual Formation	.703	.713

*Only one factor: Component 1 = Catholic Intellectual tradition.
[a]Cronbach's Alpha = .858 on 11 items, [b]Cronbach's Alpha = .905 on 11 items

Table A2.4   Factor Analysis Pastoral Dimension Traits

Pastoral Item	Factors for Indicated Component*			
	Desirable		Existing	
	1^a	2^b	1^c	2^d
Understand the Ministry	.917	.049	.619	.370
Understand Responsibility for Catholic Identity	.909	.195	.696	.324
Discern Signs of Times for Mission	.727	.514	.765	.136
Understand Responsibilities of Bishop for Coordination	.378	.426	.680	.071
Responsibility for Spiritual Life of Ministry	.576	.504	.801	.056
Inspire Common Purpose	.572	.435	.488	.526
Selecting Future Governors	.247	.822	.679	.265
Forming Future Governors	.402	.791	.654	.273
Understand Organisational Systems and Dynamics	.044	.819	.171	.865
Call Leaders to Account Appropriately	.654	.558	.113	.815

*Component 1 = Catholic Identity and Mission. Component 2 = Formation for Canonical Governance
[a] Cronbach's Alpha = .890 on 7 items, [b] Cronbach's Alpha = .821 on 3 items
[c] Cronbach's Alpha = .821 on 8 items, [d] Cronbach's Alpha = .747 on 2 items

Appendix 3

Interviewee Codes and Attributes

A   Lay person, member of a Public Juridic Person (PJP)

C   Lay person, member of Trustees of a PJP

D   Member of a religious institute leadership, formator

E   Lay person, member of a PJP

F   Priest involved in oversight and advising on PJPs

G   Bishop, canonist

H   Congregation leader of religious institute; member of a PJP health ministry

I   Lay person, member of a PJP

J   Member of a religious institute leadership; member of a PJP health ministry

L   Lay person, theologian

N   Congregation Leader of religious institute; member of a PJP health ministry

P   Member of religious institute; theologian; formator in PJP formation

R   Member of religious institute, theologian, formator in PJP formation

T   Lay person, theologian, formator in PJP formation program

V   Member of religious institute; theologian; formator in PJP formation

X   Priest, theologian, formator in PJP formation

Z   Member of religious institute, social worker, formator in PJP formation

www.ingramcontent.com/pod-product-compliance
Lightning Source LLC
Chambersburg PA
CBHW052103230426
43671CB00011B/1917